Eat Your Heart Out

Eat Your Heart Out

Food Profiteering
in America

JIM HIGHTOWER

VINTAGE BOOKS
A Division of Random House
New York

VINTAGE BOOKS EDITION, August 1976

Library of Congress Cataloging in Publication Data

Hightower, Jim.
  Eat your heart out.

  Bibliography: p.
  Includes index.
  1. Food industry and trade—United States.
2. Supermarkets. 3. Grocery trade—United States.
I. Title.
[HD9006.H46 1976]   338.4'7'641300973   76-15229
ISBN 0-394-72094-6

Manufactured in the United States of America

Known in the 1890s as "The Kansas Pythoness," Mary E. Lease was an old-time populist orator and fighter for common people. When American farmers were laid low by a farm depression in 1892, she took to the stump to urge them "to raise less corn and more Hell."

This book is dedicated to that spirit, and to all the spiritual heirs of Mary E. Lease.

ACKNOWLEDGMENTS

Much of this work is lifted wholesale from the minds and efforts of people who have been involved over the past four years with the Agribusiness Accountability Project. The Project is a public-interest organization in Washington, D.C., and it exists to monitor and challenge the abuses of corporate power in the food economy.

To call the Project an organization implies much more structure than actually exists. Rather it has been a loosely coordinated enterprise of a few headstrong and capable people. Their ideas, research and experience— as well as my own—are reflected in this book, and I am indebted to each of them.

I owe Susan DeMarco most of all. As co-director of the Project, her incisive mind has been the single most valuable asset of the Project. She has helped me conceptualize this book, has encouraged me to write it and has developed many of the thoughts that I express here. Short of forking over a share of any royalties that might accrue to me, there is no way that I can thank her enough for her contribution.

My debt is especially heavy, too, to four other exceptional people who have been mainstays of the Project's work: Martha Hamilton, Al Krebs, Nancy Mills and Susan Sechler. I have drawn heavily from their work, and if this book sells, I owe each of them a beer.

Friends like Fred Harris have encouraged my work and helped to shape some of my thoughts, and that friendship is deeply treasured. Also, invaluable support and counsel have been given by Leslie Dunbar, Chuck Frazier, Jim McHale, Weldon Barton, David Ramage, Mike Jacobson and Jim Patton—all of whom are long-standing friends of the Agribusiness Accountability Project.

Thanks, too, to Bob Sherrill, who has cared enough about my work to help me get it published. He introduced me to Ed Barber, who is as fine an editor as a writer could hope to have. Not only is Ed exceptionally good at what he does, but he also is a person who cares about people's issues and understands viscerally what people like me are trying to say. It is that kind of relationship that makes a book possible. I also owe him a beer.

In preparing the book, it has been my good fortune to have had the research and administrative assistance of Helen Lichtenstein, Julie Marshall and Leona Levine, and I am thankful for their valuable support.

There is no way to pay back a father and mother, but at least I can acknowledge the debt. They saw to it that I was loved, fed, clothed and sent to college, but they also made certain that I understood that book-learning is inferior to common sense, and that even big bankers and government officials are no better than regular people. That lesson is an integral part of this book.

Jim Hightower
Washington, D.C.

Contents

CHAPTER I. Bigger Is Better, and Other American Myths 3

CHAPTER II. Guess Who's Coming to Dinner? 11

CHAPTER III. Consumers: Footing the Bill 48

CHAPTER IV. Biting into Oligopoly 88

CHAPTER V. Ads, Gimmicks and Shelf Space: Barriers to Competition 135

CHAPTER VI. Farmers: Death of American Gothic 154

CHAPTER VII. Limousines in the Fields 189

CHAPTER VIII. Government: A Helping Hand 218

CHAPTER IX. Business As Usual: Corporate Influence on Government 210

CHAPTER X. Eat Your Heart Out 228

Appendices 307

Sources 317

Notes 325

Index 349

Eat Your Heart Out

CHAPTER I

Bigger Is Better, and Other American Myths

Economic smallness is more efficient, more productive, more innovative and generally more enriching to our lives than economic giantism. Boil down all the following pages and statistics, and that thought is the author's message. It seems almost heresy to say it, but there it is: Bigger is *not* better.

That statement grates against our received wisdom, bigness has been pursued reflexively and without questioning throughout most of our country's history. Even today, when the dangers of a growth philosophy are all too clear, chambers of commerce everywhere urge their towns to get bigger. Woe to the corporate executive who cannot tell shareholders that their company grew bigger during the year. Some automobile makers even claim that their small cars are bigger than other small cars.

Behind this attitude toward bigness is a presumption that a grander scale means a grander life. That presumption has not paid off. Although bigness has grown to hugeness, and now to giantism, although institutions and systems are surpassing human scale, few would claim that life is more rewarding than it was when things were simply big. Government and business, cities and buildings have grown bigger, but we human beings have not.

This is no plea for a return to the simpler days of 40 acres and a mule. Rather it is a plea to assess where we are headed and to question why we are going that way. There is a point at which bigness turns on us, begins to work against rather than for us. We are passing that point.

In food, more than in most areas of our lives, we have assumed that bigness is necessary, and we have stood silent while corporate food interests and governmental agencies have worked together to build a food economy modeled on industrial giantism. The mom & pop stores were declared "inefficient" and were displaced by supermarkets; today, the few national chains that control grocery sales in most cities are taking us even farther, beyond mere supermarkets to immense "superstores" and "hypermarkets."

The small farm was declared "obsolete," and three million of them have been eliminated during the past thirty years, replaced by ever-larger units of production. Now, the remaining family farmers are being told that they must subjugate their independent operations to the handful of processors and distributors that monopolize food markets. That is making the farmer a contract employee of totally integrated corporate food systems.

Town produce markets, dairy deliveries and other local marketing systems were judged "illogical," so food distribution was regionalized, and then nationalized. At present, the food-marketing system is being expanded to a worldwide basis, with multinational conglomerates putting the world food supply up for bid by Japanese, Western European, Russian and American consumers.

This mindess pursuit of giantism makes no sense for

the consumer. Certainly, there are economies and efficiencies to be achieved by some expansion beyond the lowest scale of business operation, but there are just as many diseconomies and inefficiencies that come with remote, top-heavy, bureaucratic giantism. And that says nothing about what giantism has done to product quality and to our sense of human and community values.

HAS ANYONE SEEN MOM & POP? "What do you want to do," snickered a big business executive, "bring back the mom & pop stores?" Yes. It makes sense to focus food retailing on well-run mom and pop stores, co-op stores and small supermarket chains, locally owned and managed.

The "supermarket revolution" began back in the 1920s, when these high-volume enterprises lowered their profit margins and proceeded to displace local grocers. By the 1950s, with small competition effectively eliminated, the chains slackened their price competition and raised their profit margins. Steadily gaining monopoly strength, the giant supermarkets of today have margins equal to or higher than those of the small competitors they displaced.[1]

In the last ten years, there has been a very significant development in food retailing. The biggest growth has come via an explosion of "convenience" stores, such as the 7-Eleven chain. In 1960, there were only 2,500 convenience stores in the country. By 1970, their numbers were over 13,000 and increasing steadily. These stores are now a tremendous force in the food industry, and the Department of Agriculture had glowingly described their appeal to the public, which they say "is based on convenience of location, quick service and long hours"— though they have higher prices, less brand selection and higher profit margins.[2]

Read that description again. What they have described is the old mom & pop store! We have not done away with the mom & pop store at all—we have only done away with mom & pop.

Standing where they once stood is a plastic replica, mass-produced and centrally-controlled. Southland, the parent firm of 7-Eleven, operates a third of all convenience stores in the country and makes half of all convenience-store sales. Operating in 41 states and the District of Columbia, their pervasion through American neighborhoods is practically as complete as suggested in their advertising: "If it's not around the house, it's just around the corner."

These imitations do not sell food more cheaply than the original. In fact, their prices frequently are higher than those in the few real remaining mom & pop stores, and they have not lowered their margins—Southland's profit rates generally run 50% to 100% greater than those of supermarkets. It makes sense for genuine mom & pop stores, with their low volume, to have a bit higher margins than chain stores, but 7-Eleven is a *chain*, with $1.4 billion in sales a year. That makes it the tenth largest grocery retailer in the country—not exactly a low-volume corner store.

The presence of 7-Eleven on the corner means more than high prices and high profits. It means surrendering some measure of community control to food giantism. The company advertises that it is your "good neighbor," but 7-Eleven is headquartered in Dallas, Texas. Instead of paying our food dollars to thousands of independent moms & pops, living and competing in our own neighborhoods, those dollars are shipped off to Dallas. Southland took $23 million worth of profits out of American communities in 1973.

Real mom & pop stores were flexible enough to obtain products that fit the unique character of local residents, and they would respond directly to the needs and complaints of the neighborhood. Southland, however, makes food choices in Dallas for all of us, and any local complaints have to be put on a form and submitted through corporate channels.

The power of giantism to affect our lives is not always dramatic, but sometimes more like the act of erosion. For example, 7-Eleven manufactures many of its own food products; increasingly those are the only choices available in their stores. Someone popping into the neighborhood 7-Eleven for a Dr. Pepper on a hot day is unlikely to find it in the cooler. There may be cartons of Dr. Pepper unrefrigerated, but to get a cold drink you have to buy the 7-Eleven brand. Your choice is to take what the chain offers or to drive out of your neighborhood to find what you want.

THE EFFICIENCY BUGABOO. Even if we accept cold efficiency as the sole criterion by which our economic performance ought to be judged, there is no justification for giantism. Ironically, the efficiency argument has been used as a screen to allow food corporations to expand their organizations and their market power to the point of virtual monopolies, and it is the nature of monopoly to be exceedingly inefficient.

Economic efficiency on the farm, in the processing plants and at the retail level is achieved at a surprisingly small scale of operation. In 1969 the staff of the Federal Trade Commission concluded that a local supermarket chain of only five stores and one warehouse can achieve practically all the efficiencies of bigness in food retailing.[3] That verified the findings of the National Com-

mission on Food Marketing, which found in the mid-
sixties that small chains of no more than ten stores were
efficient, profitable and competitive.[4]

In the world of supermarketing, a chain of 5, 10 or
even 50 stores is tiny. Safeway, A&P, Kroger, Lucky
and other giants that dominate grocery sales are massive, far-flung organizations. Safeway, the largest of
these cumbersome giants, has 2,300 stores, 42 warehouses, 24 distribution centers, dozens of food-processing facilities—and annual sales of some $7 billion a
year. Yet, the supermarket industry itself admits that all
economies in retailing can be achieved by a chain that
is less than 10% of that size.[5]

As staff attorneys at the Federal Trade Commission
wrote in a 1969 memorandum, monopoly and food do
not mix efficiently:

> Our point is this: Even if there were no sociological
> mandates from Congress for maintaining small retail
> businesses, and even if there were no value in preserving
> the small merchants as a seed-bed for future competition
> at some expense of present efficiency, even then, in terms
> of present competition, there is no excuse for allowing
> monopoly concentration under the mistaken idea that
> it is a price to pay for efficiency. We can have both effi-
> ciency and atomistic competition, with the former as-
> sured by the latter.[6]

Top-heavy and unresponsive, such giants as Safeway
are unable to get the efficient performance that aggressive owner-managers or cooperative enterprises produce
in their local stores and small chains. A key ingredient
of efficiency is competitiveness, and the big chains are
not interested in that. Not only is giantism too inflexible
and too remote to achieve high levels of efficiency, but
it also acts aggressively to restrict competition. Today's
dominant chain stores did not become dominant because

they were more efficient and competitive than small business, but because they had the raw financial power to buy up the smaller firms. By making stock offers that simply could not be refused, the big chains were able in one blow to increase their strength and decrease competition.

These giants are in fact a mockery of "free enterprise." They have the purchasing power to command discount prices from their suppliers and the economic power to control the marketplace. They are in a position to be inefficient and noncompetitive, yet stay in business, profit handsomely and expand their organizations. It is not survival of the fittest, as we have been taught to expect, but survival of the fattest.

We have been sold a bill of goods. Smallness may appear inefficient when put beside a model of perfect efficiency, but that model exists only in the minds of economists. In the real world, efficiency and competitiveness are products of economic smallness. Compared with the performance of giantism, smallness looks awfully efficient.

In any case, we need to remind ourselves that strict efficiency is the lowest measure of economic performance. It is not for itself that the economy exists, but for people. We must ask more of our food economy than input-output statistics—it is fair to expect that our economic system be arranged in such a way that will maximize human satisfaction.

Giantism falls far short of that higher level of measurement. You do not have to be an economist to recognize that small stores are more geared to individual relationships than the national firms. In its landmark study of food retailing in 1966, the National Commission on Food Marketing pointed to the human advantage of small enterprise: "These individuals are typically a part of the community they serve, they know their customers personally, and they are able to observe, understand, and respond to their particular environments with much more sensitivity than is typical of chain store organizations."[7]

We have grown too accustomed to thinking of any small enterprise as debris in the path of efficiency and progress. But sentiment is not the small operator's only defense. In fact, family farms, mom & pop stores, independent processors and local restaurants can feed us better than giantism can. Far from better, bigness, is inferior. It has failed in the fundamental sense that it has not achieved even the little that it promised. Few would argue that food is better or cheaper that it was before small enterprise was declared obsolete. As Susan DeMarco of the Agribusiness Accountability Project asked a symposium of business professors, "If bigness cannot even guarantee efficiency and better prices, then why should we guarantee bigness?"

CHAPTER II

Guess Who's Coming to Dinner?

Food monopolies are muscling their way toward the dinner table. Most people think of dinner as something that farmers grow for people to eat. Not quite. Farmers grow food for corporate middlemen, who then sell the food to eaters. That arrangement has prevailed in this country for decades, and it would hardly be worth a raised eyebrow now if it were not for one increasingly prevalent characteristic: The middle sector of our food economy is growing monopolistic.

Behind the phantasmagoria of food brand names presented on television and in modern supermarkets, there are fewer and fewer processors and marketers gaining more and more control over dinner. There are, for example, some 32,000 food-manufacturing firms in America—a highly competitive number at first glance. But just 50 of those companies already make about three-fourths of the industry's profits—a degree of market control that draws tighter every year. These are the brand-name giants, powerfully situated between millions of growers and millions of eaters, and they have become what economist John Kenneth Galbraith terms "the decisive part" of the food economy.[1]

America's new dinner is the stuff of "total food systems," owned and directed by such outfits as Del Monte, Safeway and Ralston Purina. These systems are highly industrialized, thoroughly integrated, richly capitalized and comfortably concentrated. Anyone who likes what Detroit's Big Three have done for automobiles will be pleased with these emerging food systems, for the same quality, price competition, choice and product reliability is being built into the food we eat. As A. C. Hoffman, retired vice-president of Kraftco, confided to a Senate investigating committee in 1973, "basically the food industries show the same characteristics of corporate giantism found in most other parts of the economy, for the same reasons, and with even greater potential danger to the public because of the critical importance of food."[2]

The Conglomeration of Ma Brown's Ol' Fashun Pickles

Walk into any major supermarket and you are confronted with thousands of items. If, by some queer leap of the mind, the question of food monopoly were to occur to you as you walked in, the sheer number of brand names in the store would put your mind to rest. "This," you might understandably exclaim, looking down the aisles, "is a competitive economic system."

But look again. There is much less competition than meets the eye. Many of the old, established brand names have been corralled by conglomerate creatures called "consumer product companies." Push your shopping cart along the aisles, picking up some La Choy frozen egg rolls, a Lambrecht pepperoni pizza, or a Rosarita frozen enchilada dinner; stop at the dairy section for a quart of Meadow Gold Milk, a pint or two of Louis Sherry ice cream and your favorite flavor of Dannon yogurt; push on for some Rainbo sweet gherkins, a jar of Aunt Nellie's pickled beets and a can of Gebhardt's tamales; pick up a pack of Fisher's mixed nuts, a bag of Kitchen Fresh potato chips, a can of Kobey's shoestring potatoes and a jar of Lowrey's beef jerky for snacks; at the bakery section get some Sunbeam hamburger buns, a loaf of Butter Krust bread, a box of Lara Lynn saltines and a Burny Bros. cake; try to pass up the Milk Duds, the Chocolate Pollywogs and the Clark candies; don't forget to go back to the meat counter for the Eckrich sausage links.

When you check out with this cart-full of products, you have not supported 21 independent food firms. You have supported only one: Beatrice Foods Company, a $3-billion-a-year, multinational food conglomerate headquartered in Chicago. Beatrice manufactures some 5,000 food items, marketing them under more than 100 different brand names.

Procter & Gamble, Unilever, Consolidated Foods, American Brands, United Brands, American Home Products, CPC International and Standard Brands are among the handful of consumer-product giants like Beatrice that now hold most of the processed and heavily advertised grocery brands. Even the old, established names, like General Foods and Pet, have become multiproduct conglomerates, reaching across many product lines. H. J. Heinz, known for its 57 varieties, now has about 1,250—including such anomalies as Star-Kist tuna and Ore-Ida potatoes.

Since there is no legal requirement that the food package list the parent company, it is not easy to know who you are buying from these days. You cannot know as you buy it that Lipton tea, for example, is owned by the British-Dutch conglomerate, Unilever. But it is possible on some items to make your own small test, for some firms voluntarily put their names on all their packages, even if in small print. Check the Borden brand.You expect to find it on cheese and other dairy products, but you might be surprised to notice it also on these well-known items:

BORDEN

- Aunt Jane's pickles
- Bama jellies
- Campfire marshmallows
- Cracker Jacks
- Drake's cakes and snacks
- Frosted Shake
- Kava instant coffee
- NoneSuch mincemeat
- Old London potato chips
- ReaLemon reconstituted lemon juice
- Sacramento tomato juice
- Wise potato chips
- Wyler soup and drink mixes

Even industrial conglomerates have found a place on grocery shelves. Wonder Bread, Morton frozen pies and dinners, Gwaltney Smithfield ham and bacon, Pearson candies and Hostess Twinkies and other snacks are all products of ITT, the largest conglomerate in the world. You also buy conglomerate food from the likes of Ling-Temco-Vought (Wilson meats), Tenneco (Sun Giant vegetables and nuts), Greyhound (Armour meats) and R. J. Reynolds Industries (Chun King, Hawaiian Punch, etc.).

Wines? Many of those old-world names appearing on the labels are no longer the signature of proud and independent family operations. Increasingly, they are the aliases of very large corporations: Monsieur Henri is just another way of saying Pepsico; Four Monks is owned by Joseph Schlitz Brewing Company; Inglenook, Lejon and Italian Swiss Colony are products of Heublein; Sauverain is partially owned by Pillsbury; Beringer Brothers is in the Nestlé family; Almadén is owned by National Distillers and Chemical Corp. Even the venerable Mogen David now is the stuff of Coca-Cola.

If competition is not what we have assumed it to be in the food industry, old-style promotional gimmicks remain the same. Few brand symbols are more popular than down-home names and faces—mom, dad, grandma and all the rest smile benignly at us from the shelves. And no wonder. What makes granny smile is that she is on a handsome retainer to a major conglomerate:

Brand Name	Owner
Ma Brown's Ol' Fashun Pickles	Beatrice Foods
Grandma Molasses	American Brands
Dad's Root Beer	Illinois Central Railroad
Aunt Fanny's Pastries	Pet, Inc.
Pepperidge Farm Bread	Campbell Soup
Sara Lee Coffee Cake	Consolidated Foods Corporation
Mrs. Butterworth's Syrup	Unilever

We have been deceived by appearances. Even the trusted family firms that produce ethnic foods now have turned their recipes over to conglomerates—Hebrew National Kosher, makers of Jewish specialties, is a subsidiary of Riviana Foods; Old El Paso Mexican foods are made by Pet, Inc.; and San Giorgio Italian products are produced by Hershey.

Not only is this brand-name concentration mildly interesting—perhaps even fun to learn—but it also is significant. These few multiproduct firms are eliminating independent competition and are gaining monopoly power over the makings of dinner.

Let Them Eat Oligopolies

An "oligopoly" is what you have when a few sellers of a product are in a position to control the amount and price offered to a large number of buyers—in short it means that competition among the makers and sellers of this stuff ranges from little to none. And that most likely means the price of the product is higher than it ought to be and that quality is lower than it would be if real competition existed.

If as few as four companies control more than half the production or sales of a product, those firms generally are considered to form a high-level oligopoly. Put another way, the four companies share a monopoly. Virtual monopolies exist, for example, in such U.S. products as automobiles, telephone equipment, computers, razor blades and photocopying, and "tight" oligopolies control such products as tires, drugs, soap, washing machines and typewriters.[3]

It is no big surprise to be told that automobiles and soap are controlled by shared monopolies. But it is not generally understood that the food industry is coming within the grasp of the same power. In his well-regarded book *Market Power and Economic Welfare*, Dr. William G. Shepherd reports that the average market share of the four leading firms in any given food-product line is 55%—an industrywide average that ranks food products right up there with the other shared monopolies.[4] By this calculation, there is more monopolistic concentration in food than there is in the rubber and plastics industry, the fabricated-metals industry, the textile industry and most other industries.

In fact, the extent of food monopoly is much greater than the industry average suggests. Consider the *single*

TABLE II—1

Product	Company	% of Market
Baby food	Gerber	65%
Canned diet food	Diet Delight (Calif. Canners & Growers)	60
Canned soup	Campbell	90
Coffee	General Foods	41
Dried soup	Lipton (Unilever)	70
Reconstituted lemon juice	ReaLemon (Borden)	80–90
Spaghetti sauce	Ragù (Chesebrough-Ponds)	60
Tea	Lipton (Unilever)*	50

* On December 16, 1773, the Boston Tea Party took place to protest the British monopoly of American tea sales. Two hundred years later, as we prepare to celebrate the bicentennial of our freedom from British control, we find that Unilever—a British-Dutch company—monopolizes American tea sales.

companies that monopolize specific product lines shown in Table II–1.

These are virtual monopolies. A further and very wide range of food products are only a little less tightly held: Dole (Castle & Cook), United Brands and Del Monte share 85% of the North American banana market. Eighty-nine percent of soft-drink sales are controlled by Coca-Cola, Pepsico, Royal Crown and Seven-Up. Three national firms—Anheuser-Busch, Schlitz and Pabst—produce over 50% of all the beer sold in the country. Borden, National Dairy and Carnation control 60 to 70% of the market for dairy products.

Next time you are in the supermarket, take a moment to learn about the oligopoly you eat for breakfast—prepared cereals. At least one aisle will be given over to them, stacked high with dozens of brands, from Boo Berry to Buc Wheats, Corn Flakes to Crispy Critters.

Looks good, competitively speaking, until you make a count of the number of brands that are owned by Kellogg's, General Mills, General Foods (Post) and Quaker. Their brands will add up to more than 80% of the total, and the Federal Trade Commission reports that this Big Four makes 91% of the breakfast cereal sales.

Such statistics are difficult to come by. The concentrated food industry, practically immune to public inquiry, keeps the lid on as tightly as possible. Food executives, backed by a chorus of governmental apologists, never cease their refrain about the competitiveness of their industry. But just as steadily, they fail to let the public check their figures. We are left to piece it together from occasional references in the industry press, from congressional and federal-agency reports, from the probings of private and public-interest organizations, from the infrequent antitrust cases that are brought by the government and from the published studies of academics. In the last category is Dr. Shepherd's listing of market shares controlled in 1966 by the four leading firms in various U.S. manufacturing industries (Table II–2).

Even these impressive numbers fail to reflect the full depth of monopoly power for which consumers pay at the checkout counter. For example, the big four fruit-and-vegetable canners are shown to have 40% of that market, a significant level of concentration, but classed as a "low-grade oligopoly" by the economists. Break that category down into the items you actually buy, however, and the level of monopoly among fruit-and-vegetable canners is elevated considerably. The four leading canners sell 60% of the fruit cocktail, 57% of the applesauce, 82% of the canned figs, 52% of the canned sweet corn, 58% of the tomato paste, 58% of

TABLE II—2

Product	% of Market Held by Four Largest Firms in 1966
Creamery butter	50%
Natural cheese	60
Condensed and evaporated milk	50
Ice cream	70
Fluid milk	60
Canned specialties	80
Canned fruits & vegetables	40
Dehydrated fruits & vegetables	50
Frozen fruits & vegetables	40–50
Flour meal	45
Cereal preparations	87
Rice milling	45
Blended & prepared flour	75
Wet corn milling	67
Bread & related products	50
Biscuits & crackers	70
Raw cane sugar	50
Cane sugar refining	40
Beet sugar	40
Confectionery products	40–50
Chocolate & cocoa products	85
Chewing gum	88
Malt liquor	65
Wines & brandy	41
Distilled liquor	55
Flavorings	63
Shortening & cooking oils	80–90
Food preparations	60–70

Source: William G. Shepherd. *Market Power and Economic Welfare.*
New York: Random House. 1970. Appendix Table 8, p. 263.

the vegetable juice, 53% of the canned peas and 72% of the tomato sauce.

In 1973 testimony before the U.S. House Subcommittee on Monopolies, Ralph Nader presented data on food monopolies that he drew from two unpublished doctoral theses at the University of Wisconsin. It showed staggering market power controlled by the four leading makers of such items as baby food (95%), baking powder and yeast (86%), instant coffee (81%), dessert mixes (86%), refrigerated doughs (87%), and ketchup (81%).

A significant point is that the same giant food firms have a way of cropping up at the top in several of these food categories. Dr. Russell Parker, assistant to the director of FTC's Bureau of Economics, told the Joint Economic Committee of Congress in 1974 that "just 50 food manufacturing corporations control most of the important producing positions in all of the individual food industries and product classes."[5] The Federal Trade Commission examined the 1963 market structure of the food industry by breaking it down into 116 different product categories. Of the top four market positions in each of these categories, 62% were held by only 50 companies.[6]

Think of it this way: There were 464 rooms at the top, and the 50 food giants held 288 of them, an average of 5.7 each.

Though comparable data is not available, it is clear that increasing market concentration and the rash of corporate mergers since 1963 would give the big 50 a much bigger share of the top slots today. In 1963, there were 32,153 food manufacturing corporations. Of them, the 50 largest owned nearly half of all food manufacturing assets and made 61% of the industry's profits. Dr. Parker told the Congress in his 1974 testimony that asset concentration by the giants "has continued to increase to where I estimate that the current 50 largest companies may account for close to 60% of total food manufacturing assets."[7]

Profit concentration has progressed accordingly, probably putting nearly 75% of the industry total in the pockets of the 50 big boys, leaving the other 32,103 "competitors" to scramble for the gleanings. What that boils down to is food oligopoly—no more than 50 brand-name food giants in charge of the food you eat.

So what? Does it hurt to have four-firm oligopolies dominating the grocery shelves? Indeed it does. Heed these words from the final report of the National Commission on Food Marketing: "When a few large firms dominate a field, they frequently forbear from competing actively by price; competition by advertising, sales promotion, and other selling efforts almost always increases; and the market power inescapably at the disposal of such firms may be used to impose onerous terms upon suppliers or consumers."[8]

That is precisely what is happening with dinner. As the few largest food corporations have extended their reach across several food lines, then reached downward within those lines to dominate sales and profits, competition within the food industry has become ludicrous.

The independent firms that are being merged into the large corporate structures are not failures, not inefficient competitors on the verge of folding. Quite the contrary, they are being bought by the giants precisely because they are competitive, innovative and exhibit favorable growth potential. Frequently the companies that are bought are the leading producers of their respective products.

These merges have been under way since the mid-1950s and continue apace today, heightening the already dangerous concentration of food power in fewer companies. As the Federal Trade Commission wrote in 1968, "Merger activity in the current merger movement has been concentrated among the largest food manufacturers. The 50 largest food manufacturers were especially active acquirers."[9]

Why do food companies diversify to become food conglomerates? Because by holding market strength in several food lines, a large company with a heavy advertising budget can begin to squeeze out the competition in any one food line. For example, Borden, which now dominates the market in reconstituted lemon juice, could use its power there to expand its market share in potato chips, using various strategies. One way would be to give buyers of ReaLemon a coupon worth 10¢ on the purchase of a bag of Wise chips. And because of Borden's size and diversity, it can afford to lose money on Wise for a while. Independent potato-chip manufacturers do not have these advantages.

The National Commission on Food Marketing has made a massive and very valuable structural study of the food economy, issuing a final report in 1966 that was promptly ignored. Noting the ability of these emerging food conglomerates to survive their own incompetence and to use their market power across product lines, the Commission warned: "Food conglomerates are likely to grow, to reduce the number of independent competitors in the industry as a whole, and to force the various segments of the industry more nearly into a single system characterized by the kind of nonprice competition in which they excel."[10]

By holding a great many cards, these consumer-products corporations are in a position to expand their market control over practically any food item they choose. It is not unlike the parlor game of Monopoly,* in which a wide range of property is bought around the game

* The game of Monopoly, perhaps instructively, is a product of Parker Brothers, now a wholly owned subsidiary of General Mills, Inc.

board before deals are made among the players to establish monopolies over selected holdings. The final
step—dealing for monopolistic control—is what business executives mean by one of their euphemistic terms:
"internal expansion." Beatrice Foods, for example, is
making that play now, according to a 1971 address by
the company's president:

> We have made a number of acquisitions over the years,
> and we will make more. However, the primary emphasis
> in our company is on profitable growth from within
> through new products, through greater penetration of
> existing markets, and through expansion into new [geo-
> graphic] markets. . . . Internal growth—this is where the
> future of Beatrice lies.[11]

There is a widely held misconception about competition: a vague assumption that competition is its own
regulator, that competition somehow begets competition. Hardly. Think of that game of Monopoly—the
ultimate purpose of competition is to *eliminate* competitors.

Of course, the gathering of brand-name food products
into fewer and fewer conglomerate hands is not happening by chance. Borden did not buy Wise just to be able
to list a potato-chip company among its assets. It intends for Wise to expand its share of the potato-chip
market and to become *the* potato-chip company. The
objective is not to hold a bunch of brand names, but
to hold a bunch of *powerful* brand names.

Supermarket, Superpower

Corporate food power gets hold of you the minute
you walk in the door. Not only are your supermarket
shelves stacked with oligopolies, but there is strong
likelihood that your supermarket itself is an oligopoly.

There are more than 200,000 grocery stores in the
United States, making sales of about $98 billion a
year.[12] Mr. Clarence Adamy, Washington lobbyist for
the National Association of Food Chains, is fond of
surveying such a structure and pronouncing it good.
"My position," he assured congressional probers in
1973, "is that the food retailing industry of the United
States today is the epitome of competition."[13]

Not so fast. There's a measurable competitive difference between the market punch of the local grocer and
the likes of Safeway, A&P and Kroger, which rank as
the 15th, 16th and 28th largest corporations in America. In 1973, the top 20 national supermarket chains
put more than $40 billion of grocery sales into their
coffers—41% of all grocery-store sales that year and
73% of all the sales by grocery chains (see Appendix
A).[14] "Well," you might say, "twenty chains taking only
41% of national grocery sales is a highly competitive
situation, or I'm a pink leprechaun!"

You're a pink leprechaun. The degree of supermarket
oligopoly cannot be measured on the national level for
the simple reason that folks do not buy their groceries
on a national level. When you head out to do the week's
shopping or to pick up a loaf of bread, chances are you
will not leave town to do it. You will stick within a geographic range no wider than a metropolitan area. Economists call that the "relevant market." You would call
it common sense.

It is at the local level that supermarket concentration
is significant—and severe. In a special 1967 Census
Bureau tabulation, the four largest food retailers in 218
local markets were found to share an average of 51.1%
of the grocery sales—a level of economic concentration
generally conceded to reduce price competition.[15] In the
Census Bureau count, market control ranged from a low

of 24.6% by the four leading grocers in Fresno, California, to a high of 80.7% of the market cornered by the big four in Cedar Rapids, Iowa.

Through a private survey, the grocery industry obtains its own yearly analysis of grocery distribution in the top metropolitan areas. This analysis includes an estimate of market shares held by grocers in each city surveyed. The 1973 edition shows oligopoly control by supermarkets to be much tighter than the government had found in 1967. In many areas of the country, the dominance of the big four is shown to be overwhelming, and it is the large multistate supermarket chains that hold nearly all the top spots. Out of 120 positions of market control in the 30 cities listed in Table II—3, the giant chain-store supermarkets held 101, with co-op groceries and independent stores scrambling for the remaining 19 slots. Safeway, A&P and Kroger held 34 of these positions of superpower.[16]

A good chunk of this market monopolization is the result of mergers—large chains buying out competing stores and local chains. A major spate of grocery mergers occurred in the decade beginning in 1955, with the top 20 chain stores doing most of the buying. In that period, the big chains picked up 272 stores and smaller chains, giving them 2,600 more grocery outlets throughout the country and adding nearly $3 billion worth of grocery sales to their balance sheets.[17]

Again, these were not "sick" local businesses being saved by out-of-town grocery knights. For the most part, they were local and regional grocery chains, averaging about 10 stores each, operating efficiently and competing vigorously.[18] The Federal Trade Commission examined 55 local chains that had been purchased by such outfits as National Tea, Kroger, Winn-Dixie, Mayfair and Food Fair. The Commission concluded that the

TABLE II—3
Supermarket Oligopolies in Selected Cities, 1973

Metropolitan Area	% of Area Volume by Top 4 Grocery Retailers	No. of Top 4 That Are Chain-Store Supermarkets	% of Area Volume by Top 2–4 Chain-Store Supermarkets
Akron, Ohio	64.5	3	49.0
Albuquerque, N.M.	74.5	2	46.0
Augusta, Ga.	59.3	all	59.3
Austin, Texas	67.7	3	51.5
Binghamton, N.Y.	51.0	all	51.0
Charlotte, N.C.	65.4	3	51.9
Cleveland, Ohio	62.7	3	53.5
Cocoa, Florida	96.0	all	96.0
Columbia, S.C.	74.0	all	74.0
Denver, Colorado	74.3	3	62.8
El Paso, Texas	77.0	3	59.0
Eugene, Oregon	57.4	3	52.2
Fort Worth, Texas	68.5	all	68.5
Greenville, S.C.	70.0	all	70.0
Indianapolis, Ind.	59.4	all	59.4
Johnstown, Penn.	79.0	3	68.0
Las Vegas, Nevada	57.0	all	57.0
Little Rock, Ark.	86.1	3	66.1
Louisville, Ky.	62.1	3	53.9
Miami, Florida	60.5	all	60.5
Portland, Oregon	74.7	3	55.7
Poughkeepsie, N.Y.	71.0	3	61.0
Raleigh, N.C.	63.3	all	63.3
Sacramento, Calif.	62.5	3	51.4
San Antonio, Texas	75.9	3	66.6
Scranton, Penna.	77.5	3	61.5
Seattle, Washington	88.2	2	68.0
Washington, D.C.	71.8	all	71.8
West Palm Beach, Fla.	70.3	all	70.3
Wilmington, Delaware	64.5	all	64.5

Source: "1973 Grocery Distribution Guide." Metro Market Studies, Inc. Lakewood Circle North, Greenwich, Connecticut. Copyright 1973.

locals had been "effective competitors" and that many
of the mergers "probably hurt potential competition."

What it did was to expand the national chains into
almost every area of the country, to make the national
chains much bigger and to squeeze out local competition.[19] And less competition means more profits for
the supermarketeers.

In a legal case against the National Tea Company, it
was shown that in cities where this supermarket made
under 5% of the sales, its gross profit levels averaged
14.9% of sales. As National Tea gained more control
of the local market, it gained more profits for itself—
when it made more than 35% of a city's grocery sales,
its profits climbed to 17.3%.[20]

That's costing you money. And it is not even money
that stays in your neighborhood, your city, your metropolitan area or your state. Safeway pulls profits of more
than $86 million a year out of some 2,300 stores around
the country, banking them at headquarters in Oakland,
California. This company takes another $4 million from
American neighborhoods each year just to pay its 61
corporate officers and directors. Also, the decisions
about what varieties of food Safeway will offer are made
in Oakland, with no particular regard for the uniqueness
of your community. Each year, the few big supermarkets like Safeway reach further into American communities and increase their share of total grocery sales,
eliminating local competition and digging deeper into
your pocket.

Womb to Tomb

As any "consumer-affairs executive" for any big food
corporation will tell you tirelessly, the food industry
actually is a whole mess of industries. Appearing with
soothing regularity at the local businessmen's luncheons,

these corporate consumerists usually unfurl a chart, with acetate overlays, showing how the farmer buys the fertilizer to grow the crops that are sold on the "free" market to the processors, who put the crops in cans and sell them at a fair profit to wholesalers, who have them transported to urban warehouse centers where grocerymen and restaurateurs come to procure them for final sale to you, taking only the slimmest of profit margins.

It is a logical, competitive structure of the food economy that they diagram—one of food being passed along from one separate industry to another, from the field to your table. If it were a television ad, Euell Gibbons probably would play the farmer and Anita Bryant most certainly would be the happy eater.

But in reality, only one character is needed to play all the middle parts, and that character might even be able to play the farmer's role. That is because the various functions within the food economy are being collected under the corporate umbrellas of the food giants. It is an economic phenomenon termed "vertical integration," which means one firm performing several successive economic functions. In practical terms, it means that a grocery chain like Safeway processes its own ice cream for sale in its stores, or that a turkey processor like Swift owns its own turkey farms.

The idea of vertical integration is to "coordinate" the various steps involved in getting dinner to the table, letting the big processors and retailers put all these steps under their own roofs. Looked at another way, the idea is to allow those big firms to eliminate the fuss of having to buy from independent suppliers and of having to compete among each other for those supplies. It is suggested that these integrated food corporations will achieve cost savings that they will pass on to consumers. This assumption has several flaws. First, there is considerable doubt among reputable economists that vertical integration achieves much saving; second, consumers will be forgiven their skepticism if they question whether today's oligopolistic food economy will allow even slight corporate savings ever to show up as lower food prices; and finally, when and where was it decided that either the consumer or the public interest is better served by big-firm "coordination" than by independent competition?

In any event, it is vertical integration that the food economy is getting. The largest food corporations have been particularly aggressive in developing a concept of "total food systems," as they like to call them. Increasingly, single companies are gaining the power to exert tight control over all aspects of making and delivering food, "from inputs through retailing," as a U.S. Department of Agriculture cheerleader puts it.[21]

Look down on the farm today and you will see the heavy hand of processors and marketers. Coca-Cola's Minute Maid subsidiary is the biggest grower in America of oranges for processing. The largest U.S. chicken farmer is Holly Farms, a subsidiary of Federal Company. Not only does this chicken giant grow, process and package chicken, but it also ships them to market in its own trucks and even fries up a batch of them every day in its Holly Farms chain of eateries, which are a joint enterprise of Holly Farms and Safeway Stores.

Cargill is the largest grain-trading corporation in the world, but it also is in a position to sell seed to grain farmers, then to put the harvested grain in its own railroad cars for transport to its own grain storage elevators. From there, its own oilseed processing plant can convert the grain into vegetable oils, or Cargill's own turkey hatcheries can use it to feed more than 2 million birds a year, or its Burrus Mills subsidiary can process the grain into flours and meals, package it in bags that they make, and sell it to you under their "Light Crust" and "Drinkwater" labels.

Several of the brand-name processors make their own packages—Borden not only makes its own cans but has created a consulting subsidiary that will advise other firms on creating "captive can shops," as they call them. Most of this movement into container-making, according to findings of the Federal Trade Commission, "has been limited to only the very largest food manufacturers."[22] Their interest in making cans might be related directly to the fact that there is money in cans—the FTC said, "The oligopolistic structure of the canmaking industry, plus its history of high profits, suggested that the large canners may have anticipated sharing in high oligopolistic returns from production."

Del Monte Corporation, the largest processor of fruits and vegetables in the world, is so pervasive in its food sphere that it claims in a magazine ad to be able to meet your needs "from womb to tomb." It is worth reviewing the vertical structure of a firm with such Orwellian potential.[23] (See pp. 32–33.)

This chart does not include other in-house incidentals at work for Del Monte, such as its own land-and-office-development subsidiary, and its own lobbyist to meet the company's need in Washington. Enormous economic power exists in a corporate structure of such vertical inclusiveness. If you wanted to enter into competition with Del Monte, perhaps processing and selling canned pineapple, you would find this degree of integration overwhelming. Your product might be better in taste and nutrition, and it might be more efficiently produced, but you would not have your own pineapple plantations in Kenya, nor would you have such advantages as several label-printing and can-manufacturing plants, exten-

sive transportation and storage facilities, a national sales
force to assure your product prime shelf space in supermarkets, a $16-million-a-year advertising budget, and
even your own marketing outlets through airlines,
schools and restaurants.

That kind of punch knocks out both current and
potential competitors. Del Monte not only is the biggest
canned fruit and vegetable manufacturer, but its rev-
enues are greater than those of its next two competitors
combined—Libby, McNeil & Libby, and Stokely Van
Camp. And if there is any question whether Del Monte
has the economic power to take care of you from womb
to tomb, they also have a private protection subsidiary,
which Del Monte claims to be the "best trained private
police force in the country." Maybe that is what the
guy in Del Monte's television ad means when he tells
the kid, "Eat your peas."

Supermarkets, too, are vertical integrators, especially
the big ones. We hear a great deal in the news about the
wholesale price index, and grocery retailers especially
are quick during times of high food prices to point to
the wholesale cost of food as a squeeze on their profits.
Supermarketeers, however, frequently turn out to be
their own wholesalers. A group of economic analysts
reported in 1972 that "four out of five firms in the
supermarket industry have their own central warehouse
or else are affiliated with a retailer-owned cooperative
or a wholesaler-sponsored voluntary chain."[24] The biggest four supermarket chains all have their own warehousing and distribution networks established throughout the country.

The largest chain stores also have become major
processors of several food items. Seven-Eleven manufactures 73% of the milk sold in its company stores, and
it makes a wide range of the other products it retails,

Del Monte Corporation
(1974 sales of $1,042,608,000)

SEED FARMS

FARMERS
10,000 U.S. farmers under contract

FOOD AND AGRICULTURAL RESEARCH

$7,500,000 annual budget
500 full-time employees
6 research and new-product development laboratories

AGRICULTURAL PRODUCTION

55 farms, ranches, plantations and orchards
132,700 acres of Del-Monte-farmed land in the U.S., Canada, Kenya, Latin America and the Philippines
Unknown number of beef feedlots in the U.S., the Philippines and South America, and fishing fleets in the Pacific and Atlantic Oceans.

PROCESSING

(In 15 states and 9 foreign countries)
59 canneries
3 dried-fruit plants
15 snack-food, specialty and frozen-food plants

INPUTS

15 can-manufacturing plants
2 label-printing plants

TRANSPORTATION
21 air-freight forwarding stations
5 banana-transport ships
9 tuna seiners and transport ships
Salmon boats
1 ocean terminal
7 trucking operations

STORAGE & DISTRIBUTION
15 distribution warehouses
1 tuna freezer-storage plant

ADVERTISING
$16+ million annual budget for national network TV, radio, magazines, etc.

MARKETING
1,220 salespeople in 58 sales offices throughout the U.S. and abroad
250 independent brokers
Market research staff

FOOD SERVICE
712 food-service accounts (United Airlines, nursing homes, hotels, school lunch programs, industrial plants, etc.)
409 food-vending accounts (3,000 Del-Monte-owned vending machines)
28 public restaurants catered by Del Monte

BRANDS
Argo canned seafood
Award frozen foods
Del Monte
Dew Drop asparagus
Grand Tour frozen foods
Granny Goose snacks
Perky meat and fruit pies

from orange juice to pantyhose. In 1963, Safeway, A&P, Kroger and Jewel Stores manufactured 63% of the bread and 52% of the coffee sold in their stores. Food manufacturing by the big retailers has grown considerably since then, with Safeway, for example, reporting in 1973, "We operate our own milk plants, bread plants, ice cream plants; we roast and pack our own coffee, manufacture jams and jellies, detergents, soft drinks, luncheon meats, vegetable oils, and other products." The company's director of supply operations considers all this "an unmatched resource that Safeway enjoys."[25]

It is frequently argued that, while entry into food processing by the giant chain stores may result in less competition among grocery retailers, it gives a badly needed competitive charge to the food-processing industries. Unfortunately, no. Borden, Swift, Wonder Bread, Del Monte, General Foods, Coca-Cola, Unilever and other food-processing powers are more than able to hold their own markets against the "house brands" of the retailers; it is the little guys that get bumped off the shelves. As the Federal Trade Commission concluded, "The chief impact of retailer integration into food manufacturing appears to have been a weakening of smaller manufacturers relative to larger ones."[26]

Someone's in the Kitchen with Dinah

In a position to grow food, process it, package and ship it, wholesale and retail it, the same corporations now are taking the final step for you: cooking and serving it. Like farming, the restaurant business has been one of the last refuges of small, independent entrepreneurs—a spot in an economy of goliaths where an individual family could establish and distinguish itself. Using big capital and heavy advertising, food manufacturers increasingly are integrating forward to take over the kitchen (see Table II–4):

Not to be left out entirely, a couple of the biggest grocery chains also have moved into the restaurant business. Lucky Stores recently purchased Sirloin Stockade, a chain of more than 100 restaurants in the Midwest, and Safeway operates 25 fried-chicken restaurants in a joint venture with Holly Farms.

The movement of monopolistic food giants into the high-volume, high-margin restaurant business will expand their profit potential, but it will not make your dinner any cheaper, make it taste better or cause it to be any better for you. Souzen Deavers, writing in *Nation's Restaurant News,* suggested that those big food firms were out to "flex the same big marketing muscle and apply the same selling savvy to feeding operations as demonstrated in their manufacturing and processing businesses."[27]

In any event, the giants are there in the kitchen, many of them able to harvest dinner with one hand and serve it to you with the other. You still have the prerogative of chewing it.

Profits: Suite Sweets

The tighter the oligopoly, the sweeter the profits. In its 1966 study of the food-manufacturing industry, the Federal Trade Commission delved into the relationship between market structure and profits. The Commission found that profits climbed dramatically as the level of competition fell. In this important study, the food corporations that operated in competitive markets averaged net profits of 7.5%, while those that operated in highly oligopolistic markets doubled that level, averaging net profits of 14.2% (see Appendix B).[28]

TABLE II—4
Some Corporate Cooks

Food Manufacturing Company	Primary Food Brands	Restaurants Owned
AMFAC, Inc.	Pacific Pearl seafood products; Lamb-Weston processed foods; Wilhelm processed beef products; sugar.	Fred Harvey Restaurants
Borden	Borden; Drake's; Wyler; Lambert's; Aunt Jane's; Bama; ReaLemon; Wise; Cracker Jacks; None Such; Campfire; etc.	Borden Burger
Campbell Soup	Campbell; Bounty; V-8; Franco-American; Pepperidge Farm.	Clark's Restaurants Herfy's Restaurants Hanover Trail Steakhouses
Campbell Taggart	Rainbo bread; Manor bread; Colonial bread; Kilpatrick's bread.	Rainbo Donut Shops
Carnation	Carnation; Contadina; Coffee Mate; Splender; Spreadables; Chef Mate; Special Morning; Albers.	Carnation Ice Cream Restaurants
Consolidated Foods	Sara Lee; Shasta soft drinks; Booth seafood products; Kahn's meats; Lawson's dairy products; Hollywood candies; Bryan meats; Union sugar; etc.	L-K Restaurants Lyons Restaurants Manners Restaurants Big Boy (some franchises)

CPC International	Skippy peanut butter; Bosco chocolate syrup Hellmann's mayonnaise; Mazola corn oil anc margarine; Thomas English muffins; Best Foods grocery products; etc.	Dutch Pantry Restaurants Bressler's Ice Cream Shops Dean Foods (Hoffman House)
Esmark	Swift meats; Butterball turkey; Peter Pan peanut butter; Allsweet margarine.	Dipper Dan Ice Cream Shops
General Foods	Maxwell House; Sanka; Yuban; Post cereals; Bird's Eye processed vegetables; Jell-O; Shake 'N Bake; Cool Whip; Swans Down; Kool-Aid; Stove Top; etc.	Burger Chef
General Mills	Betty Crocker; Bisquick; Gold Medal; Tom's snacks; Slim Jim Sausage snacks; Cheerios; Wheaties; Total; etc.	Red Lobster Inns Betty Crocker Tree House Restaurants
W.R. Grace	SeaPak frozen seafood; Leaf candies; Wayne Bun candies; Morton snacks; Nalley's snacks and convience foods; W.R. Grace canned foods.	Chain of 87 steak houses and coffee shops, individually named
Great Western United	GW sugar.	Shakey's Pizza Restaurants
Green Giant	Green Giant; LeSueur; Clark soups; Jolly puddings; Ovencrock beans; Dawn Fresh mushrooms; Holloway House frozen dinners.	Henrici's Restaurants Holloway House Cafeterias Ontra Cafeterias Red Balloon Restaurants

Food Manufacturing Company	Primary Food Brands	Restaurants Owned
H.J. Heinz	Heinz; Ore-Ida potato and onion products; Star-Kist tuna.	Chain of fast-food restaurants on West coast
Heublein	A-1 steak sauce; Escoffier sauces; Grey Poupon mustard; Regina wine vinegars; Ortega Mexican foods; Snap-E-Tom tomato cocktail; Inglenook wines; Italian Swiss Colony wines; Smirnoff liquors; etc.	Col. Sanders Kentucky Fried Chicken restaurants
International Multifoods	Kretschmer wheat germ; Robin Hood flour, mixes and bread; Sun Country Granola; IMCO eggs; Reuben processed meats; Hickory Farm of Ohio cheese and specialty items; Rose pickles; Kaukauna Klub cheeses; etc.	Mister Donut Sveden House Restaurants T. Butcherblock Steak Houses
Kane-Miller	K-M meats and grocery products; Monarch wines; Bayshore poultry; Lumberjack meats.	Mayflower Coffee Shops Calico Kitchens
Kraftco	Kraft; Breakstone; Sealtest; Breyers ice cream; Parkay; Light 'n Lively; Velveeta; etc.	Sealtest Flavorland Shops
Labatt Breweries (Canada)	Labatt beer and ales.	Mannings Restaurants
LaTouraine-Bickford's Foods	LaTouraine coffee; Bickford's grocery products.	Bickford's Pancake Houses Zeke's Restaurants
Lawry's Foods	Lawry's spices, mixes, salad dressings, etc.	Several restaurants in California and elsewhere, individually named

Nestlé (Switzerland)	Nestlé candies; Libby, McNeil & Libby processed fruits and vegetables; Beringer Brothers wines; Stouffer frozen dinners; etc.	Stouffer Restaurants
Ocean Spray Cranberries	Ocean Spray cranberry products.	Five restaurants in Massachusetts, individually named
Ogden Corporation	Tillie Lewis processed fruit and vegetable and meat products; Flavor Pict Food products; Anderson gourmet soups; Tasti-Diet grocery products.	Nedick's Restaurants
Pet	Pet; Heartland cereal; Old El Paso Mexican foods; Funsten nuts; Musselman's apple products; Sego diet foods; Downeyflake flour; Whitman's Sampler candies; etc.	Stuckey's Restaurants
Pillsbury	Pillsbury; Poppin Fresh; Funny Face drink mixes.	Burger King Restaurants Poppin Fresh Pie Shops
Quaker Oats	Quaker; King Vitaman; Life; Cap 'n Crunch; Willy Wonka; Aunt Jemima flour and mixes; Flako pie crust mix; Celeste frozen pizza; etc.	Magic Pan Restaurants
Ralston Purina	Ralston Purina; Checkerboard poultry; Chicken-of-the-Sea tuna; Ry-Krisps; Chex; Freakies; etc.	Jack-in-the-Box Restaurants

Food Manufacturing Company	Primary Food Brands	Restaurants Owned
Riviana Foods	Hebrew National kosher foods; Austex Mexican foods; Wolff's specialties; Shady-Lane specialties; Hill's diet foods; etc.	Lum's Restaurants
Smithfield Foods	Smithfield meats.	Fass Brothers Fish Houses
Squibb Corporation	Beech-Nut chewing gum; Life Savers candies; Table Talk pies.	Dobbs House Restaurants Toddle House Restaurants
Unilever	Lipton tea and soups; Good Humor ice cream; Wish Bone salad dressings; Luck Whip topping; Knox gelatine; Mrs. Butterworth's syrup; Imperial margarine; etc.	Good Humor Ice Cream Shops
United Brands	Chiquita bananas and lettuce; Morrell meats; Ostrow meats; Inter Harvest fresh vegetables; Broadcast canned meats; etc.	A & W Drive-In Restaurants
Zion Foods	Zion kosher meats; Squire meats; Vermont meats.	Smokehouse Restaurants

Sources: *Nation's Restaurant News*, April 30, 1973, p. 1.
Telephone interview with Souzen Deavers of *Nation's Restaurant News*, July 3, 1974.
Directory of Corporate Affiliations, 1974: Who Owns Whom, Skokie, Illinois, National Register Publishing Company.
Individual annual reports to stockholders of the various corporations.

In March of 1974, following a solid year of phenomenal rises in the prices of food, President Nixon pointed to the money that American farmers were making— "the farmers," he asserted in a press conference, "have never had it so good."[29] Farm people did not take at all kindly to that presidential assessment, suggesting that it was the verbal equivalent of stepping in a fresh cow pattie. At the time that Nixon was pronouncing his judgment of the food economy, the *farm* price of food was falling for the sixth straight month. But the *supermarket* price of food still was rising.

There is no question that farmers made money in 1973, finally getting their income up to where it had been in 1952. But even in that peak year, farmers took only 46¢ of the consumer's food dollar." The rest went to the corporate middlemen separating farmers and consumers. After Nixon spoke, even before spring was over, the farmer's share had fallen below 40¢, and consumers still were not getting relief at the checkout counters.

If the President had said that oligopolistic middlemen never had it so good, he would have been more on target. The lobbyists for food corporations, as well as Department of Agriculture officials, regularly downplay the profit levels of food corporations, usually by practicing the deception of lumping all food-manufacturing firms together. For example, 1973 was not that great a year for the average of all 32,000 food-manufacturing firms. But the 50 or so oligopolistic firms that dominate the industry and collect about 75% of all the profits had "a year to remember," as *Business Week* put it. The big food makers whined all that year about government price controls squeezing their profits, but Table II–5 (page 42) shows a group that whined all the way to the bank.

Food retail chains were particularly vocal against

TABLE II—5

Food Company	1973 Profits	% Increase over 1972
Anderson-Clayton	$24.8 million	40%
Campbell Soup	80.7 "	23
Castle & Cook (Dole)	26.9 "	52
Del Monte	32.9 "	35
Federal (Holly Farms)	12.4 "	80
Green Giant	9.2 "	25
International Multifoods	11.6 "	23
Kane-Miller	9.5 "	147
Pillsbury	26.2 "	39
Ralston Purina	80.4 "	23

Source: *Business Week.* "1973 Profits: A Year to Remember."
    March 9, 1974, pp. 89–90.

government price controls, and throughout the 1973 period of skyrocketing food prices, chain-store officials and lobbyists assured a skeptical public that their profits were cut right down to the bone. But *Business Week* later listed the 1973 profits of 27 of the biggest chains and found that they averaged a profit increase in 1973 of 32%.[31]

The power of food processors and retailers was made particularly clear late in 1973 and early 1974 over the matter of beef. The price of meat climbed ruthlessly in 1973, leading the general rise in prices. Cattle ranchers did very well early in 1973, but so did such Wall Street cowboys as Iowa Beef Processors, with a 66% profit increase over the previous year, and American Beef Packers, with a 288% profit increase. In August, however, the ranchers' price began to plummet, falling in the spring of 1974 below what it cost them to produce cattle. But the middlemen did not get hurt as the cost of beef fell—Iowa Beef Processors, for example, had another 50% profit increase through the third quarter of 1974.

It was the supermarkets, however, that were doing especially well in the beef business. In September of 1973, the cattleman's price for a pound of beef fell 17¢, but the supermarketeer's price rose 17¢.[32] That's 34¢ worth of fun for the middlemen. While cattlemen were going out of business, oligopolistic grocery chains were going to the bank—*Business Week* figures showed that the biggest chains increased their profits another 48% through the first three quarters of 1974. Even U.S. Agriculture Secretary Earl Butz, no harsh critic of food corporations, had to chastise the chains: "If retail stores would reduce their profit margins to something like normal levels, they could pay the farmers more, or charge consumers less, or both," he said in March 1974.

What about the constant refrain from supermarkets that they make no more than 1% profit on their sales? What they avoid telling you is that they make that profit every time they turn over their volume, which happens about 10 to 20 times a year. Consider it this way: A farmer invests $50,000 to grow sweet corn, which he sells later in the year to a processor for maybe $52,000—a 4% annual profit. A supermarket chain invests $50,000 to put cans of sweet corn on its shelves, pricing it at cost plus a 1% profit ($50,500). But it sells out of the sweet corn in a month. So it takes its 1% profit off the top ($500) and uses the same $50,000 to put another batch of sweet corn on the shelves. Again, the supermarket sells out within a month. At the end of the year, the same $50,000 has been reinvested 12 times, earning the store $6,000—a 12% annual profit. The economist's phrase for that *actual* profit rate is "return on investment."

In 1973, USDA Secretary Butz told an ABC television newsman that high profits for food middlemen in that year were only a temporary phenomenon, that the reporter would only have to look back over the past four or five years at the average return-on-investment figures to see that the food business was not all that profitable. But if you check up on the Secretary's assertion, you will find that the big companies were quite profitable over that period. In fact, food and drink ranked sixth out of 30 industries graded in the January 1, 1974, issue of *Forbes* magazine, with a median return on investment of 12.9% for five years. That level of profitability ranked the big food manufacturers higher than such industries as banking, electronics, energy, chemicals and steel.

The published profit figures of food corporations generally understate the actual earnings that the giants take. For example, some "profits" never show up as such because they have been pocketed by top corporate officers as salary increases and bonuses. While farmers began to go out of business at the end of 1973, and while consumers clutched their pocketbooks and cinched up their belts, top food executives in the biggest corporations quietly boosted their own salaries. Perhaps they needed the boost in order to buy food.

Published profit figures also fail to account for the extent of vertical integration among the largest companies. A great many "expenses" subtracted from earnings by vertically integrated food corporations in fact are paid to themselves, including a profit margin for the self-service.

An official of Supermarkets General Corporation participated in an industry press briefing in Washington in 1973 to correct "a host of erroneous judgments" that he felt the public was making about the supermarkets' role in high food prices. He offered this version of truth in food-industry profits:

From every dollar that the customer spends, 78.7¢ goes to our suppliers for the goods they sell us. 9.6¢ goes to salaries of our employees. 3.2¢ goes for rent, utilities and maintenance. 2.6¢ goes for warehousing and transportation. 1.8¢ goes for supplier and other expenses. In 1972, only 1.3¢ was left for taxes and profit.[33]

That's a pretty grim picture, until it is remembered that Supermarkets General, Safeway, A&P, Kroger, Jewel, Lucky, Southland, Winn-Dixie and the few other dominant giants supply a sizable portion of their own goods, thus paying themselves some of that 78.7¢. The 9.6¢ for salaries includes more than $100,000 each for the head honchos of these eight supermarkets, with five of them making more than $200,000 a year. And most of these big eight pay rent to themselves, have their own warehousing facilities and operate their own transportation systems. Up in the executive suites of the biggest food firms, things are nowhere near as tough as they would have you believe.

Who's in Charge Here?

The monopolization of the food economy is not occurring because of the immutable march of some economic imperative. It is occurring because corporations want it to, because government has been obsequious to corporate desires, and because the general public either has not noticed that it was happening, or has noticed but not demanded to see the manager about it.

Until 1973, Robert W. Long was serving as the Senior Vice-President for Agricultural Loans at the Bank of America, the world's largest bank. His bank finances half of California agribusiness. Mr. Long was not born on a farm and never operated one, though a 4-H club did name him an honorary farmer once. But he has been a prime mover in shaping the structure of California's corporate agriculture. His vision of the total food economy is just as corporate. While at the bank, Long urged "consolidation within the food industry to present a solid front to the consuming public," and in 1968 he wrote ominously that "new laws may be required to legalize a better marketing system which would call for a considerable interlocking of interests among people in the food industry."[34]

In 1973, Robert Long was invited to bring these views to Washington, there to serve Earl Butz as an Assistant Secretary of Agriculture. At his confirmation hearings in the Senate, held in the Agriculture Committee's incongruously ornate meeting room, the tall, well-dressed Long looked every inch the banker he is. It is not uncommon at these public hearings for visiting groups and tourists to view the proceedings, and at Long's hearing, a group of Midwest Farm Bureau members were in attendance. Midway through, having listened to the banker's views on agriculture and the food economy, one farmer leaned to another and whispered, a little disgustedly: "He don't know a damn thing about farming."

True, but it was the farmer who missed the significance of the appointment, not Long. The new agriculture is not calling for farmers, particularly not in decision-making positions. It is calling for the profit-sensitive executives of giant corporations.

The impact of food monopolies is only just beginning to be felt. Having established positions of power, there is a corporate confidence that the rest is just a mopping-up activity and that the future of dinner is theirs to remake. "Adapt" to the new Total Food Systems "or die," Earl Butz has coldly informed American family farmers, "resist, and perish."

What does that leave for consumers? Early in 1973, Department of Agriculture economists predicted that "multi-product processing firms will probably assume even greater control over the food system," and the economists talked unemotionally of structural changes in the food economy, describing them as a "shift from a commodity production orientation to a consumer product merchandising orientation."[35]

Translated from bureaucratese, that means you can expect less of nature's own stuff and more conglomerate concoctions sold to you by means of brand-name identification. *Business Week* magazine reported in July 1973 that the giant consumer-product merchandisers are gearing up their food-manufacturing and merchandising capacity to grind out more convenience foods, snack foods and fast-food chains. Those are the areas where there is the most growth potential for corporate profits. That promises consumers a food future modeled on Mr. Wonderfull's Surprize, Lucky Whip and Jack-in-the-Box.*

* Mr. Wonderfull's Surprize is a new cereal creation by General Mills. The big surprise, in addition to the toy inside the box, is that the contents are 30% sugar and 14% fat, and it costs $1.40 a pound. Lucky Whip is a fabrication of Unilever's imagination, containing only water, vegetable oil, sugar and more than a dozen chemicals, for which you pay more than you would for real whipping cream. Jack-in-the-Box is the fast-food hamburger chain owned by Ralston Purina.

CHAPTER III

Consumers:
Footing the Bill

Eaters have been the last to know about oligopolies. Up to the 1970s, Americans paid little attention to dinner, except to eat it. With prices low, with food abundant, with brand names too numerous to count and with advertising drumming a steady beat, it simply did not occur to most people that any change was taking place in the food economy—at least none that appeared to affect them. Sure, farmers were going out of business, but government and industry were quick to assure us that it was "inevitable"—after all, the mom & pop store had succumbed too, hadn't it? In fact, few economic structures have changed so radically as the food system with so little notice or protest.

Early in 1973, a group of public-interest organizations in Washington, D.C., teamed up to launch a "Food Action Campaign," hoping to reach the consuming public with the information that concentrated corporate power was making a grab for dinner. To help articulate the issue, FAC called on a few people with particular credibility to join as advocates, to travel around the country for a few months talking to people about

48

the alarming power and impact of food corporations—a Del Monte, for example.

The campaign thought it would be a good idea to ask Bess Myerson, who had just resigned as New York City's consumer-affairs director, to be an advocate. The request went through Ms. Myerson's staff, and they promised to bring it up with her and get back to FAC. After days passed, word finally came that Ms. Myerson felt she could not assist in the campaign because (1) she did not want to get involved in any campaigns at the time, and (2) she had never met anyone named "Adelle Monte."

With that, the Food Action Campaign realized that it had a long way to go to make people aware of corporate food power. Consumers were asleep at the switch.

But not for long; in 1973 food shoppers across America were jolted awake. All it took was the sharp pinch of the fastest- and highest-rising food prices in memory. Not only did the people yelp, but many of them found themselves out on the streets demanding that somebody do something. Predictably, the first reaction by startled officials was to dodge the issue. Food corporations responded in their inimitable fashion by hurriedly appointing "consumer advisors" and by trotting out every piece of window dressing that they could muster—Del Monte Corporation touchingly even dedicated its 1973 annual report to consumers. Government, in its way, responded dully by assuring folks that everything was just fine—the Agriculture Department rushed out the first of several versions of a 24-page pamphlet basically telling people that food is cheaper in the United States than it is in Tokyo, Bonn and Rome.

To practically everyone's surprise, however, consumers did not quiet down and slink off. Nor did they just stand there and shriek mindlessly. Instead, consumer organizations began to study food issues, to harden their demands and to do something for themselves. To the chagrin of food officialdom, consumers began to ask hard questions about food economics. Someone even shook Congress awake—1973 and 1974 witnessed four major congressional investigations of monopoly power in the food economy. Worse, yet, from the perspective of vertically integrated food powers, consumers and farmers began to talk to each other.

What finally will come of this new dawn is unknown, but at least it is brighter than we've had in a while, and it is sending folks off in the right direction. The issues of food prices, nutritional quality, taste and choice of foods finally boil down to the economic structure that produces and delivers food. It is the oligopolistic structure behind dinner that must be examined and challenged.

What's Happened to Food Prices?

With the price leaps of the last few years, few food shoppers would be surprised to see supermarkets have to get bigger cash registers to calculate the bill and hold the money. Food prices soared by 16% in 1973, another 16% in 1974, and are expected to rise another 15 to 20% in 1975. In short, food prices have gone up by half in just three years. The government's response to the food shopper's plight was curious:

—With heavy overtones of Marie Antoinette, the Secretary of Agriculture publicly welcomed rising beef prices as "the best way to insure a good supply of the better cuts of beef that I prefer."

—The Chairman of the Federal Reserve Board recommended that consumers switch from beef to cheese, apparently unaware that cheese prices also had risen out of sight.

—The President assured Americans in his State of the Union address that they "are living more abundantly than ever before," even though the buying power of the wage earner's paycheck had been falling for some time.

—The White House advisor for consumer affairs rushed out to advise people to "shop harder in grocery stores," and she suggested in lilting tones that such low-cost by-products as liver, kidney, brain and heart "can be made into a gourmet meal with a little imagination, some seasoning and by cooking them a little longer."

—The Secretary of Labor thought that people might plant victory gardens.

—The Chairman of the Council of Economic Advisors insisted in March of 1973 that prices might rise for a couple of months, but that it was a "temporary situation."

—The Undersecretary of Agriculture asserted with a straight face that food prices were not too high, because if they were "the housewife would back out of the marketplace and the cost would go down," though he offered no insight into how one backs out of the market for food and lives to tell about it.

While food shoppers were being driven to the wall by food prices, and being driven up the wall by the statements of government officials, executives of the dominant food corporations were being driven to the bank in the company limousines with handsome profit increases. "That food and its cost is naturally important to all does not mean the basic objective of the industry is to keep profits so low that nobody is happy to be part of the food industry," admonished one grocery official, smiling inscrutably.[1] What was going on?

Government and corporate officials point to shortages in basic foodstuffs as the cause of higher prices, blaming such factors as worldwide weather abnormalities, the unreasonable demands of American consumers, the disappearance of anchovies from the fishing waters of Peru, the appearance of beef-eating in Japan, the Russian wheat deal and even the increased food demand brought about by American poor people using food stamps. These factors, they note, combined in 1973 to push up the price of raw farm commodities.

Quite right. But there is another factor that went unmentioned: the power of shared monopolies. As *Consumer Reports* noted in an article assessing the price increases: "Since competition determines price in the

Blaine. The *Spectator*. Canada. Reprinted with permission.

classical scheme of things, it follows that the consumer interest demands healthy competition among food middlemen. But available indicators suggest that competition is generally ailing in that giant industry."[2]

It is true that 1973 and 1974 were abnormal crop years, generally raising the price of farm commodities skyward. But farmers, who are highly competitive with each other, rise and fall from year to year as production goes from shortage to surplus. The same ought to be true of the middle sector, but it is not. That is because of the market dominance of a few corporations—the middle sector of the food economy is rife with oligopolies. These firms are in a position to pass along any cost increase that they incur, plus adding on a little extra for themselves; and as the cost of the raw product falls, oligopolies are in a position to hold consumer prices high. Increasingly, it is a power that food middlemen can exert year in and year out. In a food economy characterized by shared monopolies, prices steadily go up, and they do not come down.

Consumers in 1974 spent over $125 billion to take food home. Raw farm commodities—the production of farmers—account for only 40% of that food tab. The other three-fifths of the total goes to food processors, distributors and retailers. Not only did the middlemen in 1973 and 1974 pass through to the consumer all of the increased prices of raw commodities, but they also added a 6.5% increase to their own bill in 1973 and another 21% increase in 1974. That is the pricing power of food oligopolies, and that is the power that an FTC official pointed to in 1973: "I believe," Dr. Russell Parker told a Senate committee, "that a very significant cause of high food prices is monopoly and oligopoly in U.S. food industries."[3]

The Cost of Business

When you lay down a dollar for food, what do you buy besides food? According to the textbooks, you buy processing of the food, you buy transportation from the fields to the shelves, you buy the wages of those who process and distribute the food, you buy the package the food comes in, you buy advertising that informs you of the product's existence, and you buy the profits of the processors, distributors and retailers. Fair enough.

But in an oligopolistic food system, business basics are distorted and prices are inflated. You can throw out the textbooks. Instead of competing on the basis of price, efficiency or product quality, oligopolies tend to compete on the basis of advertising. No longer is the advertising message informative; it is reduced to slogans and gimmicks.

Examples abound but a couple will do here for illustration. Canada Dry ginger ale is not advertised as being cheaper or better, but on the idea that it "tastes like love." Borden is entering the peanut-butter market, using the Cracker Jacks label. It will not advertise that its peanut butter is more efficiently produced or more nutritious than other brands, but that it is the only peanut butter with a prize inside. The high cost of such fluff is added into the price you pay.

There are other little extras that you pay for at the checkout counter, and none of them adds anything to the value of the food. The hardest to swallow is "image advertising" by corporations. These are television and print ads that attempt to tell you how "good" a corporation is—U.S. Steel is "involved," they insist; Weyerhauser plants more trees than it cuts down; ITT is engaged in medical research to help mankind; Exxon is spending night, day and lots of money looking for oil. Related to image ads are "goodwill" expenditures—such things as sponsoring a golf tournament, entering a float in the Rose Bowl parade or presenting a public-interest television program. The cost of it all is a cost of doing business, and you are the one who foots the bill.

The latest move by food companies is to show their oneness with consumers. There is hardly a big food processor or a major supermarket chain that is without a consumer advisor these days. "She's the voice of the consumer at the management level and the voice of the supermarket to the consumers," declared Armour's director of consumer services. There are so many such advisors in big business that they met in 1973 to form the Society of Consumer Affairs Professionals in Business. They met, appropriately enough, in Disneyland. There is no truth to the cynical rumor that Mickey Mouse chaired the session. But it is true that everytime you buy an Armour ham or practically any other brand-name food, you pay a little extra to cover the consumer advisor's salary.

That salary is the cheapest one you pay for. Food executives seem never to cease complaining about the cost of labor, and they are constantly in the market for any piece of technology that will replace working people. But it is in the executive suites that nests really are being feathered. In 1973, food-industry workers had wage increases of only 6%.[4] Upstairs, however, there was much less restraint—executives of the big food processors increased their salaries by 18%, while the executives of the big grocery chains were taking home a 24% pay boost.[5] Table III–1 shows about $64 million in executive salaries that you picked up in 1973.

There is a wide range of additional costs of business that add to your bill, including such items as main-

TABLE III—1

Executive Pay Levels in 25 Major Food Corporations, 1973

Food Corporation	Total Remuneration of All Officers And Directors	Number In Group	Total Remuneration* of the Top Executive Officer 1972	Total Remuneration* of the Top Executive Officer 1973
1. Anheuser-Busch	$ 1,943,277	34	$350,000	$342,000
2. Beatrice Foods	2,768,602	34	313,000	320,000
3. Borden, Inc.	2,075,204	27	329,000	335,000
4. Campbell Soup	2,442,933	40	157,000	228,000
5. Coca-Cola	2,731,480	52	300,000	306,000
6. Consolidated Foods	3,514,303	41	223,000	261,000
7. CPC International	2,166,173	35	210,000	236,000
8. Del Monte	3,220,908	44	165,000	438,000
9. General Foods	3,724,318	47	260,000	190,000
10. General Mills	2,525,311	31	279,000	316,000
11. H. J. Heinz	1,895,829	18	296,000	368,000
12. Heublein	2,598,265	29	311,000	394,000

13. Jewel Stores	2,036,483	39	213,000	284,000
14. Kraftco	1,972,605	28	264,000	321,000
15. Lucky Stores	2,197,852	30	297,000	300,000
16. Marriott	2,643,405	35	121,000	150,000
17. McDonald's	2,245,012	33	175,000	175,000
18. Nabisco	2,577,217	40	301,000	170,000
19. Oscar Mayer	2,653,669	31	219,000	227,000
20. Pillsbury	2,912,128	54	186,000	131,000
21. Quaker Oats	2,752,316	40	213,000	284,000
22. Safeway Stores	3,881,888	61	204,000	217,000
23. Schlitz Brewing Co.	1,968,750	40	301,000	300,000
24. United Brands	1,952,077	37	200,000	248,000
25. Winn-Dixie Stores	2,361,547	27	235,000	236,000

Total Sum for 25 Corporations: $63,730,552   Medians: $235,000 $284,000

* Total Remuneration includes salary, bonuses, deferred compensation and director's fees.

Sources: Forbes. "Annual Directory Issue." May 15, 1973, pp. 186–223.
Forbes. "Annual Directory Issue." May 15, 1974, pp. 168–203.

taining lobbyists in Washington, making a fleet of limousines and drivers available to corporate executives, creating additional administrative bureaucracies to manage diversified holdings, paying corporate "bonuses" to executives that end up as campaign contributions to favored politicians, and even the increasing frequency of such executive-suite crimes as embezzlement, kickbacks and theft of merchandise. These executive crimes, says a New York management consultant, costs $10 billion a year and is increasing at the rate of 15% a year: "We saw it happen because of increased mergers, acquisitions, decentralization of operations, computerization and displacement of owner-managers."[6]

Americans effectively pay double for the cost of business. Not only are all of these costs tabulated and added to the price of the food you buy, but they also are subtracted from corporate income when it comes time to pay taxes.

Processing, Packaging, Pricing and Profiteering

"The old simple concept of food as a staple, basic commodity and of a sovereign consumer with a clearly defined demand for food," wrote three economists recently, "is being cast aside."

> Industry seeks to create consumer demand for differentiated products and then to tailor the marketing and production processes accordingly. This is a process that has been used effectively in the production and marketing of automobiles, television sets, and numerous other consumer items.[7]

It gets down to this: Processing and packaging of food are becoming more important pricing factors than the food itself.

Why would food corporations rather sell highly proc- essed and packaged food than the much simpler matter of selling basics? Because processing and packaging spell profits.

First, the more you do to a product, the more chances there are to build in profit margins—Heinz can sell tomatoes for a profit, or it can bottle the tomatoes for a bigger profit, or it can process the tomatoes into ketchup for still more profit, or it can add spices to the ketchup and sell it as barbeque sauce for a fat profit, or it can add flavors and meat tenderizer to the barbeque sauce for the fattest profit of all.

Second, processing and packaging allows artificial differentiation of one company's product from that of another—in other words, selling on the basis of brand- names. Potatoes can be sold in bulk, or they can be put in a sack and labeled Sun Giant, which will bring a higher price and more profit.

Third, processing and packaging allow the use of additives to keep the same item on the shelf much longer, and they allow for shipment over long distances, thus expanding the geographic reach of a corporation.

Fourth, processing and packaging separate consumers from the price of raw food, allowing oligopolistic mid- dlemen to hold up the consumer price of their products even when the farm price falls. When the spinach crop is so abundant that spinach prices tumble at the farm level, the supermarket price of Stouffer's frozen spinach soufflé does not go down.

Although processing of food can range from simply brushing the dirt off raw potatoes to the complexity of taking potatoes apart and putting them back together again, very little food is available anymore that has not been handled at least slightly by a processor. American eaters no longer see much resemblance between the packaged food they buy and the whole foods that came off the farm. Some kids are growing up thinking that chickens have six legs, because that is how many come in a package. Already, more than half of the total turkey production in the country is either cut into parts for sale (17%) or even further processed for sale (36%).

We are eating more processed food both because consumers have sought more convenience built into the food they buy and because processing fits snugly with the profit plans of oligopolistic food manufacturers.

"The processor is guided by the wants and desires of the consumer," intoned a Department of Agriculture publication, "and the consumer's demand for food is shifting from raw commodities to more sophisticated products."[8] That is not quite the rock-solid truth that USDA believes it to be. Clearly, few people want to churn their own butter anymore, or take time in the morning to make coffee cake from scratch, but just as clearly, few people are so lazy as to insist that Kraftco make a margarine that can be squeezed ready-melted from a plastic bottle, nor did people surround General Mills and holler until Betty Crocker came out with Breakfast Squares. The only demand that this stuff responds to is the inner voice of the corporation whispering, "Profits."

Business Week magazine identified six consumer-product markets with the greatest growth potential for corporate profits—three of them were food markets: special foods, fast-food chains and beverages. "On the surface, the grocery business would seem an eminently avoidable market," stated *Business Week*. "But within the vast food and beverage sector, where consumers poured $145-billion last year, manufacturers have identified segments, and segments within segments, that they expect to outpace growth in disposable income."[9] As listed by the magazine, those segments are snack foods, candy, convenience foods, specialty foods, pet foods and ethnic foods.

There can be no doubt that the corporate enthusiasm for profits has much to do with the shift to "sophisticated" food products. In 1971, the chief executive of Del Monte Corporation talked of his firm's "continuing shift in product emphasis, from such staples as canned tomatoes, peaches and fruit cocktail, to higher-profit formulated or 'manufactured' products." Citing Del Monte's pudding cup desserts as typical, he asked: "What do they have to offer? Among other things, above-average profit margins and little or no dependence on agricultural commodity prices."

Increasingly, the cost of processing and packaging is greater than the cost of the food in the package. That is true even with some fresh produce, where processing amounts to cleaning it off and boxing it—a 43¢ head of lettuce, for example, pays 4¢ to the farmer and 6¢ to the processor.[10] As processing becomes more involved, the processor's share of the consumer's dollars grows. With fresh tomatoes, farmers get 13¢ and the processors get a nickel. When the processors put the tomatoes in cans, however, the relationship is reversed—a 24¢ can of California tomatoes in 1972 contained 2¢ worth of tomatoes and 14¢ worth of processing.[11]

With a little added processing and a lot of advertising, food oligopolies can rake in profits. Consider two mainstays of General Mills' breakfast cereal line-up. Wheaties, "the breakfast of champions," costs around 53¢ for a regular-size box. Yet, there is no more than 2¢ worth of wheat in Wheaties; the box costs more than that. In fact, it has been suggested that eaters could do about as well nutritionally by chopping up the box and adding milk as they can do with the Wheaties. In any event, General Mills also produces Total, a cereal that is heavily advertised as being both good and good for you. What Total is, is Wheaties sprayed with half a cent's worth of vitamins.[12] The additional cost to General Mills for making a regular-size box of Total is half a cent. The additional cost to you for buying Total rather than Wheaties is 22¢.

POTATO GYPS. The potato has been one of nature's bounteous and good foods, widely cultivated and eaten in numerous civilizations over the centuries. It has been easy to grow, cheap to buy, healthful to eat and easy to prepare in an interesting variety of ways.

But now, oligopolistic processors have zeroed in on the spud. "We've got to sell convenience," Secretary of Agriculture Butz lectured an interviewer:

It's good that more potatoes are going to processors because it shows we are keeping up with changes in the market. The trend to convenience foods is obvious and inevitable. Anyone in the business of producing and marketing food must recognize and conform to the trend if he wants to capture a share of the market.

Such food processors as Heinz, Procter & Gamble, General Mills and French's are buying potatoes cheaply, doing as much as they can to them, and selling them to you at fancy prices. In 1960, the average American ate 108 pounds of potatoes, 85 pounds of which were bought fresh. In 1973, Americans were eating about the same amount of potatoes, but 57% of them were processed. Most potatoes today are coming to us frozen, fried, mashed, dehydrated, chipped or reconstituted. While the processors are handing us such makings with one hand, they are lifting our wallets with the other— the cost of processed potatoes is staggering. John Feltman, writing in *Organic Food Marketing* in 1974,

TABLE III—2
The High Cost of Food Processing

	Package Size	Price	Price per Pound
Fresh potatoes	20 lb.	$1.99	$ .10
Fresh potatoes	5 lb.	.79	.16
Sliced, canned potatoes	1 lb.	.25	.25
Frozen French fries	1 lb.	.35	.35
Frozen potato puffs	1 lb.	.35	.35
Frozen French fries (extra crisp)	10 oz.	.35	.56
Instant mashed potatoes	1 lb.	.71	.71
Potato sticks	7 oz.	.47	1.07
Potato chips	10 oz.	.69	1.10
Tuna Helper (potatoes and artificial mushroom flavor sauce)	7.5 oz.	.59	1.26
Crisp-i-Taters (potato snack)	6 oz.	.55	1.47
Hamburger Helper (potatoes with a sour cream and beef flavored sauce)	7 oz.	.67	1.53
Instant potato soup mix	5 oz.	.49	1.57
Munchies (potato crisp snack)	5 oz.	.53	1.70
Chipsters (potato snack)	4.75 oz.	.51	1.72

Source: *Organic Food Marketing.* "What Processing Has Done to the Potato." John Feltman. February 1974, pp. 6–7.

offered a sobering tabulation of potato pricing (Table III–2).

The latest gimmick of the potato processor is the reconstituted potato chip. This is a process developed by Procter & Gamble, which has been working on it since the midfifties.[13] Rather than slicing and frying potatoes, like other potato-chip manufacturers, P & G peels the potatoes, cooks them, mashes them and *removes* the water from them. Using this dehydrated mash, the company then *adds* water to them, adds a good dose of chemicals (mono- and diglycerides, sodium phosphates, sodium bisulfite and BHA preservative), adds sugar and vitamin C, sprinkles in some salt and pours the whole mess into molds that are shaped precisely as hyperbolic paraboloids. They are not finished yet. The concoction moves in its molds along a conveyer belt through hot oil, which solidifies the stuff into what P & G advertises as "perfectly shaped chips." These things are then mechanically stacked, as *Fortune* magazine marveled, "neatly on top of one another in a hermetically sealed container that resembles a tennis-ball can."

Such toying with the simple potato explains why P & G's product, called Pringle's, costs you up to 50% more than potato chips.

Why do they bother? "With the existing product," propounded P & G's chief executive, "the housewife was getting 25% of the product crumbled or broken. The packages were bulky and difficult to handle."[14] *Fortune* gushed that "the development of Pringle's is a classic case of recognizing a need in a consumer market and then painstakingly working away to meet it."[15] That's what big business tells the public, and maybe they even convince themselves of it.

The idea that American potato-chip eaters are worrying about some broken chips in the bag is silly, to put it politely. There are people who *prefer* smaller bits and will crunch whole chips in order to get them. Either way, the issue of broken chips does not weigh heavy on the mind of the American public. And the suggestion that a four-ounce bag of chips is bulky and difficult for anyone to handle is so silly that P & G stockholders might wonder about their chairman's touch with reality.

The reality is that there are enormous profits in Pringle's. The potato-chip market has been relatively competitive over the years, with many local companies operating efficiently and profitably. What P & G engineers have done with Pringle's is to devise an acceptable chip-like structure that makes potato-chip oligopoly possible for the first time. Because of the fragility of potato chips, they rarely are shipped more than 200 miles. And because they are made fresh, without chemical additives, they have to be replaced at least every couple of months.

The Pringle's innovations are (1) that they can be shipped across country, thus allowing P & G to exert its conglomerate financial resources* against local chip manufacturers; (2) that they make national advertising of potato chips possible for the first time—Procter & Gamble spent $5.4 million to advertise Pringles's in 1973 alone; and (3) that they can sit on a shelf for at least a year without tasting stale.

That is why they bother. It has nothing to do with consumer demand. Not only is a Pringle much more expensive than a potato chip, it also is nearly 40% fat (the same as regular chips) and relies on chemical additives to preserve "freshness." Pringle's are no boon to potato farmers, since the year-long shelf life allows P & G to buy potatoes on their terms at the cheapest time of year, and since the reconstituting process allows them to use cheaper "field grade" spuds. And neither consumers, nor farmers, nor independent potato chip companies can feel very comfortable with the monopoly potential of Pringle's.

LIFE IS JUST A BOWL OF BOWLS. Never mind what's in the food package. The act of packaging, or the pack-

---

* Procter & Gamble is a widely diversified consumer-products company (Tide and Cheer laundry detergents, Duncan Hines cake mixes, Pampers diapers, Folger coffee, Ivory soap, etc.) making $4 billion a year in sales. Its profits on shareholder investment averaged 18.3% over the past five years.

age itself, is what many food oligopolies are selling. Nearly 20% of the price of Pringle's goes to pay for the hermetically sealed can they come in. The cost of packaging some TV dinners is greater than the cost of the dinner. You pay more for ice cream that says "hand packed" on the package, but all it amounts to is a worker holding the carton under the filling machine— "We say hand packed, not hand dipped," pointed out one ice-cream executive, beaming at the cleverness of it.

The most significant packaging trend today is the practice of wrapping fresh fruits and vegetables. "It's much easier for a woman to pick up a package of oranges than to pick up individual ones," said a Stop & Shop executive in a mind-boggling twist of logic. Logical or not, fresh-produce sections throughout the country are offering their fruits and vegetables in styrofoam trays, wrapped in plastic film. No more sampling the cherries before buying, no more squeezing the grapefruits, no more pinching the corn, no more sniffing the ripeness of the peaches, no more picking over the tomatoes. Instead of buying one or two nice tomatoes out of the grocery bin, the shopping option is narrowed to buying a package of three or more, usually of varying quality.

Admit it: Consumers do not need prepackaging of their fresh produce. Not only does it restrict choice, but it adds to the price—styrofoam trays, plastic wrapping, wrapping machines and the time to operate the machines do not come free. The effort to put a sheet of plastic between shoppers and the food they buy has not been accepted meekly, and the New York Consumer Affairs Department is responding to shopper complaints by considering a regulation that will allow the customer to open produce prepacks and pick out individual items.

Nonetheless, wrapped produce is steadily taking over

the grocery bins, and the industry press reveals a clear resolve among brand-name produce sellers and supermarkets to have their way—"the consumer will accept it," one grocery official said with finality. In an oligopolistic food structure, the consumer may have to.

Packaging of fresh produce increases corporate sales by requiring bulk purchases by consumers, it allows the grocer to move low-quality produce packed together with the better stuff, it cuts down on bruising and spoilage of produce, and it allows marketers to attach their brand names to fresh produce and sell for a higher price. Stated directly, packaging adds to profits.

The selling of packaging rather than food may have achieved the apogee of profitability with the introduction of such products as Hamburger Helper, another terrific idea from General Mills. There are several brands of these "add-meat" meals, and most tend to be packages of packages—usually a box holding a foil pouch of noodles or grain, another pouch of spices and maybe a small can of sauce. One of the primary thrusts in the advertising of Hamburger Helper is that its ingredients will help hamburger go further, allowing you to use less meat. That's a fine idea, except that Hamburger Helper sells for $1.50 a pound. You can buy lean hamburger for $1.00 a pound, or you can buy the ingredients of Hamburger Helper for about 40¢ a pound.

Packaging in oligopolistic food lines is becoming the major means of differentiating one product from another, and not only does the package cost consumers more than the food it contains, but increasingly the package carries the burden of advertising. "Now you can squeeze the mustard you love," says French's in a magazine ad touting its plastic squeeze bottle.

But the ultimate ascendancy of packaging over contents has been reached by margarine makers. Mrs. Filbert's and Kraftco both are advertising the plastic bowls that contain their soft margarine, rather than the margarine itself: "We call 'em Rainbowls," goes the lead in Mrs. Filbert's advertising, "but you can call 'em custard cups, rice bowls, snack dishes, ice cream cups, sugar bowls, gelatin molds or anything you like." Apparently, it doesn't matter whether you like the margarine.

Less for More: Another Way to Inflate Prices

In 1974, Hershey and Nestlé both increased the size of their chocolate bars; Hershey expanded its by 11% and Nestlé got 20% bigger. At the same time, however, they discontinued their 10¢ price, going to 15¢ a bar— a 50% increase.[16]

In fact, Hershey has messed with the size of its bar 24 times in about as many years, and Nestlé and other chocolate-candy producers have been frequent manipulators of their bars. Over the years, this effort has gradually cut the chocolate bar down to size. Even though it is 20% larger than the last model, Nestlé's new 15¢ bar still is smaller than the 10¢ bar of 1968. It is hard to keep track of it, but all this adding and subtracting is leaving you way behind; you simply pay more for less.

It even causes adjustment problems for the candy companies. A University of California plant geneticist told a television interviewer that his tax-paid research department bred a smaller almond for Hershey, because the regular-size almond made Hershey's shrinking bar look as small as it was.[17]

Chocolate eaters are not the only ones to be short-changed by product inflation. In 1969, the staff of the U.S. House Government Operations Committee compiled an extensive list of food products that offered less content in 1969 while costing the same or more money than they had in 1964.[18] To name just a few, Libby's canned chili was down an ounce, Chef Boy-Ardee lasagna was down half an ounce, Gulden's mustard was down an ounce, Planter's peanuts were down an ounce, Sara Lee cheesecake was down an ounce, Patio beef enchiladas were down 2 ounces, and Kraft Cracker Barrel cheese was down 3½ ounces. These little bits increase prices to you and increase profits for the manufacturer.

Packages frequently appear to be more than they are. A 1973 survey in Washington State by the Food & Drug Administration showed a startling amount of "slack fill"—the amount of empty space—in processed food products.[19] For example, an 18-ounce box of Kellogg's corn flakes was found to be 22% air; an 8-ounce box of Total was 28% air; a 5½-ounce package of Jell-O instant pudding was 32% air; a 9-ounce box of Betty Crocker coconut-pecan cake mix was 36% air; and a 15-ounce package of Pillsbury angel-food cake mix was 42% air. A certain amount of legitimate slack fill results from settling of contents, but wide ranges were found in products of the same type—some cake-mix packages were completely full; others were as much as 42% air.

Shoppers usually buy packaged products without thinking that the manufacturer might have cut the contents. As long as the package remains the same size on the outside, it generally will not be noticed that there is less inside. When Carnation introduced its Instant Breakfast mixes, the box contained a certain number of envelopes. As soon as the introductory promotional campaign had established the product, the number of envelopes was decreased, while the box size and the price remained the same.

Consumer organizations have sought legislation over

the years requiring food canners to list the drained weight of the product—for example, the actual weight of the peaches in a can, minus the weight of the water or syrup. Just by thinly slicing the weight of food going into each can, replacing it with more water, a company can add up a considerable profit increase. In surveys of drained-weight contents, the nationally advertised brand names have a way of coming up short. The Department of Agriculture, in 1969, surveyed drained weights at the request of a congressional committee, and a congressional staff member, Peter Barash, presented some of the results at a public hearing:

> For example, the Department of Agriculture figures suggest that in the Town House can, 15-ounce Town House can of whole-leaf spinach, you get consistently about 8 percent more spinach than in the 15-ounce can of Del Monte whole-leaf spinach. The 16-ounce can of Hanover cut green beans consistently contains, based on Agriculture's test results, 3 to 4 percent more beans and less liquid than the 16-ounce Del Monte can of cut green beans. The Town House fruit cocktail contains 4 to 5 percent more fruit cocktail and less liquid than the Del Monte can.[20]

A couple of years ago, an executive of H. J. Heinz discovered that some of that company's products were being filled as much as half an ounce over what the label called for—a practice that he said amounted to "a hell of a lot of money." The spouts were quickly adjusted on the filling machinery. One wonders whether such cost consciousness is as quick to the fore when the ketchup bottles are coming up a half ounce short, rather than over. *Consumer Newsweek* reported that the 1973 survey of slack fill by FDA showed "a substantial proportion of packages containing less than the net contents on the label, indicating considerable over-all loss to consumers and extra profit to producers."

Pricing People Out of the Market

The official line on rising food prices since 1973 has been that Americans are a people of such affluence that they can readily afford to pay the asking price. "We've been spoiled by low prices," was the reprimand from the head of the Grocery Manufacturers of America.[21] And government economists have kept up a steady barrage of statistics to show that, on the average, Americans are better off than ever before.

When he was Chairman of the Council of Economic Advisors in the 1960s, Walter Heller occasionally mentioned the six-foot-tall economist who drowned when he attempted to wade a stream that had an average depth of only four feet. That's the problem with industry and government attempts today to soothe public anger over rising prices—few Americans are average, and many are drowning as food prices rise.

A favorite statistic has been the one showing that Americans spend under 16% of their disposable income on food, which is a level unmatched in the rest of the world, according to the government. When pressed, however, officials who wave this statistic like the American flag have to concede that a family of four would need to earn more than $20,000 a year to get their food spending down to this level.[22] Fewer than a fifth of American families have incomes of $20,000 or more.

The chief executive of Del Monte Corporation went home with $438,000 in 1973. A low-income worker, doing 40 hours a week at minimum wage, had a gross income of $3,328 in 1973. The working stiff probably spent 62% of his income on food, while the corporate executive could easily have spent as little as 2% of his income on food. Figuring various levels of eating at several levels of income, the *Christian Science Monitor* came up with the following run-down on who was spending what for food in 1973:

TABLE III—3

*Food Expenditures as a Percentage
of Spendable Earnings*

Annual Gross Income	Low-cost Plan	Moderate Plan	Liberal Plan
$ 3,328	62%	79%	97%
5,000	42	54	66
7,280	35	45	55
10,000	26	33	41
15,000	18	23	28
20,000	14	18	22
25,000	12	14	18

That computation was prepared before food prices were launched out of sight, putting many foods out of reach of millions of people. It is not necessary to go very low on the American income scale before you find people who literally are being priced out of the market by food oligopolies. For people at the top, it makes little difference if hamburger doubles in price, but most wage-earners, elderly pensioners and low-income people are forced by that to switch from beef to beans.

There is no relief even there, for the price of beans has tripled. No problem, said the Secretary of Agriculture, because Americans are not bean-eaters anyway. Not the Americans he runs around with, but in the rural areas of the South, in the Mexican-American communities of the Southwest and West, and in the Spanish neighborhoods of New York City and elsewhere, beans are a staple of the diet and *the* major source of protein.

Old people, living on the fixed (and low) incomes of Social Security and pensions, have been particularly hard hit by the new day of high-cost food. "I'm strictly gone to vegetarian," an elderly widow told *The Washington Post:*

> I can't afford the meat. I'm taking vitamins and eating foods that give me the most proteins without meat. I eat a lot of cream cheese and yellow cheese. It's very bad for senior citizens.[23]

As oligopolistic food manufacturers shift toward highly processed convenience foods, they are leaving low-income people behind. These people do not want the convenience, since they cannot afford it, but increasingly they have to pay for it anyway. "Well, let them eat fresh potatoes," you might say. They are prepared to do that, but these days they have to bid against Heinz and Procter & Gamble and French's and other giant potato processors to get the raw product. These oligopolistic firms, able to pass raw-potato costs directly to the consumer, have bid up the price of all potatoes— even the fresh one that the old-age pensioner was hoping to boil for dinner.

Monopoly Pricing

It can be stated simply and directly: Food monopolies cost us money. *The staff of the Federal Trade Commission found in 1972 that monopoly power in 13 food industries had cost eaters $2.1 billion more than they should have paid,* and that was a conservative estimate (see Table III–4).

If low-grade oligopolies are counted (those where the leading four firms account for 35% of the market), some 80% of all food industries contain monopoly

TABLE III—4

The Extra Price Consumers Are Estimated to Pay Because of Monopoly Power in 13 Food Industries

Industry	% of Market Held by Four Largest Firms, 1966[a]	Some of the Largest Firms[b]	Amount of Overcharge to Consumers, 1972[c]
1. Meat packing	40%	Armour, Swift, Wilson, Iowa Beef Processors	$ 483,900,000
2. Fluid milk	60	Kraftco, Carnation, Borden, Foremost	256,700,000
3. Soft drinks	90	Coca-Cola, Pepsico, Royal Crown, Seven-Up	247,800,000
4. Malt liquors	65	Anheuser-Busch, Schlitz, Pabst, Coors	198,000,000
5. Bread and related products	50	ITT, Campbell Taggart, American Bakeries, Interstate Brands	191,900,000
6. Canned fruits and vegetables	40	Del Monte, Libby, Green Giant, Stokely Van Camp	143,600,000
7. Confectionery products	40–50	Hershey, Nestlé, Wrigley, Beech-Nut	94,400,000

8. Flour and other grain mill products	45	General Mills, Ralston Purina, Quaker, Pillsbury	88,500,000
9. Distilled liquor	55	Heublein, Distillers Corp.—Seagrams	88,300,000
10. Frozen fruits and vegetables	40–50	General Foods, Green Giant	84,900,000
11. Cane sugar refining	40	Amstar, Castle & Cook, C. Brewer	71,500,000
12. Canned specialties	80	Gerber's, Campbell Soup, Beech-Nut	71,200,000
13. Crackers & cookies	70	Nabisco, American Brands	57,300,000
Monopoly Overcharge in 13 Food Industries			$2,078,000,000

Primary Source: Paul D. Scanlon. "FTC and Phase II: The McGovern Papers." *Antitrust Law and Economics Review*. Spring 1972 (Vol. 5, No. 3). Table 1, pp. 33–36.

[a] William G. Shepherd. *Market Power and Economic Welfare*. New York: Random House. 1970. Appendix Table 8.

[b] These are not necessarily the four largest firms, since such information is not compiled in any regular or systematic way. In the cases of meat packing, soft drinks, malt liquor, bread, and canned fruits and vegetables, the firms listed are the four largest. In other cases, the firms listed would fall at least within the top eight.

[c] Calculated by the FTC staff by figuring monopoly profits and excessive costs (see Scanlon, cited above, p. 670) within industries as a percent of sales, then multiplying that "adjusted monopoly margin" by the value of the industry's shipments.

power that may be costing consumers extra.[24] Just counting the solid oligopolies, where the big four control more than 50% of the market, about half of the food industry is concentrated.[25]

Monopoly power includes the power to increase prices artificially. Ralph Nader has estimated that monopolies throughout our economy cost the consumer over 20¢ of every dollar spent. Senator Philip Hart, Chairman of the Antitrust and Monopoly Subcommittee, has put the figure as high as 40¢ of the dollar. Charles Mueller, an antitrust attorney and economist with the Federal Trade Commission, wrote in 1970, "While the economists working in this area offer much more refined (and somewhat lower) estimates of the public losses traceable to the absence of competition in these oligopoly industries, the largest of these figures, Senator Hart's, may well turn out to be on the low side if a program of serious reform is ever actually undertaken and the real extent of the overpricing in these industries exposed to the light of day."[26]

One who agrees is Senator William Proxmire, Chairman of the Joint Economic Committee. He estimated that two-thirds of the inflation in wholesale prices in 1974 was the result of "Unjustified price increases in six concentrated industries: steel, nonferrous metals, chemicals, fuel industry, and food processors and distributors."

It is reasonable to estimate that food would be at least 25% cheaper today if we were to deal effectively with the various aspects of monopoly power in the food industry.

COKE: THE REAL THING. If by that slogan they mean monopoly, they are right. The four largest makers of soda syrup are Coca-Cola, Pepsico, Royal Crown

Cola and Seven-Up. Together, they control 89% of the market. Consumers spend $5 billion a year in that market. Estimating both the excessive profits and the internal waste produced by this level of monopoly, the FTC calculated that soft-drink buyers were overcharged $248 million in 1972.

Profits within this monopoly are refreshing to the big four. While the top 500 corporations in the country were earning a 12.4% median profit from their shareholders' investments in 1973, Coca-Cola was pocketing a 22.7% profit, Pepsi was taking a 16% profit, Royal Crown had 18.6% profit and Seven-Up got away with a 21.4% profit.[27]

Not only do these soft-drink peddlers control the syrup market, but they also extend their power directly to the bottlers. The structure of the industry is such that syrup is sold to bottlers, who then sell to supermarkets and other retailers. But most bottlers are not independent—they are assigned exclusive territories by the big four. That system has been practiced in the soft-drink industry for 70 years, and it has created absolute monopolies throughout the country.[28] What it does is eliminate price competition—if a supermarket in Chicago wants Coke, it must buy it from the franchised bottler in Chicago or not at all. The price to the consumer is whatever the local Coke monopoly says it is; and increasingly the local bottler is owned by a conglomerate from out of town, including the likes of Westinghouse, Illinois Central Industries, Beatrice Foods, and General Tire and Rubber.

The Federal Trade Commission has launched an investigation of the soft-drink industry with an eye toward breaking up this monopolistic system of franchised fiefdoms. Undaunted, the hard-headed soft-drink executives marched to Congress with a bill that would exempt their industry from the antitrust laws. Laugh if you will at such audacity, but the legislation passed the Senate in 1974 without so much as a recorded vote, and it is now being considered in the House.

Far more serious to consumers, the soft-drink legislation is not sought in the name of that industry alone, but also for the manufacturers of other trademarked foods. That means that the big, brand-name food firms could engage in the same territorial franchising techniques that soft-drink companies now employ. The impact would be to destroy all but the very biggest manufacturers of food and to confront consumers with frightening monopolistic power prices.* In 1972, the former director of FTC's bureau of competition warned the U.S. Senate in vain against this attempt at monopolistic overkill:

> How much this kind of legislation may cost consumers is difficult to precisely estimate, but it would certainly be many hundred millions of dollars. . . . Since these bills would legalize territorial restrictions not only in the five billion dollar soft drink industry, but in the entire $131 billion food industry, the potential adverse effect on the consuming public could be truly enormous.

KNEADING THE BREAD MARKET. Few of the giant food firms are having to wait for the day of territorial franchises to assert market power and set consumer prices. Consider bread. The "staff of life," as it used to be called, already has become the stuff of monopoly.

If you fit the national average, 10% of your food

---

* The total food cost in America today is $160 billion, which is some 32 times larger than the $5 billion expenditure for soft drinks. Just by the crude calculation of multiplying the soft-drink industry's $250 million monopoly overcharge by 32, it is possible to get the roughest estimate of what this proposed extension of monopoly power could cost consumers—$8 billion a year.

purchases are of bread and bakery products. But chances are that the baker you patronize most is not the little shop down the street. More than likely it is ITT (Wonder Bread, Profile, Butter Tap), Campbell Taggart (Rainbo, Colonial, Manor, Kilpatrick's), American Bakeries (Taystee, Merita, Langendorf, Barbara Ann, Cook Book) or Interstate Brands (Butternut, Millbrook, Weber's Sweetheart, Hart's, Blue Seal, Mrs. Karl's, Four-S, Old World Variety).

The bread oligopoly is not especially tight at the national level, with these four largest bakers holding 30% of the total bread market in 1971.*[29] As in the case with supermarket oligopolies, however, the relevant market is local—at the city level, the four largest-selling brands are dominant. In a 1963 survey of bread concentration in 17 cities, the Federal Trade Commission found that the average market share held by the top four brands was 63%. If you live in Beaumont, Texas, 92% of the bread you buy is sold by the four largest bakers. In Charlotte, North Carolina, the bread oligopoly holds 73%, and in Omaha, Nebraska, they have 76% of the market.[30]

In local markets, one or more of the big national brands usually are present. The monopolistic power and practices of these giants are driving smaller competitors in local markets out of business, or forcing them to fold their labels and bakeries in with the dominant firms. By the end of the decade, says a vice-president of one large bakery, "there will probably be one or two major [bread] suppliers in the United States."[31] Whether

* This counts both wholesale bakers, like the big four, and supermarkets that make their own bread for sale. The latter have about 10% of total bread production. Among the wholesale bakers, the big four account for 37% of sales in 1970. Both in the wholesale market and in the total market, the share held by the big four has been steadily increasing.

or not it comes to that, it is generally agreed, even within the baking industry, that the next few years certainly will see fewer and fewer competitors holding more and more of the bread market.

One of those that will make it is Wonder Bread, a product of ITT and the country's biggest seller. Wonder Bread holds 12% of the national market. In statewide markets, its shares are considerably more, reaching 26% in Nebraska, 30% in Oklahoma and 48% in Utah.

But the true power of Wonder Bread is inadequately measured by such statistics. A U.S. Administrative Law judge, Alvin L. Berman, studied the competitive structure of the bread industry and the position that ITT holds there, and he concluded in a 1974 opinion that "the record establishes that [Wonder Bread] is indeed the price leader who sets the pattern of competition in whatever bread market it is in."[32]

Wonder used to advertise that it "builds strong bodies twelve ways." Today, it builds strong monopolies in about as many ways, not the least of which is national advertising. Judge Berman found that "advertising is the only real means to influence the buyer of bread, and the most effective advertising media for the wholesale baker is television." At a time when other bakeries have been cutting back their advertising budgets, Wonder has been increasing its, spending $5 million a year just to sell the Wonder label on national television. That campaign reaches 70% of the U.S. population—a power that no other bread-maker can come close to matching.

Secondly, ITT is widely diversified and able to apply the "deep pocket" concept, which allows Wonder Bread to lose money, but still survive, by drawing on the resources of the parent corporation. None of the other top eight bakers have such an advantage. Akin to the deep-pocket privilege is Wonder Bread's ability to link its sales with those of another product sold by ITT's bakery division—Hostess cakes. There are very few brand-name cake items on the market, and Hostess is by far the leading line. Following that lead, Wonder Bread can get into grocery markets that other bakers cannot crack.

Such power has not sat idle. Wonder Bread is in far more local markets than any other label, and both its geographic reach and its sales potential continue to expand. ITT expects its bakery subsidiary to grow 15% a year in profits, though bread alone is not expected to carry that burden.[33] Wonder can move into any market of its choosing, draw from practically unlimited financial resources to make capital expenditures in the market, intensify its newspaper, television and billboard advertising in the area, link sales of Wonder Bread to those of Hostess cakes, and be in a position to lose money while increasing its market share and growth potential. The impact will eliminate local competitors, who may be more efficient bakers, and who may produce better bread, but who do not have the financial backing of ITT or the budget to put their bread on national television.

Several years ago, in Denver, Wonder set off a bread price war among the area's wholesale bakers by undercutting the price of private-label bread sold to supermarkets. Not only does Wonder put its own label on the shelf, but about 12% of ITT's bread sales are to groceries that package it under their own label.[34] Thus, Wonder Bread sometimes "competes" with itself—sitting side by side with a store label that actually came from the same batch of dough. Local Denver bakers had provided much of this private-label bread, until Wonder moved in to undercut their prices. The U.S. Supreme Court in 1973 ruled that ITT had unfairly competed with the local bakers and had damaged two of them to the tune of $3.8 million.[35] The award of damages was too little too late for Homestead bread, which had been fatally damaged in the price war and had closed its doors.

Now, Wonder Bread is the subject of a $45 million antitrust suit in California, brought by five independent bakeries.[36] In fact, all of the big four national bakers are named in the suit, which alleges discriminatory pricing, selling below cost and other deliberate acts to put the independents out of business. One of the plaintiffs is the last independent producer of white bread left in Los Angeles, and another is the last remaining in the greater San Francisco area. The question is whether they can hang on long enough for the antitrust suit to wind its way through the courts.

For bread buyers, the elimination of local competition means higher bread prices. In the early 1960s, the four leading bakers in Seattle, Washington, controlled about 70% of the bread market. For several years, these bakers engaged in a price-fixing conspiracy. Wonder Bread, the leading seller, acted as the price leader; whenever it raised its prices, the others followed the lead, hiking bread prices the same amount and frequently on the same day.[37] When the Federal Trade Commission finally got around to finding the four bakers guilty in 1964, Seattle shoppers were paying 4¢ a loaf more than the national average for bread, and the 10-year conspiracy was figured to have cost Seattle consumers $30 million.

Campbell Taggart and three other Arizona bakers, sharing 85% of the bread market in that state, also appear to be caught in a price-fixing conspiracy.[38] In 1974, a Phoenix grand jury indicted these bakers for conspiring to hold bread prices at an artificially high, noncompetitive level. In Seattle and in Arizona the big bakers got caught. But such conspiracy cases reveal only the most heavy-handed aspects of monopoly pricing. The power of the big four bread makers, particularly the awesome power of Wonder Bread, is such that overt conspiracy is hardly necessary.

There is an antitrust injunction that now prohibits ITT from merging any more bakers into its bread empire, but that is a pitifully inadequate effort to restrain this giant. Wonder Bread does not need to buy other bakers in order to grow—like bread, it has the power to rise from within. And in many markets today, that power means that the price of bread is whatever ITT says it is.

A HALF-BAKED IDEA. There is a country song that goes: It felt so good when it stopped hurting. Big business has developed that sentiment to the point of science. The gasoline corporations, for example, profited in 1973 and 1974 from shortages that forced consumers into two-hour lines just to buy gas. It was a "crisis" that left people fuming, but finally the long wait was eliminated and people were grateful. Yet the price of gasoline in many places was raised during the crisis from 40¢ to more than 60¢ a gallon, and the oil oligopoly went to the bank with tremendous profits.

Perhaps admiring the inventiveness of the gasoline oligopoly, the big bread bakers decided in 1974 to try their hand at the "feel good" technique. Bill Mead, Chairman of the American Bakers Association, held a January press conference calling for export controls on wheat. If such controls are not imposed, said Mead, wheat prices will rise to $14 a bushel, bakers will not have enough wheat to make bread, and "many housewives could well be paying a dollar per loaf by late spring." That was big news, and for days frenzied public attention was directed toward the prospect of dollar-a-loaf bread.

The bakers kneaded it for all it was worth: "What we want to do," a solemn bakery official told a television interviewer, "is to assure that there will be an adequate domestic supply of wheat for bread this spring, so that there will be the products that the American people use every day—the hotdog buns, the hamburger rolls, the birthday cake, the pizza."[39]

In fact, there was no danger of the bread makers running out of wheat, least of all the big bakers. Mr. Mead, who had issued the dire prediction, is the head of Campbell Taggart, the second largest baker in the nation. His firm already had purchased enough flour to meet their needs for months to come. More significantly, there was no way the price of wheat could rise high enough to cause bread to go to a dollar. The cost of wheat in a pound loaf of bread is well under a nickel. Wheat could triple or quadruple in price and not push a loaf of bread anywhere close to a dollar.

Of course, the bakers were aware of that. George Anthan, the most incisive reporter in the country on food and agricultural issues, wrote in his paper, the *Des Moines Register,* that "the bakers have not emphasized that much of the increase they are predicting would go to pay for boosting markups by wholesalers and by retail stores that sell the bread."[40] While alarming the public of imminent breadlines and drawing attention to wheat farmers, oligopolistic middlemen were picking the public's pocket. A Texas wheat farmer, talking with a National Public Television reporter, saw right through the bakers' scheme:

> They sound like they're trying to prepare us, you know, for later on, maybe thinking it'll get to a dollar

and then cost eighty cents and think we're getting a heck of a deal for it, you know.

Shortly after the bakers cried wolf, the price of wheat began to plummet. The price of bread, however, rose. And the difference was pocketed by the bakers. There had been a wolf there, all right—the oligopolistic bakers themselves.

The Day of Cheap Food Is Over

In 1973, corporate and government food managers changed their tune about the food economy. "The day of cheap food is over" declared several officials at one time or other. They talked of a new food era, with worldwide demand for American foodstuffs and with a world affluent enough to buy it. "The end of the era of cheap food is the price American consumers will pay for an adequate domestic supply and for establishing the United States as a reliable source of food for hundreds of millions of people around the world" pronounced the editor of an industry publication.[41]

Such pontificating carefully ignores the fact that the day of cheap food is over because food oligopolies now have achieved a tight enough grip on the food economy to begin squeezing it.

Americans have not sought "cheap" food. They have sought food at a reasonable price. And every poll of the subject shows that consumers are eager to pay enough for food to assure that the family farmer gets a fair deal. Farmers have *not* gotten a fair deal, for the simple reason that they are competitive operators surrounded by noncompetitive corporations. That "the day of cheap food is over" does not mean that the family farmers' ship has finally arrived. Far from it. You will pay more, but less of what you pay will go to farmers.

High-cost food is here to stay because the food economy has become industrialized, corporatized, integrated and concentrated. "In summary," wrote USDA economists recently, "the food system and especially a significant part of the production sector will not only more closely resemble other economic sectors by 1985, it will be a more fully integrated part of the general economy."[42] That says that you can expect as much say over the price of dinner as you now enjoy over the price of a Chevrolet.

Food price increases early in 1973 were due in large part to worldwide scarcities of basic commodities. Late that year, however, raw commodities began to drop in price, and the cost of food at the farm level continued to fall throughout 1974 and into 1975. Yet, consumer prices kept climbing. This paradox has been due to deliberate price expansion and profit taking by corporate middlemen. Sugar, bread, meat, canned goods and practically every other food item in the grocery store has been hiked in price far beyond any level warranted by any actual increase in food cost. In 1974, for example, sugar prices soared. "Supply and demand," shrugged the big sugar refiners. Yet, supply of sugar in 1974 was greater than demand for the first time in three years. The price paid to sugar farmers went up only 30% in 1974, but sugar middlemen hiked their prices by 300%. There are profits in that kind of arithmetic—Great Western United, the largest sugar-beet processor in the world, enjoyed a 1,200% profit increase in 1974.

It amounts to an unprecedented power grab by food corporations—an attempt to ride the "psychology of inflation" to much more profitable price levels. It is being done simply because corporations have the power to do it.

Late in 1974, President Ford was demanding that the

American people cut back their consumption by 5% in an effort to control inflation. At a White House meeting on the economy, Carol Foreman, executive director of Consumer Federation of America, asked an executive of a major food corporation if his company would be willing to hold their price increases to 5%. "No," he said without hesitation. "Well," Ms. Foreman asked, "would you at least restrict your price increases to those actually required by rising costs?" He looked at her with a big smile and said, "You must be kidding."

CHAPTER IV

Biting into Oligopoly

"Good and good for you" my ol' daddy used to say as he pushed back from an enjoyable meal. But it is not so easily said anymore. As food manufacturers grow more dominant over the delivery of dinner, we are being taken further from the staples of the earth. And that is making it harder to claim that a meal is either good or good for you.

It is not that food firms are trying to produce bad food. Rather they are *not* trying to produce *good* food. Their objective is to produce profits, and food quality is at best a secondary consideration. Because of the lack of price and quality competition in today's food economy, and because of the industrialization of food manufacturing, such factors as taste and nutrition have a way of being refined out of the final product. These two components are relevant to the manufacturers only to the extent that they must exist in certain minimum amounts —either because government regulators require it or because a little taste and nutrition tossed in are good for sales.

Eating habits used to be learned from mom and dad, determined by such happenstance as the part of the country you were from or your ethnic background. To-day, television is the teacher. In 1971, food companies became the largest purveyors of television advertising, a position they still hold.[1] It is not a balanced dinner of the four basic food groups that they are pushing there, but snack foods, processed foods and convenience items. That's where the profits are. Children are taught that taste is a craving for sugar, that nutrition is no more than the vitamins added to breakfast cereal, and that choice of a meal is between Chef's Surprise at home or a McDonald's burger under the yellow lights down the street.

The approach seems to be to lure them with sweets at a tender age and to hold them with snacks through the teens. With this training, they can be expected to buy manufactured foods and convenience items for the rest of their years. It is the means of putting teeth into Del Monte Corporation's "womb to tomb" slogan. Not for nothing have the major food makers moved into public schools to corner the market for prepackaged breakfast and lunch programs. With a grant from the federal government, ITT's Hostess cake subsidiary developed "Astrofood," a vitamin-fortified, sugar-filled cake, which is now fed to schoolchildren every morning in several systems around the country, including St. Louis, Memphis, Little Rock, Atlanta, Buffalo, Los Angeles, Seattle, and New York.[2]

Nutrition: You Are What You Eat

What are little girls and boys made of? When they drink Kool-Aid, they are made of fumaric acid, sugar, monosodium phosphate, ascorbic acid, propylene glycol, artificial flavor, artificial color, calcium carbonate and dioctyl sodium sulfosuccinate.[3]

Few people have any notion of what is put into the stuff of food oligopolies, or what is taken out of it. As food shoppers, we have not paid much attention to nutrition, undoubtedly assuming that the food makers were taking care of that. Such trust has not been well placed, and it is time to start looking out for ourselves. As Dr. Myron Winick, head of Columbia University's Institute of Human Nutrition, understated it. "The profit motive in selling and packaging is not always compatible with the best nutrition." General Foods beams millions of dollars of Kool-Aid advertising at children, even urging them to replace the old lemonade stand with a Kool-Aid stand. The latter is good for General Foods' profits, but lemonade would be better for the kids.

In a 1965 survey, the Department of Agriculture found that American diets were less nutritious than they had been in 1955. Only half of the households in the country were found to have "good" diets,* and 20% of the households were found to have poor diets. Referring to this USDA study, nutritionist Richard Ahrens pointedly noted at a 1974 Food & Drug Administration conference that "from 1955 to 1965 consumption increased for soft drinks, punches and ades, potato chips, crackers, cookies, doughnuts, ice cream, and candy. Consumption of milk, cheese, eggs, flour, cereal, fruits and vegetables declined."[4]

Subsequent studies by the Department of Agriculture and by the Department of Health, Education, and Wel-

---

* A "good" diet in a household was one in which the per-person daily intake of seven nutrients was equal to or above the full Recommended Daily Allowance established by the National Academy of Sciences. The percent of good diets among American households fell from 60% in 1955 to 50% in 1965. A "poor" diet was considered to be one that contained less than two-thirds of the Recommended Daily Allowance for one or more of the seven nutrients.

fare confirm the earlier findings of declining nutritional quality in the American diet, particularly of such nutrients as iron, calcium, riboflavin, magnesium and vitamins A, B_6 and C.[5]

Perhaps the most startling realization is that most of us know so little about human nutrition. Public schools teach practically nothing useful about eating, usually relegating nutrition to a dull chapter on basic food groups in an elementary-school health text. Practical nutritional experience in school is even less beneficial— after reading about the virtues of whole grains, kids today can leave class and buy a lunch of snack foods and soft drinks from a vending machine located in the hallway. No wonder that only about half of American housewives are able even to describe a nutritionally balanced meal.

Worse yet, doctors are ignorant on the subject. In a good article on nutrition, Jane E. Brody pointed out in *The New York Times* that no more than 12 of approximately 120 medical schools in the country have full departments of nutrition, and the average medical student "learns little or nothing about how to feed a normal, healthy human being to maintain his healthiness."[6] Nutritional scientists generally have not served us well— in fact, a large percentage of them have not served us at all, but have hired out to food manufacturers. There, they come up with the concoctions that their marketing departments have determined will sell. As Dr. Michael Jacobson, a microbiologist and the director of the Center for Science in the Public Interest, said of most corporate scientists: "If the boss wants a creme-filled, sugar-coated breakfast cereal, you're going to do it."

HOW CONVENIENT. It is dictum among the leading food marketers that convenience is what people want for dinner. No matter what's in it or not in it, if it appears convenient it can be "sold in Peoria," as they say in the ad biz.

No doubt people are happy to have just about anything made easier for them, even though by accepting convenience, food shoppers have not intended to trade off nutritional quality. Nonetheless, they have.

Food packages can be found that loudly tout the existence of certain major nutrients awaiting you within. It is like the dinner guest loudly proclaiming the virtues of honesty; you are well advised to hide the silverware. Frequently, these food products advertise a few nutrients so boldly because they quietly have done away with so many more. Flaking, shredding and puffing of grain to make breakfast cereals eliminates up to 90% of the vitamin E. When wheat is processed down to white flour—the industry prefers to call it "refining" the whole-wheat grain—more than half of each of 14 essential vitamins and minerals is lost, and the "enriched" white bread you buy replaces only four of them. Such nutrients as biotin, inositol, paraminobenzoic acid, pantothenic acid, zinc, magnesium and chromium are refined out and not replaced. A nutritionist told a U.S. Senate Committee in 1970, "The milling process removes 40% of the chromium, 86% of the manganese, 89% of the cobalt, 68% of the copper, 78% of the zinc, and 48% of the molybdenum—all trace elements essential for life or health."[7]

Convenience foods tend to have less of the ingredients that are highly nutritious and more of the low-nutrition components that serve mostly as filler. Anyone who tries a can of beef soup will not confuse it with the homemade version, since the can's ratio of beef to soup is heavily weighted in favor of soup. In fact the resemblance between canned and homemade soup was so thin that Campbell's renamed some of its soups "manhandlers," implying more bulk. There was no more bulk, and people were not fooled. So Campbell's then came out with a new line of "chunky" soups. Campbell's beef "chunky" with vegetables costs a third more than Campbell's "manhandler" beef with vegetables—convenience is one thing, but nutrition comes extra.

In a particularly distasteful attempt to flak for the big food companies, the Department of Agriculture in 1974 attempted to demonstrate that the majority of convenience foods are as cheap as homemade. A Departmental economist trotted out a "study" showing that of 90 factory-prepared items, "59% had a cost per serving equal to, or less than, their home-prepared or fresh counterparts." Marian Burros, in a solid bit of investigative reporting, revealed the USDA study for the shabby fraud it was: "No attempt had been made to compare the nutritional value or the percentage of high-cost ingredients in the home-prepared versus the convenience items," she wrote in the *Washington Post*.[8]

In this report, the Department of Agriculture had compared the cost of a 10-ounce package of frozen pork fried rice and found it to be cheaper than the same amount of pork fried rice made at home. But there was only half an ounce of pork in the packaged version, while the homemade recipe called for 2⅓ ounces. Canned beef stew analyzed by the Department had beef, carrots and potatoes, while the homemade version it was compared with contained those ingredients plus peas and onions. "In the four examples tested by the *Washington Post*," wrote Ms. Burros, "none of the convenience items was the nutritional equivalent of the made-from-scratch version." If they had been, she concluded, they would have cost considerably more than the home-made.

Nutritionally, American eaters are not getting from manufactured food what they pay for. It is not a matter to be taken lightly, as is obvious from the declining quality of American diets. Already, about half of the food dollar is being spent on processed foods, rather than raw. Dr. Alexander Schmidt, Commissioner of the Food and Drug Administration, says, "By 1980 probably two-thirds of the meals in this country will be previously prepared out of the home."[9]

HOW SWEET IT IS. Sugar has always been considered a treat in this country—we even give sugar lumps to horses that do something special to please us. Sugar used to be considered a treat because it was used sparingly. No longer.

Begin to take notice of the number of food products you buy that list sugar among the ingredients. Beyond such obvious sources as soda pops, marshmallows, cakes and candy, you are getting substantial doses of sugar in such products as ketchup, onion dips, pickles, peanut butter, chicken-noodle soup and biscuit mixes. That does not count products like canned fruit and vegetables that do not list ingredients, but do contain added sugar. USDA reports that manufacturers of prepared foods and beverages have become the major users of sugar in the country, putting two-thirds of national sugar production into their products.[10]

When you make sugar cookies for the family, or scoop a heaping spoonful into your morning coffee, you know what you are getting, but with industry sweetening everything in sight, you are getting much more than you think. Even the foods you know to be sweetened likely are sweeter than you suspect:

TABLE IV—1

Product and Its Maker	Sugar as % of Product Weight
Tang (General Foods)	13%
Del Monte canned peaches in heavy syrup	12
Del Monte pudding cup	18
Jell-O (General Foods)	13
Sir Grapefellow cereal (General Mills)	40
Froot Loops (Kellogg's)	35
Post Alpha-Bits (General Foods)	40
100% Natural (Quaker)	19
Cracker Jacks (Borden)	68
Cool Whip (Borden)	24
Morton's coconut cream pie (ITT)	24

Sugar consumption is climbing dramatically, with Americans eating 125 pounds of the sweet per person in 1973. To put that in perspective, Americans ate 109 pounds of beef in 1973. The average hides the fact that children are eating *more* than 125 pounds a year. It's "a good and useful food," protests the sugar industry, backed by a hallelujah chorus of food makers that use their product. Indeed it is, but 125 pounds of it every year? An apple a day may keep the doctor away, but a dozen apples a day would bring the doctor running. And so will a third of a pound of sugar a day.

A number of health professionals and consumer groups, led by the Center for Science in the Public Interest, have petitioned the Food and Drug Administration to limit the sugar contents of breakfast cereals, pointing to evidence linking high-sugar diets to tooth decay, obesity, heart disease and diabetes. It is a reasonable request, not only from the obvious standpoint of health, but also from the standpoint of price. Sugar coatings inflate the cost of the product needlessly—Kellogg's corn flakes, for example, cost 54¢ a box, while Kellogg's sugar frosted flakes cost 72¢ for the same size box. The 33% price increase is for excess sugar and profits, both of which could stand to be cut back. As Dr. Jacobson said in announcing the petition to FDA, "Parents—not cereal manufacturers—should control the amount of sugar in their children's foods."[11]

THE FAT OF THE LAND. Another food ingredient cropping up in excess as processors remake the nation's diet is fat. We have always eaten a great deal of fat—things like buttered popcorn, fried chicken, and cream in our coffee—but now we are eating a great deal more. In 1961, the average person ate 114 pounds of fat; in 1973 that was up to 125 pounds and growing.

Clearly linked to such major diseases as heart attacks, obesity is one of the major health problems in this country, yet food makers keep ladling more fat into your dinner. On reporting the rising trend in fat consumption in 1974, the Department of Agriculture noted that "convenience and snack foods have risen sharply in popularity" and that "similar growth has occurred in the fast-food enterprise, including hamburger and French-fry franchises, and the chicken and fish carryouts."[12]

Fat serves the food industry well as a cheap ingredient that can add weight and flavor to the product and still get counted as a nutrient. Indeed, fat is a nutrient, essential to a good diet, but too much of it causes obesity and squeezes other nutrients out of the diet. Nonetheless, you can expect continued heavy doses of fat in processed foods—General Mills' new entry in the breakfast-cereal race, Mr. Wonderfull's Surprize, is 14% fat.

OUT TO LUNCH. Who's the biggest feeder in the country these days? The Army? Not any more. The Department of Agriculture, with its school-lunch and commodity-distribution programs? No. USDA comes in third. The first and second spots are held by (1) McDonald's and (2) Kentucky Fried Chicken (Heublein). With thousands of fast-food outlets, backed by millions of dollars in advertising and special promotions, these two chains took in $2.3 billion in food sales in 1972 ($1.17 billion by McDonald's and $1.15 billion by Kentucky Fried Chicken).

Along with other fast-food chains, these firms have a significant and growing share of America's nutritional health in their hands. On that score, they have not performed proudly, despite a spate of advertising pushing the few nutrients they do offer. Such meals tend to be short of vitamins A and C, as well as being short of iron and fiber.[13]

A typical fast-food meal (being a hamburger, French fries and a shake) could be better than it is. Put lettuce, tomato, and cheese on a hamburger, set out properly fried potatoes and a good milk shake, and you have offered a pretty hearty fare, nutritionally speaking. What's the problem at the fast-food places? One clue is that most of them significantly avoid saying *milk* shakes. Instead, their "shakes" are a sort of aerated foam made of serum solids, milk fat, sugar, stabilizers, imitation flavoring and artificial color.

By compromising on ingredients, fast-food profits are enhanced considerably. Instead of fresh vegetables to grace the patties, you are likely to get a blob of ketchup and mustard. And the meat in these burgers, amounting to just over an ounce when cooked, is a challenge to one's goodwill. In *Nutrition Scoreboard,* a valuable eating guide that apportions nutritional ratings to dozens of common food products, Dr. Michael Jacobson gives the McDonald's regular pattie 18 points. Alpo dog food gets 30 points.[14]

You can get more burger for your buck elsewhere.

These places use national advertising to convince you
that they are cheap, but the regular McDonald's burger,
at 30¢ apiece, is meat at more than $3.00 a pound. For
that, you ought to get nutrition.

A NUTRITIONAL MEGATION IN EVERY BITE. What does
a food oligopoly do if it is caught in the embarrassing
position of peddling low nutrition at a high price? Does
it (a) improve the quality of the ingredients used; (b)
lessen the amounts of sugar and fat; (c) use its vast
advertising resources to urge people to eat more basic
foodstuffs; or (d) lower the price? None of the above.
The food industry intends to keep manufacturing the
same sugary, fat-laden, nutritionally inferior convenience
items, but with three differences: (1) they will fortify
their stuff with a few synthetic nutrients at the processing stage; (2) they will advertise the fortified product
as better than nature's own; and (3) they will raise the
price.

This potential mother lode of fortified-food sales was
first mined by the cereal manufacturers, who had been
stung badly by national publicity on the nutritional
emptiness of their creations. The industry response was
to spray synthetic vitamins on each particle, repackage
it under a brand-name that evoked wholesomeness, and
hike the price substantially. So now we have Product 19,
Total, Special K and other fortified fabrications.

Quaker stretched the logic of the cereal-fortification
scheme about as far as it could be taken with its children's offering, King Vitaman. It is sprayed with enough
vitamins for every spoonful to qualify as a vitamin pill,
and it is advertised as such: "More than just a cereal,
it's a multivitamin and iron supplement specially formulated for children and adults alike," Quaker gloats on
the back of the box. Is it as highly nutritious as it

claims? No. All of its sprayed-on vitamins cannot cancel the fact that 50% of King Vitaman's total weight is sugar.

Following the lead of the cereal oligopoly, other food manufacturers quickly cut themselves in on the deal. ITT and Tasty Baking Company both concocted fortified cakes and went into the school-breakfast business, persuading the Department of Agriculture to redefine "breakfast" to include "fortified baked product with cream filling." Not only do these firms gain a massive new market through the school-breakfast program, but they are able there to teach kids that a meal is a brand-name, packaged goodie. After breaking into the breakfast business with its "Superkake," Tasty said in its annual report that sales of its cakes and pies soared 70%.

The floodgates were open. Research departments of food firms began to hum, and the minds of corporate scientists boggled at the new horizons open to them. Not to be left out, tax-paid scientists rushed to work on "nutrification," as they termed it. Rutgers University food technologists are fascinated by the prospect of adding protein to soft drinks and of filling ketchup with vitamin C. In a novel twist of the fortification scheme, Dr. Roy Morse of Rutgers wants to put junk into healthful foods, so that people will eat what's good for them: "We want to infuse corn and peas with sugar," he told *The New York Times*. "Then children will eat them like peanuts."[15]

Bread has been *en*riched for years, primarily because the manufacturing process *de*riches bread to the point of nutritional neuterism. The Food and Drug Administration, which is supposed to regulate fortification, proposed in 1971 that bread be enriched even further, allowing 10 vitamins and minerals to be added rather than the present four.[16] Most significantly, FDA called for tripling the amount of iron contained in bread—a move designed to meet the problem of insufficient iron in American diets, particularly among women of child-bearing age.

This strategy of making iron-clad bread points out major flaws in the concept of improving diets by forti-fying manufactured foods. First, a sizable portion of the population (especially males) would be getting too much iron, and something like five percent of the people could actually be endangered by the levels contemplated —including the millions of Americans with sickle-cell anemia. Secondly, the very part of the population that needs the iron is not the most likely to gobble weight-increasing bread to get it. Instead of boosting the horse-power of everybody's bread, and boosting the price along with it, it makes more sense to spend some of those advertising dollars to educate the public and family physicians on the need for iron and its ready avail-ability in such foods as chili con carne with beans, ham-burger, veal cutlets, lima beans, blackstrap molasses and sirloin steak—not to mention liver.

In 1974, the cereal and bread makers received the prestigious stamp-of-approval of the National Academy of Sciences, which swung its considerable weight behind fortification of industry's makings.[17] A committee of NAS's Food and Nutrition Board recommended that 10 nutrients be added to cereal-grain products, encompass-ing a range of processed food items from bread to breakfast cereals, from hominy grits to Hostess Twin-kies. Behind this scientific legitimization of corporate policy, however, was the heavy hand of the food in-dustry:

—Robert O. Nesheim, chairman of the NAS committee making the recommendation, is director of research and development of Quaker Oats Company, a major seller of fortified breakfast cereals.

—The chairman of NAS's Food and Nutrition Board, to which the committee reported, appeared at FDA hearings on vitamins on behalf of Mead-Johnson baby foods, Abbott Laboratories and Pet, Inc.—all companies with a proprietary interest in more fortification.

—Senator William Proxmire charged in a Senate speech that NAS's Food and Nutrition Board "is both the creature of the food industry and heavily financed by the food industry."[18]

The enrichment proposals of the National Academy of Sciences were generally reported in the press as the final judgment of "pure" science that fortification of our food was essential. Only one or two reporters in the country, including Judith Randal of the *Washington Star-News,* took the trouble to peek behind the cloak of scientific pretense and uncover the industry ties of scientists who "come out with findings businessmen can live with and reports designed to quiet the public's fears."[19]

The NAS findings were received with grateful deference by the Food and Drug Administration, which is the official public protector on questions of food additives. Serving the public at the helm of FDA's Bureau of Foods was Dr. Virgil Wodicka, who served Ralston Purina for seven years, Libby, McNeil & Libby for three years and Hunt-Wesson Foods for nine years prior to taking over at FDA. So industry scientists at NAS have told industry scientists at FDA that the public interest is best served by letting industry do what it wants to do, which is to put a megaton of synthetic nutrients into every bite of food.

Over the past couple of years, the Food and Drug Administration has issued a set of four final orders and

13 proposed orders for food fortification that amount
to a blueprint of tomorrow's manufactured dinner. Already approved is a proposal by Del Monte Corporation
to allow tomato juice to be fortified with vitamin C, thus
giving Del Monte the means to advertise its tomato juice
as a breakfast replacement for orange juice.[20] In ruling
for Del Monte, FDA noted that the cost of adding the
vitamin C was only half a cent, but the agency did nothing to assure consumers that the fortified version would
be only a half cent more in price.

The most sweeping of FDA's proposals is one establishing guidelines for fortifying processed foods. The
proposal is put forward as a means of preventing what
FDA Commissioner Schmidt calls "an irrational nutritional horsepower race," but its impact is to legitimize
the addition of synthetic nutrients to TV dinners, pud-
dings, drinks, snacks and other empty-calorie foods,
thus driving eaters further away from basic foods.

Your food future is being surrendered to the space-
age technologies of corporate oligopolies. Already, the
fortified wares of manufacturers are advertised as the
equivalent of the real thing—Tang ads suggest that it is
as good or better for you than fresh-squeezed orange
juice, and Betty Crocker Breakfast Squares are offered
as a nutritional replacement for a full-scale breakfast.
But the companies do not talk of tiny trace minerals, or
of the fiber and bulk that are necessary to keep a body
going. Nor do they mention that factory food tends to
be high in sugar, fat and price.

HAVE YOU HAD YOUR BUTYLATED HYDROXYTOLUENE
TODAY? Adding vitamins and sugar to food is one problem, but that's not the half of it. There are about 2,500
different substances that industry puts into the American
food supply, from monosodium glutamate (MSG) to

butylated hydroxytoluene (BHT), from Red Dye No. 2
to sodium nitrite.[21] In fact, the average American is eating 6.7 pounds of food additives a year, and this unknown component of the diet is increasing at an alarming rate (see Table IV–2).

These chemical and natural additives are the glue
that holds manufactured food together. Acidulants ho-
mogenize the naturally tart taste of jelly, antioxidants
keep canned tomatoes on the shelf for months without
getting rancid, preservatives allow beer to be trucked
thousands of miles without spoiling, artificial colors
make chocolate ice cream look chocolate without the
expense of chocolate, artificial flavor puts the lemon in
frozen lemon pies, enzymes bleach the flour in cake
mixes, stabilizers keep processed cheeses firm for long
periods, nutritive agents give food value to breakfast

TABLE IV—2
Current and Estimated Food Additive Markets (1971–1980)

| | Millions of $ | | |
Class	1971	1975	1980
Acidulants	55.84	69.92	98.19
Antioxidants	12.73	15.55	19.82
Preservatives	10.64	12.58	16.06
Colors	16.77	19.37	27.38
Flavor and flavor enhancers	254.00	326.90	476.40
Enzymes	21.63	27.84	40.84
Stabilizers, etc.	98.8	128.40	151.3
Nutritive agents	61.11	91.40	146.60
Surfactants	53.71	62.05	71.64
Miscellaneous	50.74	56.18	60.58
Totals	635.97	800.19	1,108.81

Source: "Prospects in Food Additives." Unpublished speech by Dr.
Ferdinand B. Zienty (Manager of Food Research & Development, Monsanto Company) before the American Institute
of Chemical Engineers, March 19, 1974.

cereals and surfactants bind the ingredients of peanut butter together.

Should you cry in your beer, that would raise the list of additives to 60. In 1973, seventy congressmen proposed legislation that would require breweries to list on their labels any use of food additives, 59 of which have been okayed for beer.[22] Various breweries add such stuff as propylene glycol alginate to stabilize the foam; everything from ethyl acetate to juniper berries are added to artificially flavor beer; to give it a robust look, such coloring as caramel or FD&C Yellow No. 5 are added; and to prevent too much gusto, heptyl-para-hydroxybenzoate is added. Wine lovers should not be quick to gloat, for there is similar tampering with the natural state of many favored wines.[23]

David Hereth. 1973. Reprinted with permission.

Additives are everywhere. Most of them are generally
harmless, but several have been linked convincingly to
serious (and fatal) diseases, others adversely affect only
certain people and many more are big question marks.
If you have been relying on government to protect you
from dangerous food additives over the years, you will
be distressed to learn that Violet No. I, a food coloring
used for 22 years by USDA to stamp meat as "prime"
or "choice," was banned in 1973 by FDA because it
was linked to cancer. MSG, several million pounds of
which are put into a wide range of foods each year, was
finally banished from baby food because of evidence
from animal studies that it could damage the infant's
brains—yet babies and the rest of us continue to eat
large amounts of MSG in other foods. Up to 1966,
breweries could control the foam in beer by adding
cobalt salts, but at least 47 beer drinkers learned the
hard way that the combination of cobalt and alcohol is
fatally toxic.

There are thousands of people with allergies to such
freshness preservatives as BHT, BHA and EDTA, but
hundreds of food products contain these additives, without listing them on their labels. Dr. Claude Frazier, editor of the *Journal* of the American College of Allergists,
estimates that 12 to 15% of the U.S. population is
allergic to food additives.[24] Another distinguished aller-
gist, Dr. Ben Feingold, has linked hyperactivity in many
children to the heavy doses of synthetic flavorings and
colorings that are pervasive in today's manufactured
food supply. In a 1974 article written for the *Washington Post,* Dr. Feingold noted, "Six separate studies in-
volving over 200 children have demonstrated food colors and flavors to be the cause in conservatively 50%
of the [hyperkinesis and learning disabilities in chil-
dren]."[25]

Most serious is the fact that hundreds of these chemicals have not been tested enough to know with any certainty that they are safe to eat, nor is there any real knowledge about how these 2,500 ingredients react to each other when they come together in the stomach. *Fortune* magazine, in a 1972 article favorable to the use of food additives, had to admit that there is room for public concern:

> The anti-additive camp clearly has its share of cranks, conspiracy theorists, and exaggerators for effect, but there is also a deep and serious logic behind their crusade. Plenty of thoughtful scientists are concerned about the proliferation of strange new chemicals to which humans are exposed these days, and not only in food. Knowledge about the consequences has been slow to accumulate. And there have been some alarming discoveries over recent years suggesting that quite a few substances can react with, and thereby alter the composition of, the DNA molecules that make up the vital genetic blueprints for all living species.[26]

Despite public concern and inadequate scientific knowledge, the public continues to get more chemical additives with dinner. Even when a chemical is admittedly dangerous, the economic interest of food manufacturers can prevail over the health interest of eaters. Hot dogs, the all-American food, are a major threat because they contain sodium nitrite and/or sodium nitrate. You can expect these chemicals to be listed on the packages of 99.9% of all hot dogs, bacon, hams, bologna, salami, corned beef and other processed meats. The major reason for including these additives is to give color and flavor to the meat, and in recent years the meat industry has claimed that the chemicals are necessary as a preservative. In 1971, however, conclusive evidence showed that these chemicals combined with other chemicals in the stomach can form nitrosamines, powerful cancer-producing agents.

The Department of Agriculture and the Food and Drug Administration responded by creating an expert panel to examine the problem and recommend appropriate action.[27] A six-person panel was appointed, but the only nitrite expert was the director of research and development for Swift & Company, the nation's largest meat packer and a major user of the chemicals in question. No consumer representative was appointed, and when consumer organizations sought representation, they were refused. More curious was the failure to appoint an Oak Ridge National Laboratory cancer researcher who is widely recognized as a leading authority on nitrites and nitrates. There may be a clue in the fact that this eminent researcher considers nitrites and nitrates to be among the most powerful cancer-causing agents known, and he favors a substantial reduction in their use.

The government-industry panel thought otherwise, however, and it recommended in 1974 that there be only minimal reduction in the use of nitrites and nitrates. Hot dogs will continue to be dangerous to eat, but at least they will still look red and have that good, nitrite taste.

There may be a need for additives, and there are many natural substances to meet much of that need. But there is not a need for the mass of chemicals that are poured recklessly into food at the whim of manufacturers. In his 1974 book, *Coping with Food Allergy*, Dr. Claude Frazier concludes that most additives are used merely to benefit the food corporations. Dr. Feingold underscores that point, writing that artificial food colorings have no nutritional value and are hardly essential: "Their sole function is cosmetic. Without them, nothing would be lost."[28]

Too many additive users are compensating for poor manufacturing quality, and they are attempting to make a product look or taste like something it is not, or trying to keep a product on the grocery shelf longer than is reasonable. Nor is it any comfort that a company's product conforms to the safety standard set by government, since many of those standards are set by food-industry personnel who temporarily are holding government positions.

The calm willingness of food firms to experiment on American eaters is quite extraordinary. Almost all of them, and all of the big ones, continue using questionable colorings and flavors on the grounds that consumers have failed to show conclusively that the chemical is harmful to wide segments of the population. They have it backward. The burden of proof ought not to be on the eaters, but on the makers of food—not, "show me absolutely that this chemical is dangerous," but "show us absolutely that this chemical is *not* dangerous, and *is* essential to the manufacture and sale of a necessary food product."

NUTRITIONAL PARANOIA. One measure of how sensitive food makers are to charges that their food is nutritionally inferior is the length to which they have gone to discredit the organic-food movement. Both government and industry officials fall into fits of verbal excess at the mere mention of organic methods. Agriculture Secretary Butz, for example, became almost wild-eyed in his assertion that the specter of organic food production promises starvation for 50 million Americans. Henry J. Heinz, Jr., branded the organic movement "food faddism," and he wrote that its advocates "are persuading thousands to adopt foolish and costly eating habits."

What is prompting such a reaction? Organic-food production and marketing is a small cottage industry, with a few thousand family farmers and a few hundred small retail outlets producing and selling food that is free of synthetic chemicals and excess processing. It is a food-production technique predicated on the notion that nature can do a pretty good job with food without requiring the addition of artificial nutrients and flavor enhancers. Organic enthusiasts approach food as a basic, operating on the conviction that the less done to food the better.

Sales of organic food are about $500 million a year. That is a mere four-tenths of one percent of the total $161 billion food industry, which is tightly controlled by a few major companies, including the one headed by Mr. Heinz. To put the dollar figure of organic sales into perspective, it is less than the combined advertising budgets of the six leading food advertisers.

In 1974, a few academics and government officials assembled in San Francisco under the prestigious auspices of the American Association for the Advancement of Science. They convened themselves as a panel on "The Food Supply and the Organic Food Myth," and they vociferously denounced the small organic movement as "dangerous nonsense." Among the "nutrition experts" who led this curious attack was Dr. Thomas H. Jukes, the convener of the session. Jukes spent 20 years in chemical research at American Cyanamid, where his work helped make it possible to add synthetic vitamins to food.

Another panelist with a career bias against organic concepts was Dr. Emil Mrak, former chancellor of the University of California, who has served on the board

of directors of Nestlé Foundation, Sugar Research
Foundation, and Universal Foods. The Department of
Agriculture and the Food and Drug Administration
also sanctioned this industry-oriented conclave, sending
top officials to speak against organics. No speaker for
the organic side of the issue was allowed to intrude
into this kangaroo court. And the whole thing was so
heavy-handed that the American Association for the
Advancement of Science took special care afterwards
to point out that while the panel had been a formal part
of their annual meeting, it had been arranged by Jukes,
not by the Association itself.

Why all this ado over so little? Not because organic
food threatens to become a significant factor in major
food markets, but because the very existence of naturally produced, basic foods causes people to think
about the manufactured stuff they are getting from the
brand-name food companies. Think! My god! Don't
think, just buy! With billions of advertising dollars
spent to develop an image, the food goliaths are not
anxious now for eaters to start questioning it all. Dr.
Jukes confessed as much in a later Michigan speech,
saying that the organic-food movement "brings about a
mistrust of the present food supply." Widespread public
thinking about food quality could lead to widespread
public demand for more information on food products
than an assurance on television that something is "lip-
smacking, whip-cracking, patty-whacking good."

Big corporations tend to be extremely cautious institutions, run by extremely cautious managers. For example, it is not unusual for a corporate executive to
make a political contribution to both sides in a particular race, just in case. The same mentality infects a
firm's approach to business. On one hand, food makers
have sought to discredit the organic concept, but on the

other hand some of the biggest food firms have rushed out new products and promotions to cash in on the recent public longing for natural foods.

On the front cover of its 1974 annual report, General Foods pictures a very appealing display of raw foods—things like peas still in their pods, a crock of natural rice, rolls of cinnamon bark, corn in its husk and a wedge of aged cheddar cheese, all on a background of basic burlap. "Those are General Foods raw materials on the Report's cover," the company writes inside, "almost two dozen samples of the kind of ingredients the company needs to make its products." Of course, the reality is less down-home than the image. Not pictured are the adipic acid, sodium citrate, fumaric acid, artificial color, artificial flavor and BHA that go into the company's Jell-O, nor do they show the polysorbate 60, sorbitan monostearate, guar gum, artificial color and artificial flavor that help make up their Cool Whip Swiggle.

Yet, having criticized "natural food faddists," the big companies have gone into competition with them. A characteristic of oligopoly is the demise of innovation. With no competitive pressure, the big companies are able to stop worrying about product improvement, relying instead on artificial changes in their existing product. This has been the case in the breakfast-cereal industry, where "innovation" has amounted to new colors, new package designs and new giveaways ad nauseam.

Then came a real innovation—not from the four major companies that control 91% of the market, but from the tiny organic marketers that do not even register on the oligopolistic meter. Their innovation was to make a breakfast cereal that is both good and good for you, using stuff like whole grains, coconut, raisins and nuts.

No colorings, flavorings, additives, prizes, advertising—just cereal. Unheard of, but it caught on with the public.

Enter the oligopolists. Now there is "100% Natural Cereal" from Quaker, "Heartland" from Pet, "Country Morning" from Kellogg's and "Nature Valley Granola" from General Mills. With a barrage of advertising featuring old photographs and scenes of the old home place, the corporate food makers have exercised their monopoly techniques* to take over the natural-cereal market from the innovators. Even in the "good food" market, however, the big firms cannot break old habits —many of their just-plain-cereal offerings are loaded with sugar. At least their advertisements are pleasing, and you can reread those as you wait your turn at the dentist's office.

THE BREAKFAST OF CHAMPIONS? The first responsibility of food makers is to supply wholesome food. They fail to do that. Nutrition has not been deliberately trimmed by the food firms that dominate the market, but it has been inadvertently lost as those firms have emphasized cheaper processing techniques and the cosmetic aspects of food. Their interest is in selling, and nutrition is important only if the firm's marketing division can use it as a promotional point. If processing has destroyed all the nutrients, and if the public is kicking up a fuss about "empty foods," just fortify the stuff and turn it over to the advertising boys. And if there's a governmental problem with the use of chemical preservatives, get the Washington office to talk with Virgil over at FDA.

* Among these techniques, discussed later, are national advertising, premium offers to consumers, discounts to supermarkets for superior display space and deep-pocket financing of the venture, plus the fact that the risk of innovation and cost of test-marketing basically were borne by the small innovators.

What does that leave you? It leaves you eating the image advertising, the synthetic nutrients, the chemical preservatives, the artificial flavor and colors, and the high price of manufactured food—the inevitable results of oligopoly.

In an industry advertisement directed toward supermarket executives, four big food makers gave details of a major promotion that they would launch in October 1974, featuring "The Good Old-Fashioned Hearty Breakfast." This one ad offers a rare insight into the Big Sell techniques of food oligopolies, telling supermarket executives what they would be telling you.

It assured the supermarket chiefs that their eye-catching October promotion would reach 43 million adults—one of every three shoppers—and those people would be lured even closer by inclusion in popular magazines of more than a page of money-off coupons to tempt you to buy the advertised food products. And if that was not enough, the coup de grace would be to hit the suckers with a premium offer of a waffle iron! Who could resist it? Not many, suggested the industry ad, urging the supermarkets to stock up on the brand-names being promoted in order to get in on "extra sales and *profits*."

What is the "Hearty Breakfast" that was being pushed? First, waffles made of Bisquick (General Mills), which contains bleached and refined flour, fat, sugar, salt, dried buttermilk, leavening, and both BHA and BHT—a mixture for which you pay 46¢ a pound, or more than double what it would cost you to buy the ingredients needed to make your own buttermilk baking mix. Slather on some Blue Bonnet margarine (Standard Brands), containing among other things partially hydrogenated soybean and cottonseed oils, water, mono- and diglycerides, sodium benzoate, artificial flavoring, artificial coloring, and vitamins A and D added. To pour on top of the margarined waffles is Log Cabin syrup (General Foods), which mentions in the tiniest of print that it is only 3% maple sugar syrup (making up the rest of the volume with cheaper sugar and corn syrups), and adding that it contains artificial flavor, caramel color, and both sodium benzoate and sorbic acid as preservatives.

To go along with the waffle, the promotion touts Swift Brown 'N Serve sausages, which come spiced with sodium nitrite, sodium erythorbate, BHA, BHT and citric acid. You are urged to wash it all down with Maxwell House coffee (General Foods) and Bird's Eye Orange Plus (General Foods). Orange Plus might be considered orange minus by many, since it is imitation orange juice, being diluted with water, sugar, syrup, corn syrup and cottonseed oil, not to mention gum arabic to give the drink body and sodium carboxymethycellulose to give it vegetable gum. There's more: citric acid is added to give tartness, then potassium phosphate, are put in to control the tartness. To give it the "plus" of its name, vitamins C, A and B_1 are added. To give it the "orange" of its name, artificial flavor and artificial color are added. All that for only 25% more money than it would cost you to buy the same amount of frozen orange juice.

Come and get it, folks—a "good old-fashioned hearty breakfast"!

The Taste of Oligopoly

Food advertising on television and in magazines can make a heat-and-serve dinner look like a gourmet's delight. In truth, however, the processor's assembly line is not geared for taste, and not much survives. Even raw food products today are engineered commodities, designed to meet the steel grip of harvesting machinery or to survive the long haul from Texas, California and Florida fields to northern and eastern cities. Using genetics to harden fruits and vegetables, chemicals to ripen them artificially, and treated waxes and glosses to give them longer life in the grocery bins, taste has been lost along the way. Tomatoes may be picture-book red, but they are not soft, they have no tomato smell and ultimately they lack tomato taste.

Outraged in 1972 by an Agribusiness Accountability Project report that found tomatoes designed for industry rather than consumers, the head of agricultural research at the University of Florida came before a U.S. Senate investigating committee with an armload of MH-1s—a tomato made on his campus. They were very red,* very round, very tomato-looking. He presented a sample to the staff of AAP. After the Senate hearing, a couple of the tomatoes were placed on a desk at the AAP office, where they accidentally were covered with papers and forgotten. Three weeks later they were rediscovered. They had not rotted—they were still sitting there as proud, as red, as firm and as plastic as the day they were presented.

"Tasting the fruits of progress is indeed a dreary and depressing experience," moaned *New York Times* writer Alden Whitman, "especially bitter for those of us who recollect these fruits before technology took command. Oh, where have those vine-ripened tomatoes gone, those sun-sweetened oranges, those toothsome peaches?"[29] They have gone to the laboratories of cor-

* The MH-1 sometimes is harvested green and placed in storage rooms to turn red. These rooms significantly are not called "ripening" rooms, but "de-greening" rooms. There, the tomatoes are sprayed with ethylene gas to make them turn red, but not necessarily to ripen.

porate and governmental food researchers. There virtually is no fruit or vegetable in the bins of your supermarket that does not have a scientist somewhere tampering with it, trying to adjust Mother Nature to the needs of the food makers.

Of course, all of this is done in the name of consumers. It is a point of pride with food firms and with their government colleagues that they can sell strawberries in Boston in January. "Who has decided for consumers that we want a fruit all year long if, as its

"YOU'RE BOTH TOO YOUNG TO REMEMBER, BUT IN THE OLD DAYS YOU COULD TELL THE VEGETABLES APART BY TASTE!"

Sidney Harris. Reprinted with permission.

cost, there is no season when it tastes good?" demanded the National Consumers League at a 1972 congressional hearing.[30] Answer: food marketers. Those strawberries will sell if they are engineered to look tasty, even if they are not. The old guides of buying produce no longer are accurate—pull down the husk of corn at the supermarket and the kernels look big and ripe, but back home those kernels probably will turn out to be filled with water and sugar, rather than corn taste. That is a triumph of genetics, and it's a triumph over you.

If you are lucky enough to find a small company near you that sells fresh-killed poultry, or a local beef operation that brings cattle along slowly, or a market within driving distance that offers real country ham, you still are in time to get a taste of what oligopoly has done to the meat you regularly eat. Chickens today come off the same type of assembly lines that make Greyhound buses, and the buses may taste better. Vance Bourjaily, who is both a farmer and a writer, offers this view of assembly-line chicken: "It is factory raised, indoors and immobile, chemically fed; and while I think the birds reach a kind of forced, physiological maturity, the only flavor they have is what will be absorbed from the cardboard and plastic wrappings they're presented in."[31]

A woman in Wisconsin tells of raising some chickens and taking them to a butcher. The chicken buyers in the area were amazed with the size and flavor of the birds, as well as with the leanness of their meat. Chicken breeders began to come around, wanting to buy her roosters and pressing her for the secret techniques she employed to produce such quality. Her "formula" turned out to be letting the chickens run free in the farmyard, allowing them to forage on the weeds and greens available there, and occasionally tossing out some table scraps or a little corn for them to peck.[32]

Whole, frozen turkey would seem to require very little processing, but such an assumption has not figured on the imagination of today's major sellers of this large bird, including Swift, Armour, and Ralston Purina. Consumers Union conducted tests and found that frozen turkeys contain added fat, sodium, sugar, artificial color and artificial flavor, not to mention emulsifiers, flavor enhancers, antioxidants and other chemicals.[33] If your next Swift Butterball, Checkerboard Farms Honeysuckle or Armour Golden Star frozen turkey tastes bland, that is due in part to the fact that it has been diluted with water. Processors are allowed under the law to add sodium phosphate to turkey, which causes it to hold water. The November 1973 *Consumer Reports* explains a peculiar chain of circumstances that occurs at the turkey factory:

> A turkey will (1) absorb water during processing. Therefore (2) processors gain permission to sell turkey with water added. But (3) the absorbed water seeps out. So (4) the processors use chemicals to retain at least as much water as they're allowed to add. They then (5) sell water at turkey prices, implying that (6) water makes turkey taste better.

Beef? Except for the fat, there is little flavor there. The major reason is that new breeds and new factory techniques are designed to produce weight as quickly as possible, with no regard for mature flavor. Beef is advertised as being "tender" or as having "sizzle," but those describe beef fat, not beef flavor. Confined feeding by formulas, many of which contain growth stimulants, is the fate of today's beef cattle, and they grow fast, but not tasty. A clue to industry's priorities is that it is beginning to feed cattle with something called Masonex, which is a waste product of the Masonite industry. "The cattle ate more per day when they were given Masonex than when they were given grain, indicating that Masonex contains chemicals that stimulate feeding," said a report on the process. No wonder the beef tastes like cardboard.

Until recently, ham was a way of life in the South, with considerable local pride vested in treasured cures, smoking techniques and recipes. It was a taste delight. Now, most people have never seen a real country ham, even in the South. Fewer yet have tasted one. Instead, supermarkets carry only the bland, chemically processed, water-filled, plastic-wrapped simulations of modern industry. Even the old names cover shameless counterfeits: "Smoked in the tradition of ancient Virginia," claims the label on Gwaltney hams, dressing them up in a colonial motif. The company is owned by ITT, and the ham is cured with sodium nitrite.

"By the mid-Fifties, what had always been a small business based generally on personal transactions between farmers and regular clients began developing into a multi-level technological enterprise," wrote James Villas in an excellent article on the fate of honest-to-goodness ham taste.[34] Big business moved into the ham industry, expanding well beyond the scale that makes quality control possible, and they were far too eager for profits to wait for the slow-curing process that decent ham flavor requires. Why wait, when a heavy dose of chemicals and a heavier dose of advertising will produce bigger profits than quality?

To take over the country-ham market without actually making country ham required the kind of muscle that the big food firms can flex. They went to the Department of Agriculture in 1971 and came away with a new standard for "country ham" so that the term no longer means produced on the farm or even in the country. Then they sought state and federal regulations on production techniques, requiring stainless steel equipment, precise temperature controls, exact levels of salt content and so forth. Who can meet those standards? Only the big firms have the financial resources to make such capital investments and the market power to pass through to the consumer the cost of those investments.

At best, the independent farmers that make the genuine product are forced to compromise and standardize the techniques that have been passed to them through generations of ham-making. The large corporations have no trouble reducing their process to bureaucratic standards, but the real thing is made by artists, not engineers. The proposed federal standards mean, as Villas points out in his article, that "food plants located in any city of the United States could distribute 'country ham' aged no longer than four days." No self-respecting ham producer in the country would bring anything out that had not been cured for more than four months, and the real ham eater wants one over a year old.

The final step in bad taste is being taken by brand-name food firms that are preparing frozen dinners for sale to restaurants. It is one thing to have to eat a TV dinner at home, or to have to eat the fare served on airplanes, but to go out to a restaurant and pay to get it is something else. Del Monte, Ralston Purina, Stouffer (Nestlé), Green Giant and Marriott are among the peddlers of this feeding concept, in some cases possessing their own restaurants. These dinners are manufactured, cooked, packaged and frozen at the factory for shipment to restaurants, where they simply are thawed,

heated in a microwave oven and finally browned in a
stove to give them that fresh-cooked appearance. The
whole thing does not even require a kitchen, much less
a chef. We are close to the day when you can eat the
same dinner in a Fort Worth restaurant, a Baltimore
hotel, or on a flight to San Francisco.

Is manufacturing to determine the taste norm for 210
million people? Do millions of years of taste-bud evolution come down to a Stouffer frozen chicken dinner? Or
will taste buds become, as columnist Shana Alexander
speculated, the next vestigial organ of the human
race?[35]

Taste, as manufactured by food oligopolies, is based
on a national norm, and the norm is bland—nothing
too spicy, too pungent, too salty, too anything. Regional
tastes are homogenized to conform to the national
norm. "You may not like the taste of these tomatoes,"
a USDA official told Susan DeMarco of the Agribusiness Accountability Project, "but your children will
never know the difference."

Oligopoly Choice. What'll You Have?

Cry in your favorite beer today, for tomorrow it may
be gone. Not because the kegs are running dry, nor because beer is being taken off the shelves for lack of
buyers, but because oligopoly power is squeezing the
small labels out of the market.

Beer comes as close as anything to being the American drink, and beer drinkers pour over $3 billion a year
down the hatch. For years, beer was a regional and
even local product, with 750 brands being offered as
late as 1935. It has been a family business, with a great
deal of diversity in the products. Brewing formulas
have been treasured and carefully guarded secrets of

the family, and the local beers have been points of pride throughout the country. But as more money has been spent on beer, four national companies and a handful of large regionals have shut the locals out of the market, forcing most of them to shut their doors.

In 1960, there were 170 breweries still in business; today, there are only 60. Hoffman's beer, Kips Bay, DuBois, Rice Lake and Burger are just a taste of those that have folded recently. All that remains of the venerable Piel Brothers, once an institution in New York City, is a small brewery in Massachusetts.

"Miller Makes It Right," goes the ad, but Miller doesn't make it at all. It is now made by Philip Morris and is just one of the old brands that have been merged into other companies. In Texas, Pearl Beer is an institution: "Come Home to Texas," pleads an advertisement that tugs at the heart of any Texan worth the accolade, "Come Home to Pearl." But now Pearl is the brew of Southdown, Inc., a conglomerate that also makes cement, candy and oil. Come home to Southdown? Hmmmm. Well, at least there's Carta Blanca from south of the border, or you can get a case of Jax from over in New Orleans. No, Southdown has bought those too.

It's happening all over. Meister Brau is owned by Miller, Narragansett by Falstaff, and Buckhorn and Burgermeister by Hamm's. Sometimes only the labels survive such mergers, with the formulas being destroyed and just another version of the parent corporation's brew going in the bottle. Heileman Brewing Company, for example, has bought several small brands in the Wisconsin area, but not the plants that produced the brands.[36]

Already, more than half of the national beer market is in the hands of the three big nationals—Anheuser-

Busch, Schlitz and Pabst—and their dominance is
growing. Only 30 breweries are expected to exist by
the end of this decade, and Bill Coors, president of the
largest and most powerful regional brewery in the nation, says "Our long-term strategy is to survive," adding
that "By 1990 there will be only three major companies left."[37]

Even with beer drawing more of the consumer's dollar, and with both prices and profits* on the rise, the
market power of the beer oligopoly is enough to force
competitors out of markets. The power of the giants is
the power to come into practically any market and
dominate it. Local brews exist at the discretion of the
major brews.

Backed by a nationally advertised image of premium
quality, Budweiser can zero in on the local markets of
brands like Lone Star, Stroh, Dixie and Olympia by
blanketing the area with advertising and cutting prices
for a while. Budweiser can cut its price by 5 or 10
percent in San Antonio and not feel the pinch, since
that city is only a small piece of the firm's national
sales. But San Antonio is the major market for Lone
Star, and they do not have the deep-pocket financing to
engage in a price war. Budweiser can deliver a body
blow to Lone Star with such a price promotion on one
weekend, then shift to Detroit the next weekend to
pummel Stroh.

The heavily advertised image of quality probably is
the single biggest advantage working for the national
firms, allowing them to sell their "premium" beers at a
substantially higher price than locals. The "premium"

* The median return-on-investment during the last five years
for all industries was 11.4%. Among the dominant brewers,
profitability was significantly higher, with Anheuser-Busch averaging a 17.8% return-on-investment during the past five years,
Schlitz enjoying a 16.7% return and Pabst taking 13.9%.

concept has no factual base at all, but simply is a promotional gimmick first used in the 1930s when the big breweries began to expand into distant markets. As Charles Burck explained in *Fortune,* the cost of shipping their beer forced them to charge higher prices, so they had to create the impression that theirs was a brew superior to those made locally. The idea became ingrained in the public mind, and the big companies are able even today to sell their "premium" brands at 10¢ to 25¢ more a sixpack than regular-priced beer, even though there is virtually no difference in quality. As Burck wrote, "The extra money paid for premium has given Anheuser-Busch, Schlitz, and Pabst the wherewithal to build new plants—and to underwrite bigger marketing expenditures, which in turn have kept the premium cachet alive."[38]

If advertising by such television talents as Ed McMahon and a Clydesdale horse is not enough to dominate any given market, the big companies can always resort to muscle. Coors, the fourth largest seller in the country, has been found in violation of antitrust laws for setting territorial limitations on its distributors, for attempting to fix retail prices and for coercing bars into selling no draught beer other than Coors.[39] Though it is a regional beer, Coors monopolizes much of the 12-state market in which it sells—it has 41% of the California market and more than two-thirds of the Oklahoma market.

Such market power and anticompetitive techniques put unbearable pressures on independent local beers. It is costing them their business, but the disappearance of their beer from the shelves and the bars also costs you —both in terms of money and choice. Beer drinkers paid about $200,000,000 extra in 1972 because of the demise of competition, according to the staff of the

Federal Trade Commission. To many, the greater cost is the elimination of variety.

The tastes and textures of beers used to be as varied as the areas that produced them, but local flavor is going out of the beer-drinker's life, replaced by the pale, homogenized brews that the largest marketers have set as the national taste. Try it, you'll like it. Or else. Ask for a Rheingold in a Newark restaurant, a Shiner in Houston, a Grain Belt in Omaha, a Rolling Rock in Philadelphia or an Anchor Steam in San Francisco and chances are the waitress will stare at you like you're a troublemaker before snapping that your choice is Bud, Schlitz and Pabst. Like the hustler used to say in the old shell game, you pay your money and you take your choice.

Programmed to conform to an average national taste, the makings of oligopoly take the zest out of eating. Those who savor an unadulterated country ham, those who enjoy the character of local beer, those who seek the richness of real cream are misfits in the modern food world, and increasingly they have nowhere to go: Oligopoly leaves a lot of us out.

Making Dinner: Your Food Future

The final step in manufactured food is being taken, and it is both eaters and farmers who are being stepped on. Synthetic food is here.

Having both the technological and economic power to redesign food, oligopolists are not hesitating to exercise it. "We might all be able to exist and flourish on a diet of three adequately compounded pills a day," wrote the head of Central Soya Company's Chemurgy division in an article urging a shift to synthetic foods: "This is not an intriguing prospect for most people. And so it is practical to have the soy-protein foods look like foods with which we are familiar."[40] Ah, at least he would allow us the "appearance" of the real thing, though one detects a real inclination to sell us the pills.

The new farm is the laboratory, and the American provider is a multinational, multiproduct food oligopoly. These futuristic food makers are taking you somewhere you may not want to go, but control is rapidly slipping from your hands. "Eventually, we'll have to depend on artificial foods to feed the world's population," declared an executive of ITT. "By using artificial ingredients now, we're helping in their development."[41] Coming from a major food oligopolist, that prophecy of our food future is self-fulfilling, and self-serving.

IT'S BROWN, BUT IT'S NOT CHOCOLATE. Milo Minderbinder, the amoral conglomerate-builder of *Catch 22,* got stuck with bales of Egyptian cotton in one of his deals that went bad. To cut his losses, Minderbinder came up with the idea of coating bits of the cotton with chocolate and selling them as candy. We all laughed at this scene in Heller's novel, but it forced us to the discomforting admission that big business certainly would sell chocolate-covered cotton if it could.

They have, though with a little different twist. Instead of candy-coated cotton, such favorites as Baby Ruth and Butterfinger are cotton-coated candies. Standard Brands, the food conglomerate that now makes Baby Ruth and Butterfinger, does not use chocolate to coat its bars, but ladles on a synthetic substitute derived from cotton. At least Standard Brands is using a plant derivative. Peter Paul Mounds and Almond Joys now are coated with what is termed "an undisclosed brown substance," and even the president of the company has confessed "I'm not sure exactly what it is."[42]

Counterfeit chocolate is being offered by the candy makers because it is more profitable to them, not because it is better tasting or more nutritious. "It's a more lasting coating," explained a candy official to a *Newsday* reporter, "Nice gloss, nice shine, nice snap to the product." Monsanto Corporation has announced that its chemists have developed a total candy "system" that combines an artificial flavor with a bulking agent and gives the manufacturer the means to replace not only the chocolate coating but also the chocolate filling.[43] A Monsanto executive noted that the system will offer candy makers a 17 to 20% savings. Does that mean that you can expect counterfeit chocolate candies to be 17 to 20% cheaper? No. Let that melt in your mouth.

THIS IS MERLINEX; IT IS NOTHING. International Multifoods manufacturers a material they call Merlinex, advertising it to food manufacturers as "Instant Anything." Food makers use Merlinex as a substitute for real ingredients, extruding, baking, shaping, flavoring, stretching and doing almost anything else to it. It is the silly putty of the food world that you eat as an extender in colby cheese, as phony fig paste in fig bars, as imitation strawberry filling in pastries, and as a texturizer in brownies, to mention only a few of its uses.

Merlinex is just one of the synthetics and substitutes that are the makings of the new dinner. The major users of these fake foods today are convenience food manufacturers, fast-food chains and such institutional outlets as schools, airlines, hotels, and hospitals. Among the items in your pantry now that most likely contain synthetic ingredients are baby food, pot pies, orange juice, TV dinners, hamburgers, canned Mexican food, candy, canned stews and soups, bologna, fish sticks, sausages, cream, bacon bits, cheese, turkey rolls and ice cream.[44]

Already, synthetics and substitutes hold 21% of the citrus-beverage market and high percentages of such markets as whipped toppings and coffee creamers. Imitation milk is now being marketed by two companies and is expected to take up to 10% of the fluid milk market by 1980. Pet, Carnation and Borden are brand names that once were synonymous with real milk and milk products, but today these firms are among the largest marketers of such artificial milk products as nondairy coffee "whiteners." Even the Department of Agriculture's main cafeteria in Washington recently has taken the symbolically significant step of switching from coffee milk to these whiteners.

The raw materials for fake foods are derived not only from plants and animals, but also from such nonagricultural sources as petroleum and coal. No matter what they are made of, they require a medicine chest full of additives to hold the makings together and to make them appear to be the real stuff. Synthetic milk, for example, is based on sodium caseinate, a chemical component derived from milk, and is then bolstered with vegetable fat, emulsifiers, buffers, protein, stabilizers, body agents, sweeteners, flavorings, colorings and preservatives.

Even the synthetic offerings made from high-quality vegetable proteins are unable to compare nutritionally to the genuine foods they replace. A synthetic soy-based hamburger, for example, does not approach the protein value of meat, as the Department of Agriculture acknowledged in a 1972 study of synthetics. "Because of essential amino-acid imbalance, most plant proteins are less efficient, have lower digestibility, and a lesser biological value than animal proteins."[45] Adding synthetic amino acids to the synthetic "meat" does not yield satisfactory results, says the USDA report, either because it

We've just invented a great new flavor! Counterfeit Chocolate.

GOOD NEWS!! In these days of dwindling supplies and high costs... our new COUNTERFEIT CHOCOLATE FLAVOR may answer a lot of production problems. It is imitation chocolate flavor but it's robust taste and aroma are just like the real thing! We mean the dark, expensive stuff made from imported South American cocoa beans. So if you're searching for a way to strengthen and enhance the chocolateness of your products, we may have the answer.

COUNTERFEIT CHOCOLATE. Now available in liquid or powder form. It's convenient, easy to use and economical. Try it. One taste, one whiff and you'll wonder how anything that good could be counterfeit.

is too expensive or because the additives are potentially toxic.

Nutritious or not, meat "extenders" and substitutes are taking an increasing share of the market, being used in everything from fast-food hamburgers to add-meat products you use at home. Primarily, such stuff is a material termed Textured Vegetable Protein (TVP), which generally is manufactured from soy beans by processing machinery similar to the kind that spins nylon from petrochemicals. Archer-Daniels-Midland, one of the largest grain exporting corporations in the world, is the leading manufacturer of TVP, claiming over 50% of the market. Other makers include Nabisco, General Mills, Miles Laboratories, Cargill and Central Soya. Recently, Ralston Purina has entered the market in a joint venture with Continental Can, marketing a soy-based substitute called SPF-200. "The enterprise should expedite penetration of several markets with a unique structured protein," says Ralston Purina.

Mostly, such synthetics are coming to us without our knowledge. The fast-food hamburger chains have been the earliest major outlets because their products are not subject to the same labeling requirements of other meats and because consumer expectations of quality are not so high there. The Department of Agriculture opened up the school lunch and breakfast programs to the synthetic manufacturers by allowing textured vegetable protein to replace up to 30% of the meat requirement. That will also help to get a new generation of eaters used to the peculiar taste and texture. USDA now has given the manufacturers another promotional coup by allowing them to call their synthetics "Textured Meat Alternatives," which has a more palatable sound than textured vegetable protein.[46]

The bait thrown out to reel consumers into the hands

of the meat fabricators is a cheaper price. But in terms of nutritional equivalency, it is not cheaper. And most meat products that contain synthetics do not even advertise that fact and do not sell any cheaper than solid meats. Even where there are cost differences, consumers can hardly trust oligopolistic manufacturers to hold their prices once market positions are established.

In some cases, the meat substitute is *more* expensive. Williams Foods, Inc. is a Missouri company that markets TVP directly to consumers, selling it in 4-ounce foil pouches that frequently are located at the meat counter of supermarkets. "Williams Fortified Textured Vegetable Protein," reads the label, "makes ground beef go twice as far." But it is cheaper to buy more ground beef, since Williams TVP costs $1.36 a pound.

In the new food economy, taste does not come naturally, but from a vial. Whether it is a tomato extender, a strip of fake bacon or an imitation filling for doughnuts, the synthetic is tasteless. Fortunately, consumers are still picky enough to insist that at least some approximation of flavor exist. They get less than they bargained for. "Give us your flavor problem," says General Aromatic Products, a division of the Stepan Chemical Company. "Our staff of highly trained specialists continually search for flavors and flavor systems to meet the ever increasing demands of the food industries." They offer a full line of standardized flavors, from bacon to strawberry, all of which come either as a liquid or in spray-dried form. For manufacturers of tomato soups, spaghetti sauces, ketchups and other such items, this outfit provides a Cooked Tomato Flavor with a "taste like it came off grandma's stove." For processors of tomato juice and the like, the company sells Fresh Tomato Flavor that gives "the full vine-ripened, fresh, tomato effect."

The William M. Bell Company has come up with Beef Flavor Imitation #11.001, advertising that "This is a most pleasing full bodied beef flavor and aroma, characteristic of prime roast of beef," adding that "It extrudes well in high protein foods, and is ideal in soups, gravies and other processed food where meat replacement is desired." Givaudan Corporation announced that it has responded to consumer demand for "naturally-flavored" foods, by developing a series of "scientifically, reconstituted artificial oils." The mind reels, to say nothing of the stomach.

No LEMONS, No EGGS, No CREAM. JUST PIE. Fake food is a fake. No amount of advertising copy and no amount of USDA assurances or revised standards can change that. Who is asking for these substitutes? Not consumers. Where is the consumer demand for food that is nutritionally inferior, laden with chemicals, has an artificial flavor that tastes artificial and costs as much as genuine food? Farmers certainly are not calling for it. The new food economy employs chemists, not farmers. Independent business? Synthetic food requires massive capital and enormous market power; only big and concentrated businesses need apply.

Fake food is the future because big business wants it. Read the annual reports of the big food makers and read their industry publications and you find them making massive capital investments and banking their future growth in the areas of synthetic food manufacturing. It is a question of convenience to them. The switch to ersatz allows them to buy raw materials cheaply on a relatively stable market. It allows them to reduce food to technology and systems, things they understand. The expensive, patented technology required by fake food puts up a solid barrier to competition, enhancing the oligopolistic positions they already hold. The flexibility of the raw material allows easy product differentiation for marketing purposes. Add it up and the bottom line shows market control, growth potential and profits. That is a result sure to draw applause from the board of directors and the large institutional shareholders, and it makes a manager's job secure.

The food economy used to exist to produce an abundant supply of good foods at a reasonable price. Today it exists to produce organizational growth and profits. Product quality no longer is an attitude or an organizational objective, but is just one of many corporate divisions. The concern with quality is reduced to a technological monitoring of whether the soup has enough artificial flavor and synthetic bulk to be advertised as "Zesty," or whether enough vitamin C has been added to meet FDA's minimum standards. And price is whatever the oligopoly sets. As long as dinner meets technological specifications, it is good and good for you, no matter what you say.

In 1971, National Educational Television ran a funny skit that stripped bare the pretensions of manufactured food.[47] Created by Marshall Efron and Penny Bernstein, the program showed what you would need to make a Morton's frozen lemon cream pie in your own kitchen. Donning the chef's hat, Efron acted the part of a cooking teacher on those how-to-do-it cook shows, taking the viewer step-by-step through the adding and mixing of such ingredients as sugar, sodium bicarbonate, ammonium bicarbonate, sodium caseinate, more sugar, emulsifiers, polysorbate 60, artificial coloring and artificial flavoring. "You may wonder what kind of pie we've made here," Efron said at the end of the spoof, holding up the Morton's box:

There it is. A modern lemon cream pie. I'll open it for you. Get it out of the box. Good. Factory-fresh, factory-approved. No lemons, no eggs, no cream. Just pie.

The people at Morton's, an ITT subsidiary, were not amused. The company fired out a "Sales Bulletin" to everybody in its marketing system, critiquing every detail of Efron's presentation and showing particular sensitivity to the lack of lemon in their lemon cream pie. Not so, said the memo—the pie does use artificial lemon flavor, but there also is a bit of real lemon juice mixed in with that flavoring. Consequently, Morton's decided that is was justified in changing the list of ingredients on the pie package from "artificial flavoring" to "lemon juice and other natural and artificial flavors."[48] Morton's got the last laugh.

It is not inevitable that the world will retire to the laboratory for dinner, but it certainly is going to happen if we allow a few giant corporations to continue working their will over our food economy. Nutrition, taste and choice of food are factors of the economic structure that delivers them. With little competitive pressure, with even less governmental pressure, and with no effective resistance from the public, oligopolists are abandoning farmers, abandoning nature—and leaving you to eat whatever is put before you.

CHAPTER V

Ads, Gimmicks and Shelf Space: Barriers to Competition

---

1. "The King of Beers"
2. "M'm! M'm! Good!"
3. "Good to the Last Drop!"
4. "It's the Real Thing"
5. "We're the Fresh Guys"

How many of these slogans and jingles are stuck in your mind? You probably are able to reel off the brand-name products that these advertisements promote,* and many others. That's what advertising has become—not an effort to transmit information to consumers so they can make intelligent choices in the market, but an effort to establish brand-name identification in consumers' minds, so they will unthinkingly reach for the branded item on the shelf.

What do the five samples above tell you about the products? Nothing. But although food advertising is fluff, offering no effective guidance to consumers and making a mockery of consumer sovereignty, it works well for the big advertisers. "Obviously, you think you

* 1. Budweiser (Anheuser-Busch); 2. Campbell's Soup; 3. Maxwell House Coffee (General Foods); 4. Coca-Cola; 5. Wonder Bread (ITT).

135

can influence spending patterns—or you would not spend money on advertising," Secretary Butz said in a 1974 speech before a group of food manufacturers. And as the Federal Trade Commission has found in several studies, the larger the food firm, the greater the reliance on advertising.[1]

Advertising and promotions are the lifeblood of oligopoly. The slogans above are those of the leading advertisers in each of the product categories, each of the categories are highly oligopolistic, and the products are the leading seller in their oligopolistic category. This relationship between advertising and oligopoly is repeated throughout the food industry. Back in 1963, four companies controlled 75% of the soft-drink market and accounted for 83% of soft-drink advertising; four firms held 48% of the canned-seafood market and accounted for 86% of the advertising; the four largest makers of prepared flour had 67% of that market and accounted for 96% of the advertising; and the big four breakfast-cereal manufacturers accounted for 83% of the market and 83% of the advertising.[2]

The breakfast-cereal industry has been a leader in promotional gimmickry, offering basically the same product in dozens of different colors, packages and shapes, with assorted sugar coatings and prizes. In terms of nutrition and taste, practically all prepared breakfast cereals are a waste of time and money, but the four companies that control the industry (sharing 91% of sales by 1973) use their market power and an advertising budget of some $75 million a year to sell their concoctions. Professor Willard Mueller, a respected authority on economic concentration, told the U.S. House Judiciary Committee in 1973 that monopoly power and advertising expenditures in the cereal industry "are costing American consumers in excess of $100 million annually."[3]

The FTC studied 20 major food corporations that bought out 65 brand-name food products between 1950 and 1965.[4] Prior to selling out, the independent companies spent a combined sum of $22.7 million on advertising. Within one year of being purchased by the 20 big corporations, total advertising for the 65 brands zoomed to $43 million. When H. J. Heinz, for example, bought Star-Kist in 1962, the tuna firm was spending $300,000 on network television advertising. Within two years, Heinz had quadrupled Star-Kist's TV advertising. That advertising cost does not make the tuna taste any better; nonetheless, it is passed right through to the consumer in the form of higher tuna prices.

A heavy reliance on advertising is both a result and a cause of monopoly food power. Put together, they spell high profits. In a 1969 report, the FTC found that "concentration is closely allied with firm profitability," and that a heavier dose of advertising makes profits even better.[5] In general terms, the FTC found that where four food companies held 40% of the market, they had a profit rate of 6.3%. If four firms held 70% of the market, however, they had a profit rate of 11.5%. Then, if they quintupled their advertising, they had a profit rate of 15.9% (see Appendix C).

Four billion dollars a year are spent on advertising and promotion of food products, with the bulk of it coming from a few oligopolistic food firms. In fact, in 1964 only 50 food makers accounted for more than 80% of advertising in all media and nearly 90% of food advertising on television.[6] In public forums (such as appearances before consumer groups or before congressional committees) these big advertisers downplay the impact of their advertising, but among themselves they openly admit its importance. *Supermarket News* is a major publication directed toward the chain-store executives that determine which food products get on the shelves. The brand-name food makers advertise in this industry periodical, going out of their way to assure the grocery executives that they are promoting their product widely and frequently, thus promising that consumers will climb over each other for the chance to cart the stuff out of the store:

—Gerber boasts in an ad that its "highly effective direct mail program alone reaches two out of every three new mothers, and keeps them aware of Gerber from the time their babies are six weeks old until they reach toddler age."

—"Del Monte advertising was designed to make a shambles of your displays," says a full-page ad that features a beaming grocer hauling off empty boxes from a depleted Del Monte display. "Night after night we talk to your cutomers," drones the ad. "We reach 9 out of 10 households on NBC and CBS TV networks during prime time plus local TV in the top 20 markets."

—Noting that Wyler's is the leading seller among pre-sweetened drink mixes, Borden's comforts supermarket executives with the news that it has launched a "dynamite campaign" designed to extend its lead, encompassing a "big *prime time* network TV schedule," "a great schedule of commercials on popular Saturday and Sunday children's shows!" and "a big daytime TV schedule."

—Diet Delight, headlining the boast that it has 60% of the canned diet-food business, attributes that market concentration to the fact that it accounts for "A hefty 90% of all canned diet-food advertising," telling the supermarketers that "We help *you* sell these products with our strategically placed campaigns."

—Roman Meal bread, a franchised product sold by two of the bread oligopolists (ITT and Interstate Brands), promised in a *Supermarket News* ad that it would soon "be back on network television with John Chancellor and Walter Cronkite." It seems that previous spots on these two shows had increased consumer awareness of the bread to an all-time high, caused the brand to "register" with a significant number of shoppers and increased demand sharply.

These enormous advertising and promotion expenditures of the major food makers erect an insurmountable barrier to those independent firms that might otherwise be competitors. Want to compete with Jell-O? General Foods puts $6.5 million worth of advertising into this one product. You might make a better cereal than Kellogg's Sugar Frosted Flakes, but can you amass an additional $4.6 million to match its advertising? ITT spends $1 million a year to advertise Twinkies, which is only one product of its cake line, which is only one component of its bakery subsidiary, which is only one segment of its food group, which is only one fragment of its multinational empire. Table V–1 lists the 1973 advertising budget of some of the largest food companies.

These figures seriously understate the full height of the competitive barrier posed by the advertising budgets of the big food makers, for they fail to include such additional components as special TV discounts for national advertisers, national sales forces that travel from store to store to promote products, discounts that oligopolistic companies give to retailers who are willing to allow special displays for a product, and savings to

TABLE V—1
1973 Advertising Expenditures of Some Food Corporations

Food Corporation	1973 Ad Expenditure	Advertising as % of 1973 Sales	% of Advertising Spent on Television	Rank Among National Advertisers
General Foods	$180,000,000	8.1%	85%	3
Heublein	77,800,000	5.9	67	18
Coca-Cola	76,000,000	3.5	74	19
General Mills	74,200,000	3.7	82	22
Kraftco	74,000,000	2.4	60	23
Nabisco	69,050,000	6.8	92	27
Norton Simon (Hunt-Wesson Foods)	61,700,000	5.1	57	33
Pepsico	58,000,000	4.4	78	37
Pillsbury	50,000,000	5.0	82	43
Standard Brands	50,000,000	4.5	57	43
McDonald's	46,500,000	3.1	90	48
Kellogg	45,000,000	5.4	88	49
Campbell Soup	40,000,000	3.7	61	53
Ralston Purina	38,500,000	1.6	78	56
Anheuser-Busch	36,520,000	3.9	59	59
Joseph Schlitz	34,500,000	3.9	84	63
CPC International	34,200,000	4.0	60	65
T. J. Lipton	28,000,000	6.9	72	73
Seven-Up	27,358,000	18.6	76	75
Nestlé	27,000,000	4.5	85	76
H. J. Heinz	26,000,000	1.8	74	79
Quaker	26,000,000	2.6	87	79

Source: *Advertising Age.* August 26, 1974.

oligopolists who allow smaller firms to bear the burden of innovation.

SEEING IS BELIEVING. Brand-name TV advertisers are quick to pat themselves on the back as public benefactors: "By putting up with our ads," goes the explanation, "you get free programs on the tube." Hardly. You do not have to put coins in the television set, but you most certainly pay coins for those programs every time you go to the grocery store. It is one thing to have to listen to the television commercials of Wonder Bread, but quite another thing to realize that every time you pick up a loaf of the stuff you also are picking up a fraction of the $5 million a year ITT spends to put those ads on television. Television advertising is a cost of doing business, and the advertisers figure it into the price of every food product they put up for sale.

But the greatest cost of food commercials is their contribution to food oligopolies. First, only a limited number of minutes are available to advertisers during prime time. These are the most effective advertising slots on television, and your own viewing experience will attest that the largest, brand-name companies dominate them. The major reasons that they get the best time is that they buy at the national level, they buy regularly and they buy in large amounts.

To appease these heavy spenders, the networks give drastic discounts, ranging from 30% to as high as 75% off.[7] One television executive told a Senate committee in 1966 that a small independent company would have to pay $3.50 to $4.00 per thousand households for advertising, while the big advertisers would get the same audience for a cut-rate $2.50. The FTC found that to get a big discount "commonly requires annual expenditures of $3 million or more on a single network."[8]

The discount tactic alone cuts out most would-be competitors and effectively leaves the "public" airwaves to private oligopolies. It is no small advantage, for access to national television is a major sales factor.

Fortune quoted a Budweiser executive assessing his company's 1963 switch of $7 million from billboards to TV advertising: "This put us *so* far ahead of the rest of the industry that it was like plucking a chicken."[9]

With assuring regularity, the largest food makers hammer home their brand names in the prime viewing hours. "Advertising works cumulatively," instructed an industry publication. "In fact, continuity may be the most important single factor in effective advertising."[10] That ability to come into your home again and again establishes brand-name identity without doing anything to improve the quality of the product or to lower its price. Instead of competing on product quality, the dominant firms hire Bill Cosby (Del Monte), Patricia Neal (General Foods), Ann Blyth (Hostess) or other personalities to gain your trust and sell their wares. Instead of lowering the price, they hire advertising agencies to create Tony the Tiger, Charlie Tuna or the Poppin Fresh doughboy. It is a nonproductive advantage that smaller competitors do not have.

Big advertisers do not entrust their brand-name identification campaigns solely to television, but engage in "saturation" efforts that link all media together, from national magazines to direct mail. "*Redbook* Helps Fill Your Cash Register!" claims a 1974 advertisement in *Supermarket News*. This is just one of those trusted magazines that pass themselves off as the shopper's friend but exist primarily as an advertising medium for food manufacturers. "Your customers read about Del Monte in *Ladies' Home Journal*, *Family Circle*, *Woman's Day*, *Better Homes and Gardens*, and *Ebony* month after month," Del Monte told grocery executives. Some of these magazines are sold at the supermarket checkout counters and are used by the food companies as major promotional outlets.

Good Housekeeping sells trust—yours. In industry
ads placed by this magazine to solicit food advertisers,
Good Housekeeping sells the idea that housewives trust
them and will trust anyone who advertises in their
pages:

> One of the major problems facing the packaged goods
> advertiser is gaining the consumer's confidence and get-
> ting her to believe what you say.
> This is where *Good Housekeeping* comes in.
> Thirteen separate studies prove that women have the
> most confidence in the advertising in *Good House-
> keeping*.
> And the more that women believe your ad, the easier
> it is for you to persuade them.
> Here at *Good Housekeeping,* we help put some of the
> impulse back into buying.

It is giant food firms that advertise in the pages of
these magazines, not smaller competitors. In the 1974
"special food issue" of *Family Circle* magazine, there
were 20 full-page food ads, more than half of them
touting the products of just three corporations: Kraftco
had seven ads, General Mills had two and Hunt-Wesson
had two. The others were taken by Heinz, Quaker,
Armour, Stokely Van Camp, General Foods, Campbell's Soup, Ralston Purina, Ragù and Pennsylvania
Dutch noodles. It is not that independent companies
fail to recognize the marketing potential of such high-
circulation magazines, but that they cannot afford their
rates.

In the first place, full-page color ads are expensive,
and not many small firms or potential entrants into food
manufacturing can amass the excess capital necessary to
launch such advertising campaigns. For example, a
full-page color ad run in just one issue of *Woman's*
Day costs $35,000. Furthermore, magazine advertising

rates discriminate against the small buyer, giving a major competitive advantage to those who advertise heavily and regularly. The Federal Trade Commission reported in 1966 that discounts allowed by leading magazines ranged from 12 to 17%, and "to obtain the maximum discount from some magazines annual outlays of $2 million are required."[11] It is doubtful that a small firm, just getting started in the food business, would have a total advertising budget of $2 million, much less be able to put all of it into one magazine.

Making it tougher for those audacious enough to attempt to compete with the oligopolists is the fact that the magazines allow a food maker to lump together all of its products in qualifying for these discounts. This means that a new company making nothing but salad dressing would have to put $2 million worth of advertising into a magazine before getting a discount, while Kraft could get the discount for its salad dressings at a much lower level of investment, since it also advertises margarine, marshmallows, cheese, one-pan meals, mayonnaise and a range of other foods in the same magazine.

The same advantages are available to the big firms that advertise in newspapers. A local company whose ads total a half-page a week pays up to 40% more for its space in the newspaper than does a large advertiser who takes several pages of space.[12] The intent of all of these media discounts surely is not to perpetuate food oligopolies, but such an impact is unmistakable.

OLIGOPOLY GIMMICKS. Consumers are lured to participate in marketing gimmicks that not only promote the products of oligopolies but also help to prevent the rise of competition from below. Food coupons are the most common gimmick. Twenty billion of these a year are "dropped," as the industry terms it, through news-papers, magazines, direct mail and on food packages. The lure is a few cents off on some advertiser's product. Shoppers take the bait to the tune of a billion coupon redemptions each year, "saving" the several thousand people who clip them a sum approaching $200 million. The "savings" has to be in quotes because it is illusory.

One thing oligopolies do not do: give away money. That 200 million dollars redeemed by coupon clip-pers is figured into the price of the products by the food makers that offer the coupons. All of us who buy the products pay for the coupons whether we redeem them or not. The company is out nothing—they have devised a promotional scheme that gives them good publicity, that convinces people to try their product and that is totally subsidized by consumers. In short, they are tak-ing $200 million extra from all consumers and giving it to the few who redeem coupons, while also establish-ing greater consumer identification with their brand.

Not only do consumers pick up the bill for coupon-ing, but their participation also helps to stamp out com-petition. A coupon campaign is dependent on a large advertising budget to distribute the things, and on an initial amount of capital to put the hustle into play. With limited capital, limited advertising budgets and limited access to advertising media, smaller and would-be competitors cannot match the couponing power of the dominant food makers—glance through the weekly food section of any big-city newspapers and you will see that coupon offers almost always flow from the food giants.

If a new competitor arises or an existing one makes a move on the leadership positions of the oligopolists, the latter can rush out a coupon campaign to deter con-sumers from switching to the competing product. If an oligopolist wants to introduce a new size or style of package, or if it wants to introduce a new product, the coupon is a handy tool to wield. "There's a good deal behind our new meat labels," promised Libby in a full-page color newspaper ad that announced a new package design and offered a 7¢ coupon just to make sure nobody got nervous and switched.

A barrage of coupons led the way in 1973 and 1974 when the cereal oligopoly moved to take over the "natural" breakfast food market—"Wake up to a breakfast cereal as natural as its name," drawled Kellogg when it introduced its Country Morning brand, attaching a coupon worth 10¢ toward the purchase of same.

Since the dominant food corporations in practically any food line today are multiproduct firms, they are able to use one product to sell another. Heublein can attach a coupon to its A-1 steak sauce worth a few pennies off its Grey Poupon Dijon mustard, or it can push its Ortega brand of canned chilis by linking their sales to its Snap-E-Tom tomato cocktail. This flexibility is particularly useful when pushing a new product— "We'll send you a coupon for free Minute Maid lemonade when you buy Minute Maid orange juice," advertised this subsidiary of Coca-Cola in 1974, adding, "Or, if you prefer, you can use the coupon to enjoy other great tasting Minute Maid ades: pink lemonade, limeade, orangeade or lemon 'n limeade."

A variation of the coupon gimmick is the premium gimmick—coupling the sale of a food product to a prize or gift. It could be called the Cracker Jacks syndrome. By whatever name it is called, it is widely employed today:

—Planters peanuts (Standard Brands) offers coupons worth 10¢ off on Planters and $10.00 off on a Kodak camera outfit.

—Stokely Van Camp circulated 30 million coupons offering four scenic placemats for 10 Stokely labels.

—Star-Kist's Charlie Tuna (H. J. Heinz) will send a battery-operated pencil sharpener in exchange for $4.95 and three tuna labels.

· —A ring made from sterling-silver spoon handles is yours for $3.50 and proof of purchase of Minute Maid orange juice.

This promotional technique is frequently pitched to children, with extensive advertising in funny papers. Kool-Aid offered kids a pup tent, Dole offered a banana blow-up and Baby Ruth offered baseball bats, balls and gloves in recent promotions. It is characteristic of all of these special offers that the gift carries the burden of the advertising, not the food product. What does the taste and nutritional quality of Eckrich bologna (Beatrice Foods) matter when it is the ticket to an autographed Hank Aaron baseball bat? And the price of the stuff is no object to these little shoppers, since it is not their money.

The shift to premium peddling indicates how limited product and price competition is in the food industry. The premium has become more important than the food. And the technique also works to further limit competition by tying buyers to established brand names. Plenty of small meat processors can make sausages as good as Eckrich's, if not better, but they find it mighty hard to compete with the deep-pocket advertising punch that allows Eckrich to bring in the power hitting of Hank Aaron.

TINKERING AND LITTERING. In a 1974 article on Procter & Gamble, *Fortune* reported that "Once a brand is established, P & G changes it in some major or minor way twice a year."[13] That is a dramatic example of "product differentiation," the term economists have attached to the hokey attempts of oligopolists to make products appear different or improved without actually improving them. It amounts to little more than frequent and meaningless design changes. Automobile oligopolists pioneered it by annually adding or taking away the chrome fins on their cars; detergent oligopolists do it by putting in or taking out the blue dots in their boxes; and breakfast-cereal oligopolists do it by changing the flavor and color of their makings.

It is a gimmick that allows the food makers to launch continuous new advertising campaigns designed to keep consumers reaching for products that essentially are the same old stuff. The strategy is based on advertising, and it suffocates the real improvements that a competitive economy would deliver. In fact, whenever smaller companies produce a food innovation that catches on, the oligopolists simply buy it. It is a policy of innovation by merger. Contrary to what most people think, innovation comes from individuals and small firms, not the industrial giants.

Kretschmer, once an independent company, developed a good wheat germ that could be eaten as a substitute for "empty" breakfast cereals. International Multifoods bought it when it was obvious that people liked the idea of nutrition for breakfast. Right off, International bolstered the advertising budget for Kretschmer, and next moved quickly from the basic product to offer four differentiated varieties: regular, sugar and honey, cinnamon-raisin and caramel-apple. "Kretschmer announces two new wheat germ flavors that don't taste much like wheat germ," ran a 1974 ad.

That is the level of oligopolistic "innovation"—tinkering with basics. "Sara Lee introduces All Butter

Chocolate Pound Cake. Yes. *Chocolate,*" enthused an ad of this Consolidated Foods subsidiary, with just a little touch of disbelief. Beatrice Foods has explored the outer rim of this silliness: "People like margarine," a corporate executive stated flatly. "But people also like change. And to move along with this change, we are testing flavored margarine." Thanks a lot.

Another result of differentiation is product litter— where one of a kind would do, there are several. General Foods' Shake 'n Bake, for example, comes in regular, mild, pork, fish, hamburger, Italian and the new Shake 'n Batter. Hunt's tomato sauce comes plain or with mushrooms, with onions, with cheese, with herbs, or—can you imagine it?—with tomato bits.

"We make two kinds of brownie mixes because people like two kinds of brownies," says a Betty Crocker ad pushing the new Fudge Brownie Supreme and the old Traditional Fudge Brownie. Only two? Some people might like three or six. Some are said to like their brownies spiced with marijuana—can they count on Betty Crocker for those? That would be a brownie with a difference, and if it were to become legal and the market tested good, you can bet your last brownie that Betty Crocker would be making *three* kinds of brownie mixes. . . .

OLIGOPOLY ON THE SHELVES. The bigger you are, the more advertising you do, and the more advertising you do, the greater your chances of getting on supermarket shelves. If you want to compete in the food economy, it is necessary to get on the shelves.

It is easier said than done. Even as supermarkets grow more massive, there is limited space for product display, and getting yours up there is not a matter of making the best food, but of making the best deal.

Supermarkets make their profits from high turnover —products that move off the shelves fast. Hence, they like those firms that advertise heavily and that use every promotional gimmick to get shoppers to snap up their product. At the very start, then, the smaller and newer independent food makers with limited advertising budgets have a strike against them.

Strike two against the smaller competitor is the high, hard one of "What're you offering?" This gets down to discounts, displays and deals that giant food makers and giant supermarketeers work out among themselves. The grocery industry press is full of ads with cryptic references to specials that are available to the supermarkets—"When your broker calls," says an ad in *Supermarket News* for Wyler's drink mixes, "ask to see the Wyler File." It has all the subtlety of a stage wink.

Gerber, in an attempt to move beyond baby foods (there has been a radical decline in the number of babies), has developed a line of prepared meals in single-serving packages, targeted toward those people who eat alone. To get the ball rolling, Gerber is offering supermarkets a profit margin of 41%, and promising a standard margin of about 26%.[14] That is the kind of discount that gets the attention of the supermarketeers, and it is the kind of discount that few independent firms can offer. It also is the kind of discount that is made regularly by major food corporations introducing a new product. Cargill is offering a dry-roasted soy-nut product, telling grocers that it is "45% Protein. 35% Profit." It is the latter percentage that will get it on the shelf.

Nor has the struggle ended once a product is safely on the shelf. The question then becomes "where on the shelf?" Will it be at eye level, or down in a bottom corner? A publication of the canning industry asked its readers: "Did you know that the average customer pushes her supermarket cart past an average 310 grocery items per minute?—That she makes 73 percent of her purchases on impulse?" And the writer concluded, "It is easy to see that prominent shelf space is indeed a primary factor in grocery sales."[15]

The dominant food firms have large promotional budgets to develop special displays that feature their products and contribute to fast turnover. Many of these are designed to fit at the end of aisles, smack in the middle of aisles, at the checkout counters, or in other coveted positions geared to impulse buying. Miller beer developed an eye-catching aisle display in 1974 with a summer cookout theme, offering supermarkets the extra bait of displaying their own house brands of potato chips, napkins, ketchups and charcoal.

House-brand production can be among the special deals that are cut by food makers in order to get prime position in the markets. Twelve percent of Wonder Bread's production, for example, is sold under private labels of supermarkets. Robert Ronzoni, an official of the family firm in New York that markets Italian pastas and sauces, told *The New York Times* of trying to break into other markets around the country: "It's not easy, because most supermarkets only want to carry two brands on their shelves—the market leader in their area and their own house brand." In your own supermarket you can begin to notice the trend that Mr. Ronzoni is confronting. It is a trend that solidifies oligopoly.

Strike three for the small competitor is a soft curve. As in all bureaucracies, cracking the food oligopolies is not a matter of what you know, but who you know. Oligopolists know everyone, and everyone knows them.

Big food makers and big food sellers form a business clique that is wary of outsiders—particularly innovative competitors.

The brand-name firms employ large sales staffs that roam across the country, bearing gifts of special discounts and displays, and backed by national advertising. It is an expensive proposition to match this sales punch. The Federal Trade Commission surveyed eleven national grocery manufacturers in 1966 and found that the median number of company-employed salesmen was 460.[16] Today it would be considerably higher—companies like Gerber and Del Monte, for example, have more than a thousand people in the field to push their products.

A national sales staff gives the oligopolists the power to hand-deliver a new product or a new product size or a new display case. For large supermarkets, these sales people come in weekly to make sure that their firm's display is in order and well stocked, and to assist the store's management in any little way; small stores that carry the product, however, are lucky to see a sales representative once a year. A mutual relationship develops between oligopolistic makers and oligopolistic sellers of food, and that relationship effectively shuts the door to outside competitors.

When the small firms that were the innovators of natural breakfast cereals demonstrated through health-food stores that a sizable market existed for their product, the supermarkets took them in, but they were relegated to poor shelf positions. Then came the major corporations with their sugared versions of "natural" cereals. They were backed with massive advertising campaigns, coupons for consumers, promotional allowances and discounts of 50¢ to $1.20 a case for supermarkets.[17] The national sales staffs of Quaker, General

Mills, Kellogg and the others came with special displays. Their cereal was not cheaper and not better than that of the small innovators, but their marketing power drove the granolas off the shelves.

Today's supermarket shelf guarantees oligopoly. Not only does it shut out small competitors, but also it allocates room for only a handful of brands. Even the dozen major manufacturers that offer "natural" cereals must now struggle among themselves for oligopolistic position, as *Supermarket News* made clear in 1974.

> When the introduction and promotion dust settles, retailers are expected to concentrate on perhaps four or five best-selling brands. But as the brands are introduced, most retailers will take advantage of the promotional activities. The reason for the shake-down will be tight shelf space.

Advertising, promotional gimmicks and shelf-space considerations do not make your food tastier, more nutritious or less expensive. Why then are these anticompetitive factors being allowed to determine the structure of the food economy? Because they transfer consumer spending from many products to a few, establish a brand as something valuable in itself, when it clearly is not. We could all live quite well, probably better, if the entire promotional industry were to pack up today and begin to look for honest work. Certainly, a lot less flim-flam in the food economy would be a spur to effective competition.

Left to their own devices, however, brand-name food giants most assuredly will offer more flim-flam. If there ever was any doubt of that, the chief executive of Nabisco put it to rest for good: "Some time in the future," he said, with obvious anticipation, "we'll be able to beam our advertising by satellite to four billion people, all potential customers."

CHAPTER VI

Farmers:
Death of American Gothic

Cultivators of the land, herdsmen of the livestock, protectors of traditional values—noble American yeomen!

We want to believe that about farmers in this country, and to a large extent, we do. Though farmers make up less than 5% of the population, no national or statewide campaign for political office is complete without a special nod to the farm folks—"the breadwinners of our national family," Richard Nixon hailed them in his 1972 race. Even with the highest food prices in memory sending shock waves through the American public in 1973, opinion polls continued to show unwavering goodwill and warm feelings toward the farmer. In a special poll commissioned that year by the Department of Agriculture, 69% of the people felt that the farmer worked harder than his city cousins, and 51% even thought farmers were "friendly and helpful."[1]

Agriculture Secretary Earl Butz rides the rural image for all that it's worth, and then some: "As your cowhand on the Potomac," he told a group of Nebraska cattlemen in 1972, "I've always got some fence to mend or a stray to round up, a bull to buy or a calf to clamp, a banker to corner or a trader to sell. And every time it looks like I might settle down for a peaceful night around the campfire, a dozen feisty coyotes howl in the moonlight not far away."*[2]

Those are not coyotes howling in the moonlight, they are farmers who have been driven out of business. While we have been praising them, we have been losing farmers at the rate of 1,000 a week.[3] And those that remain must increasingly give up their independence by coming under the control of the big corporations. The very politicians that are quick to laud farm people as "the salt of the earth" are at work back in Washington structuring totally integrated food systems that will leave farmers with little more than the salt in their sweat bands.

Pat Oliphant. © *The Denver Post*. Reprinted with permission of the *Los Angeles Times* Syndicate.

* Earl Butz is a "limousine cowboy" if he's one at all. Far from riding the range, at the time of his nomination to be Secretary of Agriculture, he was serving as a paid board member of Ralston Purina, International Minerals & Chemical Corporation, Stokely Van Camp and J. I. Case farm machinery company (now a subsidiary of Tenneco).

The Economical, Family-Size Package

Paradoxically, the public celebration of farmers works against them. Based heavily on nostalgia, public sentiment for the family farmer gives way every time to a deeper, fatalistic assumption that the old home place is an inefficient relic, doomed to competitive extinction by modern technology and big business systems. It is an assumption that food corporations encourage, since their agricultural aspirations are banked on the public's willingness to believe that family farmers are unable to produce food as efficiently as corporate food systems.

In April 1973, top government officials traveled to a Nob Hill hotel in San Francisco to confer with representatives of the food industry, giving them an in-person assessment of economic conditions and a personal explanation of government policies affecting their industry. Each segment of the food economy was represented —Lucky Stores for the supermarkets, Del Monte for the processors. For the farmers? Tenneco.

This oil-and-pipeline-based conglomerate, the 38th largest corporation in the country, has become the country's biggest farmer. It is at work trying to dominate the production of fresh fruits and vegetables which it markets under its Sun Giant label. At the Nob Hill session, Tenneco's man pronounced this judgment on the folks his conglomerate hopes to replace:

> The family farmer, along with mom and the flag and apple pie, is one of the cultural heritages of our nation. At the same time you find that the cottage industry that is represented by family farmers is just not capable of providing food.[4]

Nonsense. The family farm today is the most efficient unit of production in the country. Furthermore, it is the last bastion of free competition that exists in the food economy, if not in the entire economy. The Tennecos cannot hope to match the family farmers' productive efficiency, and they have no intention of maintaining the competitiveness. Our fatalistic assumption that big businesses inevitably must take over food production is based on a misperception about the nature both of big business and of family farms.

In size, today's family farms can range from a five-acre tobacco allotment in North Carolina to a 5,000-acre wheat spread in Nebraska. These are not the simple yeomen of Jefferson's ideal, and their operation is not limited to mule power and horse sense. These farmers are up-to-date managers of complex business operations—making management decisions, taking capital risks, applying scientific methods and pouring on a steady stream of old-time hard work. The concept of family farm is not defined in terms of acreage or sales, but by entrepreneurial independence—a business unit in which decision-making power is in the hands of the farm family and on which the family assumes the business risks and does most of the work. It is small-scale capitalism, alive and performing well—though not flourishing—throughout the American countryside.

Since 1952, the farmer's efficiency (output per man hour) has increased by 330%, compared with a 160% increase in manufacturing industries.[5] That record is unmatched in the rest of the economy. More importantly, the record has been set on family-size farms, not on the ponderous landholdings of the conglomerates. Experts confirm this. Dr. Roy Van Arsdall, an agricultural economist at the University of Illinois, wrote in 1969, "Evidence suggests that family farms can convert inputs into output in physical terms as effectively as any other form of business."[6]

Apologists for agricultural giantism are fond of trotting out the phrase "economies of scale," used by academics to express the relationship between size and efficiency. In agriculture, this complex phrase covers a very simple concept—for every crop there is an optimum size for efficient production. Obviously there are inefficiences if acreage is too small, but it is often forgotten that there also are inefficiencies if acreage is too large.

"Farming offers no great operating efficiency from large-size units," Drs. Harold Breimyer and Wallace Barr concluded in 1972. "Scale economy in crop production is handicapped by space and distance—there are cost disadvantages in farming acreages located far from headquarters."[7] The quick assumption that bigness brings superior efficiency to farming fails to recognize that bigness demands such cumbersome and inefficient factors as absentee decision-making, added levels of management bureaucracy, fragmented responsibilities, employment of administrative staff, increased labor bills and much heavier capital investment.

Ralston Purina Company, which has had long experience as a corporate farmer, admits that they can offer no efficiency advantage in agriculture. An executive of the corporation said in 1973, "The individual farmer or family corporation can meet, and many times surpass, the efficiency of the large units that operate with hired management." The executive allowed that Ralston Purina has developed "a very great respect for the independent entrepreneur. This respect comes not from sentimentality, but from observing results."[8]

Family size turns out to be optimum size for production of most crops. In the first official government study of the subject, the Department of Agriculture concluded in 1967 that maximum efficiency in farming generally is achieved "at a relatively small size of operation," well within the capacity of family farms.[9] Another study by the Department in 1973 confirmed the earlier results and concluded that:

We are so conditioned to equate bigness with efficiency that nearly everyone assumes that large-scale undertakings are inherently more efficient than smaller ones. In fact, the claim of efficiency is commonly used to justify bigness. *But when we examine the realities we find that most of the economies associated with size in farming are achieved by the one-man fully mechanized farm.* (emphasis supplied)[10]

It will come as a surprise to many people that inefficiencies in farming today are as much a product of agricultural bigness as of smallness. For example, in materials submitted to the U.S. Senate Labor Committee in 1972, the Department of Agriculture reported that the optimum size for a California vegetable farm was 440 acres. Yet, the average size of the corporate farms that dominate vegetable production in California is 3,206 acres—eight times larger than efficiency warrants.* Seventy-three percent of California vegetables are produced on farms that are much larger than the optimum.[11]

"The chief incentive for farm enlargement beyond the optimum one-man size," said the Department of Agriculture in its 1973 efficiency study, "is not to reduce unit costs of production, but to achieve a larger business, more output, and more total income." The corporations that are coming to farming are not in pursuit of greater efficiency, but of greater control of farm production. It is not even profits that they seek from the farm

---

* Among the big-time corporate farmers producing vegetables in California are Del Monte, Dow Chemical, Getty Oil, Norton Simon, Purex, Tenneco and United Brands.

so much as it is power—the power to control a food line totally, from the field to the table. The impact will be to shut off competition in the only segment of the food economy where any competition remains.

Economists point to family-farm agriculture as generally having the purest competitive structure of any major industry.[12] There are some 2.9 million farmers dispersed across the countryside, virtually unorganized and with no real hope of doing anything about the price at which they sell. Now, using the myth of superior efficiency, vertically integrated conglomerates and food merchandisers intend to impose their oligopolistic structures over that competitive situation.

A Way of Life

It has become a cliché to observe that "farming is no longer a way of life, it is a business." That expression, frequently delivered with a stern face, has about the same perceptive quality as the one that goes: "No one is qualified to hold office unless he has met a payroll." In both cases, experience teaches us otherwise.

People farm because they like it. It is *both* their business and their life. It is what they want to do. Chief among the likes is the sense of independence, the freedom to call most of your own shots on your own place. Another is a sense of accomplishment—putting yourself up against the weather, the bugs and the marketplace, and producing a crop that sometimes brings you out ahead.

In fact, farming involves more art than it does either business or science. Producing an abundant, high-quality crop—whether a field of tomatoes or a pen of hogs—simply cannot be reduced to impersonal factory techniques or financial flow charts. As a Montana farmer said with relish: "Most of these farm experts in the colleges couldn't farm their way out of their paper lunchbags." It's like learning to hit a golf ball. There are plenty of experts, with statistics and diagrams, who can show you on paper precisely what it takes to hit the thing smoothly, but all the expertise will not substitute for ability and enthusiasm. The professional golfer Lee Trevino used to play golf with a Dr. Pepper bottle —and win.

Even if the corporate pretenders were technically as efficient as the family farmer, their way of doing business cannot compete effectively with the intangibles that are a part of farming. Living things are growing on the farm, and they have to be tended differently from hair dryers and automobiles. Farming requires a degree of personal involvement that can't be found either in the corporate boardroom of General Electric or on a Ford assembly line. As Breimyer and Barr put it: "Farmers have a genuine love of the land, a respect for it, and a desire to protect and preserve it. This attitude is not mercenary; it has roots that are almost religious."[13]

Despite the maudlin tones of that attitude, it is a real factor of production and an essential element of agricultural efficiency. The price, taste and nutritional value of our food supply has depended on the farm family's willingness to plow a bit of themselves into the land. Confucius said it centuries ago: "The best fertilizer is the footsteps of the land-owner." No amount of chemical spray can replace it.

Another big factor of farming productivity that they do not teach future corporate managers at Harvard Business School is the enormous work load shouldered by the farm family. Jim McHale, Pennsylvania's excellent Secretary of Agriculture, tells of being consistently on the go as a dairy farmer in northwest Pennsylvania:

"My boy was 15 years old before he found out his name wasn't 'Hurry.' That's about the only way I ever addressed him on the farm—'Hurry, get those milkers! Hurry, load that truck.'"

It is this sense of personal involvement, the unique position in today's economy of being both management and labor, that the corporate "farmer" can never match. It is hard to imagine a corporate manager crawling out of a warm bed on a cold winter night to go sit up with the company sow. The director of economic and marketing research for Ralston Purina admitted as much: "It is difficult for a corporation to provide the incentives which will result in all hired managers doing as good a job as they would do if they owned the operation."[14] John Kenneth Galbraith, in his *Economics and the Public Purpose,* noted that this capacity for work is a key to the success of the independent farmer:

> Nothing regulates the hours of work of the individual entrepreneur, and nothing at all regulates the intensity of his effort. He may thus be in a position to offset the higher technical productivity of the better-equipped worker in the organized but regulated sector of the economy by working longer, harder or more intelligently than his organization counterpart. In doing so, he reduces his compensation per unit of effective and useful effort expended. He is, to put the matter differently, almost wholly free, as the organization is not, to exploit his labor force since his labor force consists of himself.[15]

Technology can be applied and management systems can be adopted, as they have been, but farming ultimately gets down to one or two skillful people who know what to do at the right time and are there all the time to do it." My kids call me an Agricultural Production Manager," said a successful Kansan, "but what I am is a dirt farmer." Corporations, of course, are able to get a crop from their assembly-line techniques, large wage force and administrative bureaucracies, but not as efficiently. And there is the same kind of quality difference that one finds between a good, family-owned-and-operated restaurant and the fast-food franchise down the street.

Live Poor, Die Rich

Well, if farmers are so damn smart and efficient, why ain't they rich? The hard fact is that there is not much profit to be had in farming. The steadily escalating costs of production, the high risk of failure, the restricted access to farm markets and the low return on investment hardly make it a glamour item on Wall Street.

The farmer operates in a highly competitive situation, with no power to affect the cost of items he must buy and virtually no power to affect the price at which he sells his produce. That's what is meant by free-enterprise competition; it is what we say our economy is all about. Unfortunately for the farmers, they are the only ones practicing it. Supply and demand forces swirl about the family farmer with the force of a Texas tornado, putting him in good shape some years, but mostly leaving him gasping. For example, it was not until 1972 that farmers nationwide finally got back up to the income level that they had been at in 1952. In the meantime, the cost of farming had gone up 110%, and the debts the farmers owed down at the bank had risen 355%.[16] Now, farm incomes are falling again, while costs continue to climb.

Congressman Jamie Whitten (D-Mississippi) is Chairman of the agricultural appropriations subcommittee in the House of Representatives. Noting the $70,000 to $100,000 investment required these days to farm, Whitten pointed out that it takes "about as much money to start a farm as to start a bank, and about as much nerve as to rob a bank."[17]

If you or your neighbors have taken to vegetable gardening recently, you know that farming is an economic version of Russian roulette. Will it be too wet to plant, so that the seeds will wash out or rot? Will the birds eat the tender shoots? Will bugs move in to lay their eggs and feast on your plants? Will a hot, dry spell hit you and parch the whole crop? Is there going to be a good market price at harvest time, assuming that late rains don't sweep in and make it too wet to harvest? If there's going to be a good market, will politicians decide to ruin it? If they do, how are you going to pay off your note at the bank? And how hard are you going to hit that son-of-a-bitch economist down at the agricultural college who says that you just have to get bigger and more efficient?

Go out to a fair-sized family farm and you will be impressed by the richness of the scene—acres of valuable land, several farm buildings and lots of shiny machinery. Hell this guy's rich. Nope. He's just got a bunch of assets, most of which are owned by the banker. Even if he owns his land and buildings and machinery, their market value is meaningless unless he sells them. Even with a hundred thousand dollars in assets, a farmer can live poor, but die rich.

This massive investment does not produce much of a return. Over the last ten years, return on investment in farming has averaged 3.9%.[18] A bank will pay you better than a 5% return just to invest your money in a savings account. Why do farmers do it? Because it offers a way of life that they like and cannot find elsewhere, and because they are able in good years to make a living from it. They hunker down in the bad years, get

© 1972 by NEA, Inc.

"We, in Washington, see prosperity just around the corner for the family farm. All you have to do is survive until the suburbs reach you, and you'll make a fortune in real estate!"

Jim Berry. © 1972 by NEA, Inc. Reprinted with permission.

more efficient and productive, and wait for the good years. The price and quality of the American food supply is directly derived from the willingness of the farm family to make that kind of commitment.

Farm families make their commitment on their own, without getting the special incentives that big business seems to require. Oil corporations tell us that their abnormally high profits are warranted as an encouragement to them to produce more oil, and they fight tooth and nail for the oil-depletion allowance that gives them an annual tax cushion against the risk of failure. The chief executives of General Motors, Ford and ITT are paid in excess of $800,000 a year, a sum that includes "incentive bonuses" of more than $200,000 each. One wonders what they would do without that incentive pay—show up late for work? Not take work home at night?

Any objective view of the farm family has to conclude that they have done all that has been asked of them—they are efficient, competitive, productive and enterprising. But he who lives by the free-enterprise ideal apparently dies by the free-enterprise ideal. Farmers are going out of business, at least in the entrepreneurial sense. It is not happening because they are obsolete, but because they are being squeezed out by monopolies. On one hand, farmers have to buy supplies from monopolistic sellers; on the other hand, farmers have to sell to monopolistic buyers. It is economic murder by strangulation.

Farming the Farmer: Input Oligopolies

"It used to take many" sings Ralston Purina in a corporate paean to the American farmer, "now just a few, to accomplish much more than the many could do." Chevron Chemical Corporation awards a plaque and $100 prize to the three top winners in its annual "Speak Up for Agriculture" letterwriting contest, asserting that it hopes to be "a vehicle for agriculture to bring its views before urban dwellers." The farm editors of newspapers receive awards, called "Oscars in Agriculture," from DeKalb AgResearch, Inc. The Agricultural Council of America sponsors a series of television ads that "tell the farmer's side of high food prices."

Who are these friendly advocates, so eager to stand by the farmer's side? They are, or they represent, corporations that sell supplies to the farmer. Ralston Purina is the leading farm supplier of animal feeds in the country. Chevron is one of the biggest farm-chemical salesmen, and DeKalb is the country's major seller of agricultural seeds. A primary financial supporter of the Agricultural Council of America is John Deere, a company known as the "colossus" of the farm machinery industry. Taking a big chunk of the $73 billion farmers pay for supplies each year, these giants have much to sing about. When such "friends" offer to stand tall alongside the farmer, the farmer is quick to put his hand over his wallet.

It is not generally recognized that farmers probably are the biggest consumer group in the country. From baling wire to barns, from pickling jars to corn pickers, the farmer seems constantly to be in town buying the necessaries of farm business. Before the first sprout breaks ground, American farm families are over their heads in debt to such corporate powers as Bank of America (production loans), Upjohn Company (seeds), The Williams Companies (fertilizer), International Minerals & Chemical (pesticides), Ford Motor Company (machinery), Firestone (tires), Ralston Purina (feeder pigs), Merck & Company (poultry stock), Cargill (feed), Dow Chemical (cartons and wrappings), Eli Lilly (animal drugs), Exxon (farm fuels), and Burlington Northern (rail transportation).

Unknown to most farmers is the extent to which

conglomerate firms are reaching into the farm input industry. When they buy a combine from J. I. Case, their check ends up in the account of Case's conglomerate owner, Tenneco. The purchase of Nutrena animal feeds actually is a purchase from Cargill, the largest grain exporter in the world. A dollar spent on Chemagro herbicides leaves this country to be banked by Farbenfabriken Bayer, the German parent both of Chemagro and of Bayer aspirin. Seeds for planting? Ferry-Morse seed company is owned by Purex Corporation; Burpee seeds are now products of General Foods; Asgrow is a subsidiary of the Upjohn Company; and Funk Bros. seeds now spring from the corporate structure of CIBA-Geigy, a chemical-based conglomerate in Switzerland.

There is a conspicuous lack of competition in most of the farm-supply industries. Economist William Shepherd found, for example, that the four leading firms control 67% of petroleum products, 71% of tires, 74% of chemicals and 80% of rail transport.[19] In specific items and local markets, the concentration is greater. DeKalb AgResearch and Pioneer Hi-Bred International supply half the hybrid seeds sold, and there are many farming areas where feed must be bought from Ralston Purina or not at all.

The tractor, a farming essential, rolls off the assembly lines of a tightly held shared monopoly, as shown in Table VI–1. In fact, the tractor oligopoly is tighter than suggested in these figures. There has been relentless pressure on American farmers over the past dozen years to expand their operations, not only to encompass more acreage, but also to use bigger machinery. Horsepower in tractors has leaped from an average of 46 hp in 1960 to an estimated 82.5 hp in 1973. Deere & Company has led in promoting the highly profitable super trac-

TABLE VI—1
The Tractor Oligopoly

Tractor Manufacturer	1972 Share of U.S. Tractor Market (unit sales)
Deere & Company	33%
International Harvester	24%
	Big Two = 57%
Massey-Ferguson (Canadian firm)	13%
Ford Motor Company	13%
	Big Four = 83%
J. I. Case (Tenneco)	7%
Allis-Chalmers	5%
White Motor Company	4%
Others	1%

Source: *Business Week.* "Riding the Farm Boom." October 27, 1973, p. 78.

tors; 75% of its tractor sales are of machines of 80 hp and over. Deere and International Harvester claim about 70% of the big-tractor market, which Deere's chief executive calls their "corporate bread and butter."[20]

Only the big four tractor makers remain as full-line producers of farm machinery, with the others offering only limited product lines or concentrating on specialized farm equipment. J. I. Case, for example, stopped producing a full line of farm implements in 1972. Further evaporation of competition is anticipated, leaving farmers pretty much in the monopolistic grip of Deere and International Harvester.

The technological barrage from farm suppliers has been a mixed blessing. There is no doubt that machinery, hybrid corn and other technological developments have contributed enormously to farm efficiency and productivity. No one who has ever plowed 40 acres behind a mule has any interest in returning to that. But there has developed an expansionist imperative, a mentality of giantism within the input industry that finally has to be questioned and checked. Bigness is pursued as its own rationale. Deere & Company, now producing 200-horsepower tractors, talks of 500-horsepower mammoths.

Yet, the big tractors are shown to be less energy-efficient than the smaller ones, and the price of the things puts them out of reach of most farmers. A Michigan State University scientist calls the big tractor the SST of agriculture, and some farmers have found too late that these manufactured mastodons are so heavy that they bog down in the fields after even moderate rain. In 1962, the top International Harvester tractor cost $3,500. Ten years later, that same-size tractor was at $10,000 base price, with no extras, and the cheapest tractors offered by the industry ran $7,000.[21]

Bigger farm machinery has required much heavier capital investment by farm families, which has demanded that they expand their operations even more just to generate the volume necessary to pay off the loan on the big machines. Much of this machinery has been designed and developed by tax-paid engineers at state colleges of agriculture, which work closely with the giant machinery corporations and accept small research grants from them. The Federal Extension Service has been an active promoter of bigness, urging farmers to accept practically every new gadget of the industry.

Robert Long, former senior vice-president of the Bank of America and now U.S. Assistant Secretary of Agriculture in charge of agricultural research and extension, is a major proponent of big technology. "We have examined the statistics on California farms," Long approvingly told Westinghouse Broadcasting just before coming to Washington in 1973, "and the average farm in California now has a total capital investment in excess of $400,000."[22] It is at this scale of capitalization that the big banks are willing to talk farm credit, and this scale of capitalization is what puts the spring in the walk of farm-supply executives.

There may be profits being made off the farm, but much bigger profits are being made off the farmer. For a sample of profit increases some major farm suppliers enjoyed in the first quarter of 1974, see Table VI–2.

These enrichments came at a time that the average profit increases for large corporations were at 16% and at a time that the prices paid to farmers were falling steadily from their 1973 peak. Looking happily forward to 1974 and 1975, an Allis-Chalmers executive gushed that his company was "pretty damned bullish."

TABLE VI—2

Farm-Supply Corporation	Farm Products and Services	First Quarter 1974 Profit Increase
Allis-Chalmers	Machinery	41%
Burlington Northern	Rail transportation	102%
Consolidated Freightways	Trucking	75%
Federal Paper Board	Cartons	100%
Firestone	Tires, inner tubes	19%
W. R. Grace	Chemicals	129%
International Harvester	Machinery	113%
International Harvester and Chemical	Chemicals	131%
Occidental Petroleum	Fertilizers, fuels	716%
Pfizer	Drugs	33%
Ralston Purina	Feed	32%
Rohm & Haas	Fungicides	30%
Stauffer Chemical	Chemicals	55%
Tenneco	Chemicals, machinery, fuel, packaging	57%
Upjohn	Drugs, seeds	32%
White Motor	Machinery	38%

Source: *Business Week.* "Profits: Better Than Expected." May 11, 1974, p. 69.

Frank Miller. © 1973 by *Des Moines Register and Tribune* Company. Reprinted with permission.

It may be a bullish market for oligopolistic farm suppliers, but it is the family farmer that is being bullied. The Federal Trade Commission found in 1972 that the lack of competition among farm-machinery manufacturers cost farmers an extra $251,000,000. And if there had been adequate competition in the animal-feed industry, dominated by such giants as Ralston Purina and Cargill, farmers would have saved $200 million, which the FTC says is the amount of that industry's 1972 "monopoly overcharge."[23]

With monopolistic power comes the ability to manipulate supplies and artificially boost prices. International grain traders and feed-manufacturing corporations profited from this power in 1973 by cornering the market in soybeans that they held from the previous year.[24] In the same 1974 press conference at which President Nixon asserted that "farmers never had it so good," he chastised grain farmers for the high price of soybeans. He missed the real culprit by a country mile.

In fact, farmers sold their soybeans in 1972 for under $4 a bushel—a good price, but not exorbitant. They sold to corporations like Ralston Purina and Cargill, which used the soybeans to make animal feed and other products. But the half-dozen companies which bought the soybeans simply sat on their supplies for a few months, well into 1973. American dairy farmers, egg producers, cattle ranchers and other users of soybean-based animal feeds were clamoring for supplies, but the corporations turned a deaf ear. They saw that a worldwide grain shortage was in the making, and they had about the only grain in town. The same soybeans that farmers sold for $4 a bushel sat in corporate storage facilities and inflated in value to more than $12 a bushel.

Reuters news service reported that Ralston Purina "was able to put together a nice lump of inventory profits—using cheap soybeans to make oil and meal that had quadrupled or better in price."[25] The corporate feed manufacturers reaped windfall profits, the grain farmers took the blame, animal and dairy farmers were faced with skyrocketing feed costs and consumers were stunned by the wildest price spiral in the memory of American eaters.

The grain and feed firms are hardly alone in their appreciation of supply manipulation. "We've learned how profitable it can be to keep inventories under control," confided Deere's chief financial officer in 1973.[26] Indeed they have. The supply of tractors, for example, has been kept under such tight control that a black market developed. The editor of a farm-machinery magazine reported in 1974 of an implement dealer who "can locate John Deere 4-wheel drive tractors and deliver them to a customer for a flat $10,000 more than the list price."[27] Since the list price is well over $10,000 to begin with, most family farmers had to make do with the old tractor.

But there also is a problem getting the parts necessary to put the old tractor in working order. In the first place, parts are expensive: "You don't need too big a truck to haul away $500 in parts," groaned an Iowa farmer. But at least he could get parts. In most farming areas, it's harder to get parts than a straight answer on the weather. In fact, parts are not available locally; they have to be ordered, with a wait of months, and no guarantee at that. In the meantime, machinery is standing idle and crops are growing.

The wheeling and dealing by Deere and its oligopolistic cohorts is making them a bundle. In 1972, Deere became the first company to sell more than a billion dollars worth of farm machinery, and in 1973 its sales were up by 34% and profits up by 50%.

But the tractor firms may be outsmarting themselves. The Belarus is coming. Just as American automobile manufacturers got fat and complacent in the 1950s and 1960s making ever bigger, more expensive cars, the American tractor manufacturers are failing to see that many family farmers are looking for a machine that will help them farm, rather than help them out of farming. Automobile manufacturers were hit by the Volkswagen; American tractor manufacturers are being hit by the Belarus, a Russian tractor.

Conservative congressman John Rarick saw it this way: "During the past two months a steady stream of fire-red farm tractors, made in Minsk, U.S.S.R., have been arriving in the port of New Orleans on their way to invade the farmlands of the U.S."[28] That is a great deal more dramatic than the actuality, which is that a few farm dealers in the Northeastern part of the country introducing the tractors are doing a fairly brisk business with them.[29] The Belarus, like the Volkswagen in the 1950s, has struck a responsive chord where it has been introduced because it is meeting a need that American manufacturers are not—to wit, the Belarus gets the job done with less horsepower and less fuel, and it costs much less. "That tractor delivers for $7,500," a dealer told *The New York Times* in 1974. "Anything comparable made in the United States would run you $15,000."[30]

The high cost of farming is eating up farmers. In 1953, farm production expenses were $21 billion. In 1974, expenses have risen to more than $73 billion—an increase of 245%. The Federal Reserve Bank of Chicago reported that production expenses in 1974 were "49 percent above the level of two years ago."[31]

At work here is one jaw of a corporate vise that is squeezing family farmers off the land and pressuring food prices up. The other jaw is the monopolistic power of food middlemen, controlling the price that farmers are paid. Despite their efficiency and productivity, farmers get caught in this squeeze with nowhere to go but out.

My cousin and her husband raise cattle and grain on a family farm outside of Rixeyville, Virginia. In 1974, while supermarket beef prices climbed, the farm price of beef plummeted. At the same time, farm-supply costs were unbelievable, as input corporations joined the supermarkets to make a killing off the farmer. Cousin Velma was one of those farmers:

June 10, 1974

Dear Jim

We took a load of steers and heifers to the cattle auction Saturday and came away so sick and disgusted that we went fishing. After catching enough fish for dinner, we came home and I compiled these figures. They are straight from the horse's mouth, and maybe the next time you feel the urge to call Butz a dirty name they will give you a little extra ammunition.

a. After waiting weeks for the ship carrying baler twine to arrive in Baltimore, we paid $31 a bale; last year it was plentiful and we paid $8.50 a bale—265% increase.

b. Barbed wire this year is $30 a roll; last May it was $12.95. The only blessing there is that you can't find any even at $30—132% increase.

c. Oats for seeding last year $5.70 a hundred; this year $10—75% increase.

d. Fertilizer for the grain fields (we don't raise corn, thank goodness) $89 a ton; last year $55.80—60% increase.

e. Of course everybody knows about gas, but farm price is now 52.9¢ compared to 32.9¢ last May—60%.

f. And then there is the friendly Production Credit Association and Federal Land Bank who are charging us 9½ % interest on our cattle note this year compared to 7½ % last spring—27% increase.

Now comes the good part!

a. Our load of cattle averaged $33 per hundred Saturday. In 1973 the average was $47 per hundred—42% loss over last year. However, we all know that last year beef prices were unusually high. So I went back to 1972: the average that year was $39—still an 18% loss. And then back to 1971 which was our first year of sales: average was $34.30—a modest 4% loss.

The clincher is that this is the last year we have in which to show a profit on the farm; otherwise the IRS says our farming operation is just a hobby and we won't be allowed to deduct any of our losses.

Love
Cousin Velma

The Farmer Goes to Market: Output Oligopsonies

This little piggy went to market
Where he brought thirty cents per pound.
But down at the store
They charge sixty cents more
Where it averages ninety, I've found.

The farmer is standing,
His back to the wall.
The housewife is serving
Hooves and all.
The little guy's deserving
A better break;

But somebody
Somewhere
Is on the take.

Ninety less thirty,
That's sixty for sure.
Still the housewife gets took
And the farmer gets poor.

Tell me, oh sage,
Where the sixty cents goes.
Nobody,
Nobody,
Nobody
Knows.

Written by Lavern Rison in 1972, this bit of grass-roots poetry may not challenge a Shakespearian sonnet in its structural beauty, but it does go right to the heart of the food-marketing structure in this country.[32] When the farm family goes to market today, they are not met by dozens of competitors eagerly bidding for their food-stuffs. "Markets are either closed or constantly threatened by closure," was the frank admission of the U.S. Undersecretary of Agriculture in 1974.[33] Having the power to restrict the farmer's access to markets, corporate middlemen also have the power to control the farmer's price.

The farmer's price bears little relation to the consumer's price. In fact, the situation in hogs is worse than Lavern Rison states it. "We buy ham at the supermarket just like everybody else," said the wife of a Maryland hog farmer in 1974, "and I'm amazed that they charge up near $2 a pound when I know that we only get 50¢." National statistics show that farmers average about 40¢ of the consumers' food dollar.[34] The other three-fifths is taken by corporate middlemen. In

fact, most farmers never see even that much of the food
dollar (See Table VI–3).

The new phrase for today is "output oligopsonies."
It may sound like a disease, but actually it's a bit of
economic jargon that expresses the situation of many

TABLE VI—3

What the Farmer Got Out of Some Food You Bought in 1973

Food Item	Cost to You	Paid to Farmer	Farmer's Share
White bread (lb.)	28¢	4¢	15%
Cookies (lb.)	58¢	9¢	15%
Corn flakes (12 oz.)	32¢	3¢	11%
Apples (lb.)	30¢	11¢	37%
Grapefruit (each)	20¢	5¢	20%
Oranges (dozen)	$1.05	23¢	22%
Cabbage (lb.)	18¢	6¢	36%
Celery (lb.)	24¢	7¢	29%
Lettuce (head)	42¢	14¢	34%
Potatoes (10 lbs.)	1.37	45¢	33%
Canned peaches	41¢	7¢	17%
Canned pears	57¢	12¢	21%
Canned beets	23¢	2¢	6%
Canned corn	25¢	3¢	12%
Canned peas	27¢	4¢	16%
Canned tomatoes	25¢	3¢	11%
Frozen lemonade	15¢	4¢	26%
Frozen orange juice	25¢	9¢	34%
Frozen French-fried potatoes	17¢	4¢	22%
Frozen peas	24¢	4¢	17%
Margarine (lb.)	37¢	14¢	37%
Salad & cooking oil	71¢	22¢	31%
Peanut butter	52¢	18¢	35%
Canned spaghetti	20¢	3¢	13%

Source: USDA. ERS. "Marketing and Transportation Situation."
MTS-192. February 1974. Table 25, pages 40–41.

sellers operating in a market controlled by a few buyers. That is precisely the plight of millions of family farmers today, confronted in the marketplace by the consolidated power of food processors and marketers. The competitiveness of family farmers does consumers little good when farm products must be funneled into monopolistic hands of corporate middlemen before being taken home by consumers.

Like the shopper in search of food to buy, the farmer with food to sell is geographically restricted. The perishability of the food and the cost of transporting it limits most family farmers to local sales points. For example, what if you grew spinach around Crystal City, Texas? This community, 100 miles southwest of San Antonio, calls itself "The Spinach Capital of the World," and it even has erected a statue of Popeye to punctuate the point. Del Monte Corporation has a major processing plant in Crystal City, and it cans all of its spinach there. But Del Monte is there alone, buying spinach from area farmers without the fuss of bidding against Green Giant, Bird's Eye, Libby or any other major spinach "competitor."[35] Spinach farmers in the area who do not want to sell their harvest on Del Monte's terms can look forward to long days of eating lots of spinach.

Why don't they organize and drive Del Monte to the wall? For one thing, farmer boycotts of processors risk economic devastation for farm communities. Like industrial plants that have abandoned Northern cities, food corporations begin to look for greener pastures when confronted with organized resistance. Asparagus growers in California, Oregon and Washington State produce most of their crop under contract to Del Monte. The growers organized in a bargaining association, and they succeeded in boosting their price from Del Monte. But this multinational processor almost immediately began to move some of its operations out of the Northwest to Mexico.

Del Monte now gets all of its white asparagus and much of its green asparagus from its Mexican operations. It is possible there to buy cheap asparagus and cheap labor, paying only 27¢ an hour to cannery workers. The Mexican government helps out by giving Del Monte a 10% tax credit on canned goods exported from Mexico. These considerable savings allow Del Monte to puchase, process and export asparagus for 40% less in Mexico than it costs them in the United States, but none of that savings is passed on to consumers—canned asparagus by Del Monte sells for the same price, whether homegrown or imported.

Mushroom growers in this country are faced with a similar situation today. Back in 1886, *The Grocers' Hand-Book* asked this question:

> Why is it nobody cultivates mushrooms in America? If anybody is in the business it must be on a very small scale. Even the wild mushrooms are seldom gathered, yet when they are brought to market they are rapidly sold at good prices. . . . The mushroom is a delicacy liked by everybody, and to raise it is an easy matter. As it is, by far the greater part of our mushrooms come in cans from France. . . .[36]

There is a mushroom industry in America today, developed by Italian immigrant families settling in Pennsylvania. Until recently, it was a competitive business, with several hundred family-owned companies involved. Now, a great deal of market concentration is taking place, as large corporations have bought out many of the small packers of this specialty item: B in B, the leading brand, and Mr. Mushroom are labels now owned by Clorox Corporation; Dawn Fresh is owned by Green Giant, which also markets mushrooms under its own name; Steak Mate mushrooms are now a product of Ralston Purina; and Castle & Cook is marketing the Erlands and Shady Oak West labels.[37]

Increasingly, the big corporations are abandoning Pennsylvania mushroom growers and getting their supplies from South Korea and Taiwan. Paying extremely low wages, the government-run mushroom industries of these two countries deliver to American processors at a cheap price. As a part of our foreign policy, the U.S. government has helped to build the mushroom industries of these countries. Meanwhile, American growers have increased their efficiency significantly, without government support, and they clearly are able today to meet the growing American demand for mushrooms. But American growers also pay labor a fair wage, and they are in no position to meet the price of the imported mushrooms.

If Green Giant and Ralston Purina are able to get mushrooms cheaply, you are not. Their cost savings is not passed on, but pocketed. Since these corporations became involved in mushroom canning over the past decade, imports have quadrupled, and one out of every three processed mushrooms eaten today is an import. Green Giant, which imports more than 90% of the mushrooms it sells in jars, admitted to the U.S. Tariff Commission that it could get plenty of high-quality mushrooms in this country to meet its needs, but the foreign imports mean greater profits for Green Giant:

COMMISSIONER ABLONDI: Is it solely economics?
MR. HABLE: That we are going to Taiwan?
COMMISSIONER ABLONDI: Yes.
MR. HABLE: It's a matter of economics from a return on capital control.[38]

American mushroom growers and workers are being put out of business; militaristic, centralized governments paying low wages to workers are being subsidized; independent mushroom canners in this country are competitively disadvantaged and being squeezed out of business; and American consumers are being left with a mushroom oligopoly and high prices. All that so a few large food firms can fatten their profit margins on mushrooms, supposedly a low-calorie item.

Farmers find it difficult to shop around for buyers, but buyers have no difficulty shopping around for farmers. The *Wall Street Journal* reports that Ralston Purina exercises "a good deal of leverage" over the price it pays to farmers for grain: "When the price of one grain rises, local buyers are instructed to switch their purchases to cheaper substitutes or to buy in nearby regions where prices are lower."[39] This corporate hopscotching allows oligopsonistic middlemen to set prices pretty much to their liking.

With an abundant crop of perishable food on their hands, farmers usually have to like it too. Idaho potato farmers tried a few years back to get a better price from the processors by withholding their harvest for several months. But the processors simply turned to their own storage houses, which were filled with spuds they had quietly grown themselves or purchased elsewhere. The withholding action was broken as the potatoes of the Idaho farmers began to rot.[40]

"It's like money in the bank for the American farmer when he brings grain into a Cargill elevator," goes the lead line in a magazine ad for the largest grain dealer in the world. The ad concludes that the efficient operation of Cargill's grain-storage facilities "means that Cargill can pay the farmer top prices for his grain." In fact, grain storage and shipping is a tightly held oligopsony, and Cargill frequently is in a position to pay the farmer any price Cargill chooses. Six multinational grain corporations—Cargill, Continental, Bunge, Archer Daniels Midland, Dreyfus, Peavey and Cook—handle 90% of all the grain shipped in the entire world.[41] Cargill and Continental alone split half of the market.

These friends of the farmers apparently asserted their market power to squeeze the last dime out of hard-pressed grain farmers across the country in 1973 and 1974. Grain is bought from farmers and stored in "elevators" by local outfits, which then sell and deliver the grain to the giant traders and feed companies. In 1973 and 1974, however, there was an acute shortage of railroad "hopper cars" used to haul the grain to the big corporations. Government investigators later discovered that thousands of these railroad cars were either owned or controlled by the grain exporters. In order to get those firms to release cars to them, the local boys not only had to pay the normal hauling costs, but also had to sell their grain to the firms for 10–25¢ a bushel under the going rate.[42] Because of this black market in railroad cars, forcing the local elevators to sell at discount rates, farmers quickly found that the price they could get was cut back accordingly.

The Big Beef

The beef industry generally appears to operate in competitive markets, with only 21% of the nation's cattle slaughter being controlled by the big four.* But it would be hard to convince most independent cattle

* In 1970 the largest four firms slaughtered 21.3% of cattle, 23.8% of calves, 31.5% of hogs and 53.1% of sheep. The five largest meat packers are Armour (Greyhound), Swift (Esmark), Wilson (LTV), Iowa Beef Processors and American Beef Packers. The last two are the largest beef-slaughtering firms in the country.

raisers that there was much competition for their beef.

Cattle-buying used to be done at sprawling stock-yards in such centers as Chicago, Fort Worth and Denver, where the cattle were brought to the buyers. There, the beef packers and processors would bid on the offerings. Now, the buyers go to the cattle. With national procurement staffs, the big firms have buyers traveling from feedlot to feedlot, and even from farm to farm. Seems like a nice service, but it effectively limits competition.

The relevant market to cattlemen is not national and usually not even statewide in scope. Few cattle are shipped more than 100 miles in search of buyers, mainly because of the trucking costs, loss of cattle weight, and risk of injury. It is in these localized markets that beef oligopsonies make their full power felt.[43]

The beef found on most supermarket meat counters today does not come from cattle roaming the open range, but from cattle that are raised in pens and fed a steady diet of grain. Nearly all of these grain-fed cattle (96%) are in 25 states, and the buying structure in those states is highly oligoponistic. The four largest meat packers in these states control an average of 62% of the cattle market.[44]

The area around Amarillo, Texas, is one of the major cattle-producing centers of the country. Within a 150-mile radius of Amarillo, sweeping across the panhandle sections of Texas and Oklahoma and into the adjacent states of Kansas, Colorado and New Mexico, cattlemen find that 78% of their market is in the hands of the four largest meat packers.[45] Just two of those corporations control half of the market.

That kind of market concentration puts considerable power in the hands of the big meat packers, and leaves independent ranchers having to take what they can get.

Competition depends on the number of buyers who are accessible to the cattleman. The handful of sprawling feedlots, with 100,000 cattle in their pens at a time, get most of the buyers' attention. The smaller feedlots get much less attention, and the independent cattlemen are lucky to get even a couple of packers to come out and bid on their cattle when they are ready for market.[46]

The few buyers are very much in control of the many sellers. If a meat packer decides to buy or not to buy, the decision will affect prices throughout the area. If a rancher or feedlot operator decides to sell or not to sell, the decision will have no effect on prices. As the Department of Agriculture understated it in 1974, "This means that the market for fed cattle is not fully competitive."

Not only are the big firms able to control the price they pay independent operators, but they also own their own feedlots. Armour, Swift, Wilson, Iowa Beef Processors, John Morrell (United Brands), American Beef Packers, Hormel, Oscar Mayer and Missouri Beef Packers are just some of the big outfits that feed their own cattle for slaughter. This ownership gives them even more muscle to affect prices paid to independent cattlemen, since in times of rising cattle prices they can turn to their own stock to cause a surplus, then reenter the open market to buy at lower prices.

Nor is it just the big meat packers that abuse cattlemen. Supermarkets, too, are major buyers of beef and have a direct impact on the price cattlemen can get. In 1974, a federal jury found the A & P chain guilty of a conspiracy to fix the prices it and other supermarkets paid to cattlemen, awarding $11 million to six ranchers for losses they suffered as a result of the price-fixing. Safeway and Kroger also were named as defendants, but they settled out of court. Seven other chain stores were named as co-conspirators in the case, but were not indicted—Winn-Dixie, First National, Colonial, Food Fair, Giant, Brenner Tea and Jewel Tea. The charge for which A & P was convicted was that the supermarket chains agreed not to compete with each other in buying fresh meats. Through the National Association of Food Chains, the supermarkets were found to be allocating buying territories among themselves and to be exchanging procurement information in order to preclude competition.

Farms for Sale, Hands for Hire

Squeezed between supply oligopolies on one side and market oligopsonies on the other, the survival of the family farm as an independent, competitive business unit is doubtful. "Twenty years ago," Michigan State University economist Leonard Kyle remarked, "almost no one believed corporate control of farming could happen; today the corporations themselves and growing numbers of integrated or displaced farmers know that corporations can succeed."[47]

That success is not a function of superior efficiency, productivity, innovation or competitiveness—it is a function of superior economic power. Corporations cannot out-farm the family farm, but they can out-muscle it. Good farmers are going out of business. And those that remain increasingly must surrender their entrepreneurship and sign on as hired hands to integrated corporate systems.

We are letting that happen in this country. It will mean monopoly control, higher prices and lower-quality food. It need not happen, but if we do nothing to control monopoly power in the food economy, it will. The Department of Agriculture, despite its bullish rhetoric about the tenacity of family farmers, already is looking beyond them: "By 1985 the contemporary transition of our food system will largely be history," observed Department spokesmen in 1973. "Internal control of the system will rest in those market-oriented agencies with the most direct access to mass consumer markets."[48]

If we allow the family farm to be foreclosed by monopolistic food firms, then we allow a bit of ourselves to be foreclosed with it. Not only are we giving up competitiveness and economic efficiency, but we also are loosening our grip on the idea that individuals can make it on their own, that human enterprise is of greater value than any security that corporate systems can promise. "The farmhouse lights are going out all over America," is the way it was put by Oren Lee Staley, president of the National Farmers Organization.[49]

> And every time a light goes out, this country is losing something. It is losing the precious skills of a family farm system. And it is losing free men.

CHAPTER VII

Limousines in the Fields

Government officials are quick to ridicule the idea that corporations are involved significantly in farming. "I remember in the 1960s the so-called invasion of agriculture by big corporations," Agriculture Secretary Butz scoffed. "These big, nonfarm corporations often were outsmarted by our family farms. Many of them got out of farming faster than they got into it."

Family farmers, however, are not so cavalier about the corporate presence. Behind the marble walls of the U.S. Department of Agriculture, officials and government economists can afford to be self-assured, but out in the isolated areas of rural America, family farmers are grappling daily with the overwhelming power of the corporations that Washington dismisses so easily.

To be sure, there have been some corporate failures, but many more have stayed, and corporations continue to move into agricultural production. These firms either become farmers themselves, or they effectively merge farmers into their integrated structure through binding production contracts that shift the farmer's entrepreneurial power to the corporation. In either case, it is the corporation that controls the farming.

While officials are making light of any corporate threat, many farmers are gazing across their fences in disbelief at the new neighbors—industrial conglomerates. Those who doubt the existence of corporate power in farming might want to RSVP to the menu of conglomerate-produced food, which could be served at their next dinner party (page 191).

These conglomerate farmers are only the more startling fragment of widespread corporate involvement in farm production. The erosion of the family farmer's position in agriculture is much more serious, much more fundamental, than either government or corporate executives are willing to admit.

The Department of Agriculture dwells on its finding that only 1% of the farms in the country are corporate farms, and that most of them are family corporations. In the first place, it appears that USDA's figures are wrong. Professor Richard Rodefeld checked up on the department's count in Wisconsin and found that it completely missed 252 farm corporations in that state: "It was found that USDA underestimated the total number of acres actually owned [by corporations] by 37 percent, acres rented by 269 percent, number of cattle fed by 80 percent, number of milk cows by 54 percent, number of sows by 216 percent, and acres of vegetables by 37 percent," Rodefeld told a Senate committee.[1]

In the second place—and far more importantly—the question is not simply who owns the farm, but who owns the farmer. A farm family might own the land and do the farm work, but not be making the decisions. Increasingly, farmers are working for corporations, producing food to corporate specifications. Marshall Harris, a University of Iowa agricultural economist, pointed with alarm in 1974 to "the trend toward off-

APPETIZERS

Sautéed Mushrooms by Clorox wrapped in
Bacon by ITT
Salmon by Unilever

SALADS

Tossed Salad of Lettuce by Dow Chemical
and Tomatoes by Gulf & Western
Avocado Salad by Superior Oil

ENTREES

Turkey by Ling-Temco-Vought
Ham by Greyhound
Roast Beef by Oppenheimer Industries

SIDE DISHES

Artichokes by Purex
Carrots by Tenneco
Potatoes by Boeing
Apple Sauce by American Brands
Deviled Eggs by Cargill
Olives by Zapata Oil

BEVERAGE

Wine by Heublein
Citrus Juice by Pacific Lighting Corp.

AFTER DINNER

Peaches by Westgate-California Corp.
Almonds by Getty Oil

farm businesses that have decision-making power but no property, and farmers who have property but no power."[2] That is the most significant development affecting the structure of agriculture since the Homestead Act of 1862, yet agricultural officialdom acts as though it is not even happening.

The Urge to Monopolize

"Why," you might fairly ask, "would high-profit corporations like Del Monte, Ralston Purina and Tenneco want to move directly into farming, which now has a profit return of under 5%?" These three giants, for example, clearly are accustomed to better things, having an average return on investment of 14.9% in 1973. There are two reasons, both requiring monopolization of the farming sector and both meaning higher prices to the consumer.

"It is difficult to justify most types of large corporations in farming by conventional economic tests of efficiency in resource use and management," observed economist Philip Raup.[3] No matter, large corporations are coming to farm anyway. What they are bringing is monopoly. These firms literally are engaged in a power play down on the farm, with the objective being to control the production of the foods they sell or process: (1) if they sell food from the farm, monopoly over production promises monopoly pricing and higher profit margins; (2) if they process food from the farm, monopoly overproduction promises steady supplies for their vertical system, with profits to be taken from the consumer of processed food.

First, consider the corporate farmers who are producing for the fresh-food market. It is important to stress again that the family-farm system, with millions of small units dispersed throughout the country, is highly competitive, thus generally unable to control markets and build higher profit margins. If a giant corporation can use its capital resources to lock up production of a food item it can corner the market and reap monopoly profits—something family farmers now are unable to do.

Either by using its enormous financial reserves to buy up farms, or by using its enormous market power to force its will on farmers, a corporation can become a major farmer in a hurry. If it can corner enough of the total production of a commodity—sometimes as little as 25%—it can find itself as the major domo of that commodity, in a position to undercut competitors and to begin monopolizing markets. "One of the paradoxes of markets," observed University of Missouri economist James Rhodes, "is that when competition drives out too many competitors then competition destroys itself."[4]

Ralston Purina, for example, during the 1960s, sought to control the egg industry in this manner. This giant feed company built egg facilities and began to integrate existing independent facilities, with the intent of controlling enough of the national productive capacity to be able to eliminate the sweeping cycles of too much or too little production that then characterized the highly competitive egg industry. If Ralston Purina could control enough production to do that, it certainly would be in a position to control prices. In short, the strategy was to eliminate the competitive structure of the egg industry by consolidating a major portion of egg production in their hands.

This consolidation was pursued in two ways. First, as the 53rd largest corporation in America, Ralston Purina has the internal capital and financial pull to buy its way in. Second, both as a supplier of chicken feed to hard-pressed independent egg producers, and as an integrated egg marketer, Ralston Purina could pull strings that effectively tied the many independents to them.

Ralston Purina bailed out of this particular effort, abandoning the egg business in 1972. It is important to recognize that the withdrawal was not due to the strategy, but to Ralston Purina's unwillingness to continue committing the huge capital required. The company had consolidated a huge chunk of total egg production, but it was not happening fast enough to satisfy certain management and financial forces within Ralston Purina who were eager to direct the firm's capital toward ventures that turned a faster profit.

Independent farmers and egg companies were displaced in the process, and they were not around to pick up the pieces of Ralston Purina's scrapped venture. Just the attempt to impose monopoly power led to a new level of economic concentration in the egg industry. That industry remains the target of corporate consolidation efforts, with such new farmers as Safeway and Kroger taking a crack at it.

Usually linked into this corporate strategy of consolidation is a marketing strategy of product differentiation. United Brands, for example, is seeking to dominate the fresh-lettuce industry today by sticking its well-known Chiquita label on some nine million cartons of lettuce that it produces in California and Arizona. The Federal Trade Commission, ruling on United Brands' absorption of nine major lettuce farms, found in 1974 that "The introduction of a successful branding program into an industry in which brand differentiation is non-existent could pose a grave threat to competition."[5]

But the Commission did not have the courage of its

convictions in this case. In one of their weakest rulings yet, the Commissioners allowed United Brands to keep its lettuce-farm acquisitions on the grounds that the company had come just short of effectively monopolizing the industry, and that its branding program thus had not been fully successful in commanding higher prices.

Tenneco, too, has been a leader in the effort to control farm production of fresh crops, then to sell the produce by establishing consumer identification with its highly advertised Sun Giant label. According to a vice-president, Tenneco hopes to do in fresh vegetables "what Del Monte has done with canned foods." The *San Francisco Chronicle* reported that Tenneco vegetables "will be pre-packaged, and each package will bear a smartly prepared advertising booklet pushing the thought that Sun Giant produce is something special." Only about 10% of Tenneco's produce is marketed that way now, but the company plans to have 70% of it branded within three years, and the firm has doubled Sun Giant's advertising budget to make sure it happens.[6]

It's a terrific system. Efficient and competitive family farmers are replaced by a monopolistic producer, price competition is eliminated in favor of brand-name hucksterism, consumers pay more for their produce and the monopoly takes a fatter profit from farming. You can count only one winner there.

Next consider the corporate farmers that are not concerned with farm profits, but are looking further up the line. "We literally begin with the seed and end at the grocer's shelf," boasted the chairman of Del Monte Corporation.[7] Del Monte seeks to control farming in order to sweeten the profits it takes from the grocer's shelf. It is a totally integrated food system. Del Monte,

Swift, Minute Maid and other brand-name processors are farming to meet their own needs, not to make farm sales.

The interest of the big processors in farming is to assure that their assembly-line food system will have a uniform flow of standardized foods, produced precisely to corporate specification. It is an effort to change a competitive arrangement to a "coordinated" arrangement, to restructure the food economy in a way that best fits their profit needs. Not only do they have the will to do it, but because of their oligopsonistic market position they have the power to do it. As Dr. Rhodes said of these vertically integrated food firms, "The vertical link is used to transmit the advantages of power from one level to another."

That these big processors do not compete directly with independent farmers for crop sales offers zero relief either to the economic condition of those family farmers or to the competitive condition of the crop they produce. The fact is, these giant firms monopolize production of crops whether they sell the produce or run it through their own processing plants. The impact on farmers and ultimately on consumers is the same— monopoly pricing at the farm level, where there used to be competition.

There is, for example, practically no open market today for a farmer producing vegetables used in processing plants. Processors themselves produce 10% of those vegetables, and another 78% are produced by integrated farmers under contract to processors.[8] That puts 88% of the crop under the direct control of corporations.

Yet, when tallying the number of corporations involved in agricultural production, the Department of Agriculture does not even count these "subsistence" farmers, since they consume what they produce and make no farm sales. Del Monte has 55 farms with 130,000 acres, and it has 10,000 farmers with hundreds of thousands of acres under production contract, but Del Monte does not get counted as a corporate farmer by the government.

Hired Hands

The Department of Agriculture is offering a special slide presentation for sale, calling it "The $150 Billion Food Assembly Line." The recorded sound track accompanying the presentation notes that the average American eats 1,500 pounds of food every year, and "to produce and market this food, an assembly line is needed—a line that runs back from retailers through wholesalers, shippers, processors and farmers."

Indeed there is such an assembly line, and not only does it run back to the family farmer, but it runs right through his heart.

Such giant processing corporations as Del Monte and Swift, such giant retailers as Safeway and Kroger, and such giant farm suppliers as Ralston Purina and Cargill are among the leaders in an industrywide move to incorporate farmers into vertically integrated food systems. The tool is a contract. Prior to planting, farmers sign a paper committing them to produce a certain amount of a food product by a certain date and to deliver it to the corporation for a certain price.

What's wrong with that? Nothing, if the two parties to the contract were dealing from equal positions of strength. But that is hardly the case. Again, in most farming areas of the country, potential buyers of the farmer's food are not numerous, and not competitive. Gene Potter, of the National Farmers Organization, went right to the heart of it when he said, "Farmers sign contracts with integrators because they are hard-pressed." When cost of supplies is high, when prices paid to farmers are low, and when the farmer's market is monopolized, the choice can come down to signing with a corporation or going out of business.

Typically, the contract is prepared by the corporate lawyer, preprinted and delivered on a take-it-or-leave-it basis. Woody Guthrie, writing about bankers fore-closing on farm mortages during the Depression, has a song that goes to the farmer's situation today:[9]

> As through this world I've hoboed
> I've seen lots of funny men
> Some will rob you with a six-gun
> Some with a fountain pen.
>
> But as through your life you ramble
> Yes as through your life you roam
> You won't never see an outlaw
> Drive a family from their home.

The robbery today is not usually of the farm itself, but of the farmer's proprietary independence. "The con-tracting firm," wrote economists Breimyer and Barr, "generally decides who shall produce the product, how it shall be produced, and how much production shall be allotted to each contractee."[10] Professor Marshall Harris, in his report on entrepreneurship in farming, refers to three empirical studies which show "that about half of the selected items of decision-making are shifted to off-farm firms under these contracts."

It all adds up to corporate control of the farmer's produce, without having to buy the farm and the farm-ing equipment, and without having to take the risk of production. Those burdens are left to the farm family. Taken from them are the heart of farming, for under

this arrangement, the farmer no longer is self-employed
—he is another hired hand on the payrolls of the food
combine.

Contractual integration represents a radical restructuring of our food system, yet it is being allowed to run
its course without serious examination of where it is
taking us. Already, 22% of the American food supply
is produced under vertical integration by corporations,
with 17% of that done by contract.[11] Not only is that
degree of corporate control increasing, but the rate of
the takeover is accelerating. The American Agricultural
Marketing Association estimates that 50% of the American food supply will be produced under corporate contract at the end of this decade, and that by 1985—just
ten years away—75% of our food will be in the hands
of the integrators.[12] For many of our basic food items,
corporate control already is a fact (see Table VII–1).

Corporate power has a tight grip on the growing of
many of the things people like best, including 95% of
sweet corn, 90% of snap beans, 50% of cantaloupes
and honeydews, 95% of tomatoes, 100% of mint and
even 90% of popcorn.[13] There are other food items
that long have been considered safe from corporate
control, but now are conceded to be within the grasp of
the big firms. Hogs, for example, presently are 98%
free of corporate production, but disease problems associated with crowding hogs into confined "factories"
now appear to be solved, and such corporations as Esmark, Ralston Purina and Babcock Industries already
are making their move on this mainstay of family-farm
agriculture.*[14]

---

* A 380,000-acre hog, cattle and grain operation is being
built now in North Carolina by a New York City trucking
magnate who hopes to produce at the unparalleled rate of a
million hogs a year.

TABLE VII—1

Corporate Control of Some Food Items, 1970

Crop	% Farmed by Corporation	% Under Corporation Contract	Total % Under Corporation Control	Some of the Corporate Farmers
Fresh vegetables	30%	21%	51%	Boeing, Tenneco, United Brands, Purex
Processing vegetables	10	78	88	Del Monte, Campbell Soup, General Foods, Norton Simon
Potatoes	25	37	62	Heinz, French's, Simplot
Citrus fruits	30	17	47	Coca-Cola, Tropicana, Royal Crown Cola
Sugarbeets	2	98	100	Great Western United
Eggs	20	20	40	Safeway, Kroger
Turkeys	12	42	54	Esmark, Cargill
Chickens (broilers)	7	85	92	Federal, Greyhound, Pillsbury, LTV, Continental Grain

Sources: USDA. ERS. "Interrelations in Our Food System." Talk prepared by William T. Manley and Donn A. Reimund. February 21, 1973. Table 1. Also, annual reports of the corporations.

It can happen fast—chickens, the first farm commodity to draw major corporate attention, went from 4% integration to 92% within ten years. The Department of Agriculture talks a good game of family-farm independence, but when pressed they name only cash grain crops, forage crops (hay) and range livestock as farm products likely still to be under independent control by 1985.[15] That leaves most things you eat in corporate hands.

It should be remembered that corporations do not need to control 100% or 75% or even 50% of a crop to have an effective monopoly. The impact of monopoly power (in this case, oligopsonistic power) is the ability to restrict competition and to set the terms of production, including price. That can be accomplished by holding a relatively small amount of total production— maybe as low as 25% in some areas. A firm holding just that amount in a growing area could be by far the largest producer and likely would be the price setter for all the other producers.

The power of these giant corporations can be devastating to the family farmer. Frequently, corporate contracts cost the farmer more than the rights of entrepreneurship—they cost him money, and sometimes his farm. The classic pattern of farm integration occurred in the 1960s when Ralston Purina led such other major corporations as Cargill, Pillsbury and Continental Grain into the South to take over production of broilers.*

* The integrators were helped by government officials, who assured skeptical farmers that corporate contracts were OK. In 1958, just after he resigned as Assistant Secretary of Agriculture and became both dean of agriculture at Purdue University and a board member of Ralston Purina, Earl Butz wrote a widely disseminated article titled, "Don't be Afraid of Integration," directed toward chicken farmers. Many farmers took his advice and then were economically devastated by the company he served.

They came when chicken prices were low, offering credit to financially-strapped farmers who could not find credit elsewhere. The farmer had to agree to use only his benefactor's feed.

Then the feed company began to supply the chicks and to buy the grown chickens, paying the farmer a piece-wage for each bird. But the farmer had to agree to build a new chicken house, to put in new equipment, to comply with the production instructions of the corporation, and to allow corporate inspectors on his property at any time.[16] Contract terms were corporate terms, as can be seen in Appendix D, which is a copy of a current broiler contract for growers in Maryland. You can find apartment rental leases between tenants and corporate landlords that give the rentor a better break than these contracts give farmers.

Harrison Wellford, in his excellent study of agribusiness methods, *Sowing the Wind,* says that a Department of Agriculture economist found Alabama chicken growers making minus 36¢ an hour for their service to the corporations.[17] In the 1960s, the National Farmers Organization worked in the South to organize chicken growers against the onslaught of the big integrators. For their effort, they got violence and blacklisting. The corporations won, decisively, and they left the chicken growers of the South with little more than fear. "Today," said an official of the Mississippi Farm Bureau, "a Mississippi farmer could not sell broilers in the market if he wanted to produce them. Only integrators now sell and produce broilers. Farmers do not own the birds. They furnish only the labor and the houses. They do exactly what they are told by integrators."[18]

The power of the integrator over the grower is total, and it is not administered beneficently. An integrated chicken grower in Alabama talked to ABC-TV news in

1973, but fear of reprisal kept her from allowing her face to be shown or allowing mention of the corporation for which she raises chickens:[19]

> INTERVIEWER: What did it cost you to put up these [chicken] houses?
>
> GROWER: It cost us $29,600 for a lock and key job. I mean, ready to put the chickens in.
>
> INTERVIEWER: And how did you raise that money?
>
> GROWER: We borrowed it.
>
> INTERVIEWER: So your home was mortgaged to pay for the houses?
>
> GROWER: Yes.
>
> INTERVIEWER: Now how about the money you've been getting for your chicks, is that working out all right?
>
> GROWER: It sure isn't. It has dropped in the last bunch of chicks I sold. I didn't get nothing for them, hardly, period.
>
> INTERVIEWER: And how about the number of chickens or chicks that you've been raising this year as compared to last year?
>
> GROWER: Well, they was six weeks between bunches of chickens this time.
>
> INTERVIEWER: Did the integrators give you any reason why they didn't deliver the chicks?
>
> GROWER: No. No, they don't.
>
> INTERVIEWER: Why do you stay in the business of chicken raising?
>
> GROWER: We have to! We'll lose our home. Our farm. Everything we've worked for.

By any reasonable definition of the independent family farm these chicken growers fall short. Nonetheless, the Department of Agriculture continues to count them as such. They have no entrepreneurial power and are at the mercy of corporate whim. "Us folks in the chicken business are the only slaves left in this country," was the much more accurate assessment of an Alabama chicken grower. The New Jersey Supreme Court ruled back in 1960 that a chicken grower there, producing under such a contract, had effectively surrendered operational control of his farm and had become a laborer employed by the corporation.[20] Nonetheless, the Department of Agriculture continues to count these contract growers as full-fledged family farmers.

Del Monte: Down on the Farmer

It is not just chicken farmers who feel the pressure of the corporate thumb. Vegetables, grown for the brand-name canners, are another commodity locked up by corporate integrators. Farmers are organizing into bargaining associations in an effort to get a better deal from the processors, but today only 9% of the country's processing vegetables are grown under contracts negotiated through these bargaining units.[21] Sixty-nine percent of processing vegetables are grown under corporate contracts signed between individual farmers and such powers as Del Monte Corporation. The imbalance in that relationship can come hard on family farmers.

Tom Ellerd, a California peach grower, is one who felt the power. He had been a successful farmer for years. "It was one of the best farms in the country, best taken care of," he told ABC news. "Even the canneries complimented us on our way of operating, taking care of the place."[22] Then Del Monte signed him up not only to produce for them, but also to expand his operation. In a deal that no longer is legal, Del Monte even loaned Ellerd the money. But the bottom subsequently fell out of the peach market and the Ellerd farm went into debt—as frequently happens to independent farmers. However, Mr. Ellerd found that he was not indepen-

dent. Del Monte lawyers had written the contract so
that the company legally was in a position to foreclose
and take the farm—and that is precisely what they did.
Mr. Ellerd thought he could get a bank loan on his next
peach crop and save his farm, but he found out that
Del Monte legally had control of the crop:

> Well, after you get started with Del Monte and they
> have a mortgage on the peaches and your crop, no bank
> or anything will touch you because they've got every-
> thing in their control. They wouldn't release the crop for
> you to get money or anything. They wanted it all.

Even with today's bargaining associations, the power
of the processor is superior, and the terms of production contracts are written with corporate interests in
mind. Asparagus growers, for example, find that their
contracts with Del Monte allow the corporation to decide what part of the crop is "acceptable." In 1972,
eight percent of the asparagus crop was rejected in this
manner. With no open market to sell on, farmers literally had to eat that loss.

In many cases, however, Del Monte will buy the rejected asparagus from the farmer—at cut-rate prices.
In 1972, the price for "acceptable" canning asparagus
was 23¢ a pound. The price for asparagus the corporation found unacceptable was .0005¢ a pound. Del
Monte has sole power to decide whether a batch of
asparagus is worth 23¢ or .0005¢, and the contract
requires the farmer to offer any unacceptable asparagus
to Del Monte. If the corporation does not want to buy
it, then the farmer can take his rejects elsewhere. But
there is nowhere else.

Why would Del Monte want to write such a provision
into its contract? Because there are windfall profits in
those asparagus culls. The farmer may have to give the

stuff away to Del Monte, but Del Monte certainly does not give it away to you. Del Monte packages and sells these rejects as asparagus soup, asparagus cuts and asparagus tips—all drawing a pretty penny at the supermarket.

Contractual integration of family farmers is a euphemism for their elimination. Farmers are stripped of their entrepreneurship and left to sell their labor and skills cheaply. It is not the concept of contractual integration that is bad, but the practice. Such integration would be acceptable if there were equal bargaining power between farmers and integrated corporations, and if there were actual competition at the consumer's level. But that is not the experience. As it is, farmers are crushed by oligopsonies, which then turn to face consumers as oligopolies and do not pass on the cheap prices they are able to extract from farmers.

It is not farmers who are causing this shift in the structure of agriculture. Summarizing the results of several polls of farmers, economists Breimyer and Barr report the obvious conclusion: "The vast majority of farmers declare they prefer to remain independent proprietors buying and selling in the open market, rather than enter into production contracts."[23] Purex Corporation, which has run into trouble in its farming effort, recently offered this perplexed analysis: "People who are used to farming do not want to adhere to corporate policies."

Want to or not, millions of farmers are being forced to. In recent years, farm groups have tried to fight back legislatively, urging passage of bills that would require corporations to bargain with farmers. That effort has flushed out the real proponents and beneficiaries of contractual integration—brand-name processors. Through their Washington lobby, the National Canners Association, the big fruit and vegetable canners led the charge against any government action that would interfere in "the processor's right to choose his suppliers and to decide with whom he will deal."[24] There still is no bargaining bill for farmers.

Always painting a rosy picture, the Department of Agriculture officially stresses the point that contractual integration guarantees a uniform supply of raw food to processors and marketers, and it guarantees farmers a market for their produce. Never mind that it is a monopolistic market. Rather than harsh terms, like "contractual integration," the Department prefers the softer sound of "coordination" or "interrelation" within the food system. Most damning, the officials of government have chosen to side with the oligopsonistic power of corporations against the competitiveness and efficiency of family farmers. Testifying before the House Judiciary Committee in 1972, U.S. Undersecretary of Agriculture Phil Campbell gave the Department's stamp of approval to corporate integration:

CHAIRMAN CELLER: Is it your view that we should encourage vertical coordination—that is the term you used—should we encourage that in every way?

MR. CAMPBELL: Coordination?

CHAIRMAN CELLAR: Yes.

MR. CAMPBELL: Mr. Chairman, the coordination that we have seen from production through processing and into marketing has come about through the free enterprise system of competition, and it has brought about in our opinion the most efficient setup possible to (1) protect the farmer, and (2) at the same time give the consumer the best possible product at the most reasonable—

CHAIRMAN CELLER: I take it, then, that your answer is "yes."

MR. CAMPBELL: Yes. [25]

Contractual integration of farmers has at best been a dehumanizing process for family farmers, and at worst it has been brutal. For consumers, it has seriously choked competition at the farm level. With friends like the Department of Agriculture, farmers and consumers need no enemies.

Deep Pocket

Corporate farmers may not bring any improved efficiency or productivity to their task, but they do bring one ability that independent family farmers do not have. The economists' phrase for it is "deep pocket."

To enter farming, practically all corporations create or buy a farming subsidiary. The deep-pocket advantage is the ability of that subsidiary to draw enormous sums of money from the parent corporation. It is not an insignificant advantage, and it clearly is unfair competition against independent farmers. The daddies of family farmers are considerably less well-heeled than, say, Tenneco, with $5.4 billion in assets to draw from, or even Ralston Purina, with a middling $1.3 billion in assets.

These corporations can dip into their deep pockets to (1) buy enormous amounts of machinery and other supplies directly from manufacturers, thus getting sizable discounts; (2) suffer farming losses, either because of business mistakes or bad crop years, without going out of business; or (3) sell farm products under market value, making up the difference in other lines of business.

At a time when the Department of Agriculture and the big food corporations are urging farmers to specialize in one product, thus risking bankruptcy with one bad crop year, the food companies are rushing pell-mell into diversification programs. The food giants see it, in the words of Del Monte, "as a means of spreading risk and sustaining growth." Some are spreading pretty far out: Pillsbury has moved beyond flour to fresh-cut flowers; General Mills now offers Lionel trains; Quaker Oats aims at the kids with its Cap'n Crunch cereal, then follows up with its Louis Marx toys; Swift is drilling for oil; Consolidated Foods is now the Fuller Brush salesman; through General Foods you can put on Maxwell House coffee or Viviane Woodard cosmetics; and Ralston Purina owns a ski resort in Colorado.[26]

The deep pocket of corporate farmers offers another financial advantage that ironically is supposed to accrue to family farmers. This is the tax-loss advantage in agriculutre. In detail it's complicated, but in concept it's simple: Lose money in farming and write those losses off against nonfarm income. That is of doubtful benefit to family farmers, but it is of big benefit to corporate farmers—mainly because corporate farmers are the ones that have a nonfarm income from which to deduct losses. If Ralston Purina has a bad year growing turkeys, it can write those losses off against the big money it is making selling condominiums in the Rockies. The farm family can do that too, if they happen to be selling condominiums in Colorado.

Food Factories

It isn't difficult to envision agricultural plots several miles long and a hundred feet wide. Equipment straddling the strip will roll on tracks or paved runways swinging around at the end to work the adjacent plot without a wheel-touch compacting the soil in the cultivated areas.

Weather control may tame hailstorm and tornado dangers. Atomic energy may supply power to level hills or provide irrigation water from the sea. Satellites and

airplanes overhead will transmit readings enabling a
farmer to spot diseases breaking out in his crops more
surely than he could by walking through the fields.

Sensors buried in the soil will tell him when his plants
need water, and automated irrigation systems will bring
it to them. He may have at hand chemical means of
speeding or slowing crop growth to bring harvests to
market at optimum times.[27]

This is a bit of farming futurism served up by Dr.
George Irving when he was a Department of Agriculture
official in 1970. Far-fetched? Dr. Irving says that these
techniques already exist in pilot projects or in the research stage.

Desirable? Only giant corporations, supported by the
resources of major banks and insurance companies, can
amass the enormous capital to implement such a vision,
and only vertically integrated, oligopolistic marketing
systems will allow the enormous cost of this technology
to be passed on to consumers. Dr. Irving's reference
in the last sentence to bringing harvests to market at
optimum times implies supply manipulation—the power
to come to market at the most *profitable* time.

In fact, food factories already exist. Fred Andrew,
the president of Superior Oil Company's farming subsidiary, told the Westinghouse television network about
his company's Arizona tomato farm that is entirely
under plastic: "We've made it such that we can control
the light in there, the light intensity, the temperature,
the heat—both the high temperature and the low temperature, the air movement and the gas exchange in
there for the carbon dioxide exchange, that the plants
need and we, we can do this operation almost any place
in the world."[28] The production of chickens, turkeys
and eggs, all highly corporatized, also has been con-

verted to factory methods, with an assembly-line process that runs from computerized blood lines in the beginning to an electric shock at the end.

The industrial methods of large corporations are less concerned with quality production than with profits. Corners are cut whenever possible to minimize input costs and maximize profits. The objective is not to produce the best-tasting tomato or the most nutritious chicken, but to produce an acceptable product at the cheapest cost to the company, leaving the rest up to the advertising departments. Breeds are selected that promise maximum yields, good shipping qualities, extensive shelf-life and proper appearance. Products are designed to appeal visually to consumers, even when that means deception—such things as injecting Xanthophyll to increase the yellow color of chicken skin, and bathing tomatoes in red fluorescent lights to increase the color of the fruit.

The firms gear their assembly lines to meet minimal standards of nutrition. Ralston Purina uses computers to determine the least expensive ingredient mix that will sneak in under the law.[29] Cost-conscious managers at H. J. Heinz do no research into the nutritional quality of the tomatoes they bottle as ketchup, asserting that "you kill the vitamins in tomatoes when you make ketchup anyway."[30]

The corporate farmer does not hold much to the Confucian admonition that "the best fertilizer is the footsteps of the landowner." If the landowner in the corporate farm is personified in the chief executive officer, he is most likely out at the country club, with little inclination to walk through any field without a golf club in his hands. The corporate crop is built on chemicals and hormones, not the personal attention and care of the landowner. Chicken factories, as described by

Harrison Wellford, are a harbinger of our food future in the hands of industrialized farmers:

> The chicken which used to run free to scratch and root in the soil until time for slaughter now spends its short life in a 12″ by 18″ cage crowded up against three other birds. His day may consist of sixteen hours of artificial light in a totally programmed environment. Crowding favors disease by creating stress and aiding the buildup of harmful bacteria and parasites, such as coddidia. The chicken's feed, therefore, is sprinkled with antibiotic drugs. Other drugs, including arsenic and antibiotics, such as nitrofurans, are fed to increase the rate at which the chicken matures and gains weight. Before going to market, chickens may also be bathed in tetracyclines (antibiotics) or sorbic acid to extend their shelf life. In addition, the bird's chemical diet may contain coloring additives to give their flesh a desired yellowish tint.[31]

A taste of industrialized farming techniques is available in the modern tomato. Beginning at least as far back as 1947, researchers of tax-supported colleges of agriculture began to tamper with nature's design of this popular fruit. The objective has been to make a tomato for industry that can withstand the rigors of mechanical harvesting, both for processing tomatoes and for the fresh market. Genetic scientists developed a hard tomato for that purpose—one with firm walls, thick flesh and free from cracks. Now they even have changed its shape to square for easier handling and packing. In order to harvest these "love apples" of industry in one sweep of their machinery, they are sprayed with ethylene gas, which causes them all to turn red at the same time.

But turning them red turns out not to be the same as ripening them. The gassed tomatoes generally lack the vitamin A and C content of nature's own beauties. A

Harvard nutritionist, for example, pointed to a tomato manufactured at Purdue University that looked great, but would have "at best approximately half the vitamin A content of the varieties of tomatoes presently on the market."[32] Taste? There's more flavor in the cellophane that is wrapped around some tomatoes. "But most people smear it up with their favorite salad dressing recipe, and they don't know the difference," shrugged a University of Illinois food specialist. Other scientists have been more sensitive to criticism about the lack of flavor in their structures, so they are out to correct the oversight. At the University of California, scientists have isolated some 70 chemicals that cause old-fashioned flavor in nature's tomatoes, and they are in the laboratories now trying to program some of those chemicals into the man-made version.

Unfortunately, tomatoes are not the only food product being redesigned to meet the needs of industrialized farming. Cantaloupes that grow on bushes, rather than vines, for easier mechanical harvesting are new from the University of California. The University of Georgia is working to breed a chicken with no feathers, so the big processors don't have to pluck the birds, and the same university had built a machine to take the fuzz off peaches: "The machine will remove the fuzz that exists on all peach fruit," the project director told ABC-TV. "It will coat the fruit with a water-soluble wax containing fungicides to prolong storage life and prevent weight loss during storage."[33]

Such technological gadgetry is designed for a highly capitalized, highly industrialized agriculture, which is just another way of saying corporate food factories. Family farmers also use chemicals, genetically altered breeds, animal drugs and other tools of industrialized agriculture, but on their efficient scale of operation such things are used as complements to the farmer's skill, not as a replacement for it.

Sentimental as it may seem, family farmers are close to their land and close to the living things that are raised on it. Without wanting to overstate the case, that closeness is an important element in the quality of food that comes off the family farm.

You won't find Tenneco entering its cucumbers and pumpkins in the county fair. On the cumbersome scale of corporate farms, with tens of thousands of acres or hundreds of thousands of livestock, bureaucratic systems and technology become essential. With rigid production schedules to meet, and with corporate headquarters to appease, factory managers cannot even consider letting a crop sit in the fields to ripen when ethylene gas is just a pushbutton away.

Food Factories Are Forever

It is tempting to dismiss the corporate farm on the grounds that its inefficiencies and its high profits will cause it to fall of its own accord. But the inclination to believe that is rooted in classic free-enterprise ideology. These firms are not engaged in free enterprise—they are mammoth, multibillion-dollar firms, diversified across several product lines, integrated from inputs through retailing, operating profitably on a multinational basis and existing *both* as oligopsonies and as oligopolies. That is more power than many governments have, and it is not the kind of enterprise that responds to classic assumptions.

Innovation? ITT did not grow so massive so quickly because it built a better mousetrap, but because it had a deliberate and successful strategy of acquisition and merger, because it bought growth that gave it more

power to buy still more growth. Efficiency? A & P has
been as badly managed as a corporation can be, even
losing money for years, yet it stays in business and continues to grow. Productivity? The major tractor manufacturers restrict their output in order to manipulate
prices and build enormous profits. Quality? The nutrition and taste of processed foods grow steadily worse,
yet the prices just as steadily go up. Private enterprise?
Giantism throughout the food economy *requires* regular
government subsidy, both in the form of direct assistance and of passive acceptance of the corporate will.

Dr. James Rhodes and Dr. Leonard Kyle, two of the
most thoughtful and respected agricultural economists
in the country, put it this way: "The capacity of the
giant corporation to grow and grow, despite the lack of
any real competitive edge over individual farmers in a
traditional accounting sense, is the crucial difference
between the corporate and the individual competitor."[34]
Boeing might be an inept potato farmer, but its ability
to apply deep-pocket capital, to merge, to vertically
integrate, to advertise and to attract government subsidy
is enough to overwhelm real potato farmers.

Behind the big Cheshire Cat smile that food firms
show to consumers, there is an awesome power and
hunger for profits that is destroying family farmers and
eliminating competition throughout the food system.

We are to be left with factory farms, and they are
forever. As family farmers are displaced, they do not
hang around waiting for the call to return. Nor are
they teaching their skills and art to their children—the
average age of farmers today is 53, and their kids are
grown and working in the city.

What will happen to factory-farm productivity when
technology fails? There is considerable evidence, for
example, that the enormous productivity of American

agriculture during the past several years has been due less to technology, as widely claimed, than to good luck with the weather.[35] Meteorologists suggest that the United States has enjoyed abnormally favorable weather for crops since 1956, but that the droughts of 1974 have begun to show a return to the normal cycles of good and bad.

Will the corporate farmers hunker down after a bad year, betting their investment on a good year down the road, as family farmers have done? Or will they choose, as Ralston Purina did in 1972, to look for greener pastures? "Our interests," said chairman Hal Dean, announcing that Ralston Purina was calling it quits as a chicken farmer, "will be better served by employing capital in areas with less cyclical profit patterns."[36] What about the public interest? With corporate eyes focused on the bottom line, can the public expect that corporate farmers will keep on producing, even when times are bad? Or is it more likely that there will be more shortages and higher prices?

Corporate executives with such conglomerates as Tenneco and Superior Oil have arrogantly claimed that the family farmer is obsolete and incapable of meeting America's food needs. That is a hard line to swallow, coming as it does from two of the oil firms that have not earned much public trust in meeting the nation's fuel needs.

Agricultural abundance over the decades, with accompanying low food prices, has not been the result of any corporate efficiency or productivity, but of family farmers. The Department of Agriculture's chief economist reported in 1974 that 94% of the increase in food prices over the past twenty years was the result of added costs by corporate middlemen—with only

6% of the rise coming from farmers.[37] It would make more sense economically to let farmers take over the middle sector, rather than the opposite path we are now on.

CHAPTER VIII

Government:
A Helping Hand

In 1971, the U.S. Senate was considering the controversial nomination of Earl Butz to be Secretary of Agriculture. The nomination was strongly contested, primarily on the basis that Dr. Butz had spent his entire professional life either directly serving agribusiness and food corporations or helping design public policies that worked in the corporate interest.[1]

No one was more familiar with Dr. Butz's record than farmers, and they were in the forefront of the fight against confirmation, particularly through such groups as National Farmers Organization and National Farmers Union. A great many farmers had traveled to the Capital to attend the confirmation hearings, and they were a part of the large crowd that overflowed the small committee room. On the second day of testimony, a farmer in the hallway was asked if he had been satisfied by Butz's earlier assurance that he would shed his corporate trappings, put his holdings in a trust and be the Secretary of all the people. "Every now and again I find a snake skin that has been shed on my farm," replied the sage farmer, "but you can bet there's still a snake out there."

Government frequently is corporate power in another form, and the helping hand of the public has a way of being extended mostly to large private interests. In the last twenty-five years, covering five presidential administrations, food policies and programs have centered directly on the interests of processing, marketing and exporting corporations. There have been substantive differences between Democratic and Republican approaches to the food economy, but the result of them all has been to encourage corporations in the middle to grow more powerful at the expense of consumers, farmers, workers and taxpayers.

To this farmer outside the hearing room in Washington, the nomination of Earl Butz was only the latest and most blatant admission by government that it has sided with the food giants against the rest of us.

The Public Trust

"It is imperative—not only to agricultural producers, but all U.S. consumers—that sufficient supplies of cans be forthcoming," Secretary of Agriculture Butz declared in a 1974 letter to steel-company executives. He was trying to get the steel firms to make more tinplate, which is used to make tin cans.

This might seen an obscure and minor action, one of hundreds taken each year by government food officials, but it offers a large insight into government service. Who needs the tinplate? Big processors, most of whom make their own cans. The wish here by the Secretary was to increase supplies of tinplate so that these processors could get it at a low price. Yet the

Secretary's letter never once mentioned the processors, who were the actual beneficiaries of this governmental action. The request was made in the name of consumers and farmers.

"Consumers" and "farmers" are terms that government officials bandy about almost reflexively, while "middleman" and "oligopoly" do not seem to be in their vocabulary. Even when oligopolists are remaking the American food economy, shaping it to fit their private pecuniary interest, every step toward the new food systems is officially sanctioned by government and rationalized as serving the public interest. Thus, farmers are not forced out of business, they are "freed" to seek more rewarding livelihoods elsewhere, according to the twisted language of the Department of Agriculture.

Left to work its will, big business can be counted on to expand its market power in the food economy and to increase its potential for profit. It will pursue its economic interest to the logical conclusion—monopoly—no matter the cost to the larger interests of the public.

The pursuit of expansion and monopoly are inherent in the structure of the giant entities. "Those who manage most big businesses are hired men," said A. C. Hoffman, a former vice-president of Kraftco: "Their performance, their self-satisfaction, even their job security are related directly to the growth of the enterprises—to increasing total sales, total profit, share of market, rate of return on capital."[2]

Some have urged that corporations be more "socially responsible," and many of the big firms have been quick to embrace the concept and wear it like a white hat. They have not done so because they *are* socially responsible, but because to appear so polishes their public image and serves their economic interests—something like the monopolists of an earlier day who tithed on Sundays but were all business the rest of the week. Somehow, we have lost sight of the fact that business *is* a social function—the delivery of goods and services to a society that needs and wants them. If we could just count on food corporations to do that—without inflating price, diluting nutrition and taste, and eliminating efficiency and competitiveness—that would be social responsibility aplenty.

The hard fact is, however, that we cannot look to oligopolistic corporations to perform even at that bottom level of public responsibility. The corporate interest, almost by definition, lies solely in increased growth and profit, and experience makes clear that the big firms will be true to that self-interest. If that also coincides with the public interest, fine; if not, well, that's business. It is futile to expect more from the corporations.

But people have every right to expect more from government. It is here that oligopoly and its abuses ought to be checked. Government is the proper champion of the public interest, logically standing as an aggressive, countervailing force to powerful private interests, particularly on a matter so basic as the food supply. But it does not. Food oligopolies flourish today, like weeds in the cornfields, because government has failed to take the hoe to them. In fact, far from keeping the field clean, government has fertilized the weeds.

Service with a Smile

The government wants to hear from most of us only on April 15th. The average person needing a helping hand from government might as well be appealing to El Salvador, for the government in Washington is not likely to go out of its way to assist a regular citizen.

But for those who pull up to government agencies in company limousines, there is curb service. It can be said straight out: government works for big business.

The services available to enhance corporate power and profits are truly awesome, ranging from direct cash payments out of the public till, to such passive subsidies as the lack of enthusiasm in antitrust enforcement. Farmers and consumers are regularly told by government that the supply of grains from this country must be put on a "free market" basis, that they must take the risk of volatile prices that stem from political and weather abnormalities in the world market. But a food corporation operating a processing plant in a developing country does not have to bear the risk of its own profit-making investment, for the government-funded Overseas Private Investment Corporation insures them against any losses stemming from abnormalities.

If a small business violates a federal standard, chances are the business will be threatened with closing and fined substantially. But if a food giant runs afoul of the law, it usually can obtain from government regulators something called a "consent order," which allows the firm to say, "We never did it and we promise never to do it again," in exchange for which it gets off free. The Federal Trade Commission is fond of handing these out to food makers that violate the truth-in-advertising laws.

Even old and established government programs, meant to benefit farmers and consumers, are now enlisted in the corporate service. For more than forty years, for example, the federal government has purchased food mainly under a program called "Section 32" that was designed to stabilize farm prices by removing surplus production from the market. A glut of peas, goes the logic, would drive pea farmers bankrupt, so the government buys the surplus to prevent that devastating result. It makes sense. The peas are then distributed to low-income people (surplus commodity distribution program) and to school children (school-lunch program).

In the 1960s it became clear that the distribution aspects of these programs were hardly satisfactory, since the poor and the kids were having to eat whatever was in surplus at any given time—gobs of peanut butter one month, and beans the next.[3] People were being left badly nourished and even hungry. Countering the criticism, the Department of Agriculture ingenuously explained that, after all, these programs were not really intended to feed people,* but to raise the income of farmers.

Since the government is the biggest grocery shopper of all, buying more than $4 billion worth of food each year, these programs could indeed boost farm income. But when the income-distribution aspects of the programs are examined, it turns out that corporate middlemen are being paid—not farmers. In her excellent book, *The Great American Grain Robbery and Other Stories,*

---

* At the tail end of the 1960s, the government made a dramatic shift in its low-income food programs, switching from an emphasis on surplus commodities to an emphasis on food stamps. In part, this was due to the embarrassing findings of hunger and malnutrition among the American people. Food stamps could deal with that embarrassment better than surplus commodities. In larger part, however, the switch to food stamps was due to the findings by giant food makers and retailers that food stamps meant more people buying more food products, and that meant more profits. That discovery removed the objections of a number of business-oriented congressmen and agency heads who previously had opposed the program as a "government giveaway." Ironically, these same officials in 1973 and 1974 pointed to the increased use of food stamps as evidence of rising "consumer affluence" that was to blame for bidding up food prices.

Martha Hamilton reports that practically all of the government's purchases are of processed food, and the big processors are the ones getting government payments.[4]

Flip through the daily announcements from USDA of food purchases that it has made, and the same familiar brand names keep cropping up. Oscar Mayer, Ralston Purina, Stokely Van Camp, Armour (Greyhound), Del Monte, Swift, Tillie Lewis (Ogden Corp.), Wilson (LTV), Cargill and Dole (Castle & Cooke) are just a few of the giants who were more than million-dollar-winners from these income-subsidy programs in 1971. What about the smaller competitors? In a random sampling of 200 meat packers located throughout the country, Ms. Hamilton found that 60% of the small companies had not even been informed by the Department of Agriculture that the opportunity existed to sell their products to the government. The larger the firm, the more likely it was to receive a request for bids from USDA.

USDA says that it relies on middlemen to relay the benefits of these programs back to farmers, but the government makes no attempt to determine whether this ever happens. Del Monte Corporation sold canned tomatoes, tomato juice, canned peas, canned corn, dried prunes and canned apricots to USDA in 1971 for a total tab of $2,121,112. It's not likely that this federal payment to Del Monte did much for the farmers who sell to the corporation. A 1973 Del Monte publication shows that a 29¢ can of its tomatoes returned 3¢ to the farmer.[5]

Unable to demonstrate that these corporate payments ever trickle down to family farmers, USDA has retreated to the position that the program offers them a "psychological boost." The Texas conglomerate Ling-Temco-Vought (Wilson meats) got $17 million from this program in 1971—money which it can haul to the bank. Farmers, in whose name the program was created and in whose name it continues to be funded, must find their psychological boost mighty cold comfort.

NOBODY HERE BUT US CHICKENS. The corporate bailout has become a governmental specialty. Whether it is Lockheed, Penn Central, Franklin National Bank or TWA, corporations have recently lined up before Uncle Sam with giant tin cups. The government generally has been obliging, doling out millions of tax dollars to shore up these sagging bastions of free enterprises.

In 1974, Washington was besieged with another request for emergency assistance—this one from the chicken industry. It was sought in the name of farmers, and the national press reported it that way, but the "farmers" turned out to be a handful of corporate executives dressed in overalls. It was a chicken saga that involved one mystery villain, two vegetable-oil manufacturers, five chicken processors, a flock of congressmen, 785 chicken farmers, 1,100 chicken processing workers and nine million chickens, which were dead.[6]

On a March Sunday, newspapers throughout the country reported that the federal govenment had ordered the destruction of millions of chickens being raised on Mississippi farms. The chickens had eaten feed that contained traces of Dieldrin, a powerful pesticide made by Shell Chemical and used much like DDT. It kills pests, but it also has the potential to kill people— Dieldrin's link to cancer is so strong that it was banned in late 1974.

Dieldrin was not used *on* chickens. It was applied to field crops such as corn. But in today's technological agriculture, something done to corn has a way of cropping up later in someone's box of fried chicken. In the Mississippi case, the chicken contamination was traced back to two local manufacturers of vegetable oil, which is mixed into chicken feed to make the chickens grow faster. No one seemed to know how the Dieldrin got into the oil.

In any event, the chickens ate the feed that contained the oil that contained the Dieldrin. The Department of Agriculture's periodic spot check of chicken factories hit the right spot this time, finding nine million birds that had up to 10 times the dose allowed under government standards. The big chicken kill was ordered.

Rather than swallowing the bitter loss as one of the risks of doing business, or seeking damages through legal action against the negligent parties, a delegation from the Mississippi chicken industry hotfooted it to Washington seeking "indemnification" for their losses. In blunter words, they wanted the taxpayer to pick up the tab. Suddenly, Senator James Eastland was on the floor of the Senate with a bill to pay "a fair value" for the chickens and the cost of destroying them. The Department of Agriculture estimated that the indemnification would cost $10 million.

The chicken bill got immediate consideration and zipped through the Agriculture Committee in one day, without a public hearing. The committee was almost poignant in stating the necessity for this emergency assistance, noting that "many of the production employees will be without jobs temporarily, and many of the 785 growers will have empty broiler houses." All was poised in congress for a quick payoff until Senators Dick Clark of Iowa and Philip Hart of Michigan raised an extremely relevant question: *who* is being paid off?

There are 2,900,000,000 chickens produced in this country each year. Ninety-two percent of them are produced by corporations, including the likes of Holly Farms, Kentucky Fried Chicken, Wilson, Cargill, Pillsbury and Armour. The chicken farmer—in whose name the Eastland bill was put forward—is a hired hand to integrated chicken processors, and his hire is cheap. Supermarket chicken prices were running 80 to 90 cents a pound at the time the Eastland payoff was being considered by the Senate, but chicken farmers were getting just two cents a pound.

After all the talk about the hardships being worked on 785 chicken growers and 1,100 processing workers in the Mississippi case, the deal came down to five chicken processing corporations. These five owned *all* of the nine million chickens, and the 785 growers were under contract to them. It was the big five who had come to Washington for aid. Out of the total payoff, the 1,100 workers were to divide about $450,000; the 785 farmers were to divide about $585,000; and the five corporations were to divide $9,000,000. Not only were the chicken firms being covered for their total investment and the cost of killing the chickens, but also for their profits. The Senate approved the chicken payoff by a vote of 56 to 31.

Without the involvement of corporate power, this bid for relief never would have made it to the U.S. Senate. A mere 785 chicken farmers, or a small processing business would have attracted no official attention. At that small level, the free-enterprise ethic is invoked, and the little guy takes his lumps. And 1,100 workers? In the Mississippi chicken deal, USDA went out of its way to oppose any special benefits for the workers involved, noting that they have unemployment compensation ($37 a week in Mississippi) and food stamps to see them through lean times.[7]

But there is an attitude among corporate executives,

shared by government executives, that they are special citizens, somehow more worthy of public support than regular folks. Unemployment compensation and food stamps also are available to down-and-out corporate executives, but they expect better care and feeding than that, and they consider it their special prerogative to be bailed out by taxpayers.

TAX-PAID CONSULTANTS. People who run small businesses view government as a burden, for they seem always to be paying taxes or filling out endless forms for the folks in Washington. They do not have legal departments, tax departments and governmental relations departments to turn these burdens into assets, nor do they have the market power to make consumers pay the cost of the added paperwork.

Oligopolistic firms, however, have learned to live with government and like it. In fact, they have embraced government as a colleague, enlisting its support and seeking its participation in many aspects of their business. In particular, giant food firms have been able to draw on the expertise of government, keeping its officials and bureaucrats busy as tax-paid consultants to industry.

The new food economy, and even the new food, has been designed with the full advice and consent of government officials, and the economists and scientists of government have worked side by side with their corporate peers. Much of that consultation has been by researchers at state colleges of agriculture and by researchers attached to the Department of Agriculture. There are thousands of these, and they spend more than half a billion tax dollars a year in their work.

When Swift and Ralston Purina considered participating in development of a massive hog production facility in Missouri—a facility with the potential to monopolize the hog market in that part of the country—the University of Missouri's college of agriculture lent its experts to make feasibility studies. When workers began to request better wages from chicken processors, the Agricultural Research Service of USDA was quick to develop machines that cut up chickens, and cut out workers. Such examples are common. It is relatively easy to find this kind of close relationship between big business and government experts on every land-grant college campus in the country.

Some colleges specialize in service to particular segments of the food industry. Kansas State University is partial to the milling and baking industry, for example, while Texas A & M is close to the cattle interests. When the Agribusiness Accountability Project issued a 1972 report criticizing these binding ties, the dean of agriculture at Texas A & M complained publicly that AAP researchers had been on his campus but had not had the courtesy to interview him. In fact, AAP's researcher had gone first to the dean's office to talk with him, but had been informed by his staff that he was on a safari in Africa with an official of the King Ranch.

Cornell University enjoys a special relationship with supermarkets. It was here, for example, that researchers developed a machine to test how hard one needs to squeeze a grapefruit in the supermarket:

> Should you squeeze a product firmly or softly to determine its freshness, such as is commonly done with bread and some fruits? By using a universal testing machine, scientists have determined that a gentle squeeze, or more scientifically, a small deformation force, is much more precise in comparing textural differences than a firm squeeze or large deformation force.[8]

Cornell is especially proud of its "Food Executive

Program," which it sponsors with the National Association of Food Chains. For a $625 tuition, the supermarketeers and the big food makers are invited to spend two weeks in intense study of such subjects as "Labor and the Food Industry," Management and the Computer," and "Government's Role in the Food Industry." As the university puts it in a promotional piece on the program, "An exposure to the vast resources of Cornell, some of its most distinguished faculty, and colleagues from other food industry firms with wide and varied experiences in small formal and informal meetings will be a most rewarding and valuable experience that would take years to obtain in the normal course of business life."

Rutgers, the state university of New Jersey, specializes in food technology, and is working on the future for the food industry. Technologists there, dissatisfied with many of nature's designs, have sought to reconstruct foods to conform to the marketing needs of food firms. For example, Rutgers actually employs a Professor of Flavor Chemistry, who is busily remodelling the taste of things. He is the one who has spent time and tax dollars trying to make spinach taste like potato chips. One of the flavor professor's colleagues is quite upset by banana peels, because they let the fruit get ripe earlier than the banana oligopolists would like. So he has devised a semipermeable membrane that can be wrapped around the fruit to protect it from the open air —a sort of rubber glove for bananas. He is now working on man-made skins for tomatoes and green beans. Reporting on his work, *The New York Times* said, "Each fruit and vegetable will require a different quality of membrane to have a longer shelf life, and the specialist in packaging hopes that some day he will be able to cover them all."[9]

This is work that ought to be done by the corporations themselves, if it should be done at all. Not only is it a waste of taxpayer's money, but it is an unforgivable diversion of publicly employed expertise. These researchers could be at work on the needs of family farmers, rather than enhancing the power of oligopsonies; they could be working to improve job conditions and developing the productive capacity of workers, rather than eliminating them; they could be considering means to improve the competitive position of small businesses, rather than servicing the giants; and they could be working directly with consumers, rather than tinkering around with nature to meet the marketing specifications of oligopolies.

A BUSHEL, A PECK, AND A HUG AROUND THE NECK. International grain-trading corporations are the darlings of the Department of Agriculture, and the Department takes every opportunity to show its affection.

These international traders are giants, but it is not likely that you have heard much about them. Cargill and Continental, the two largest, are not household names, but they handle more than 50% of the world's grain shipments, total more than $6 billion in annual sales, and their worldwide dealings affect the price of groceries more than any other six food corporations combined. Both Cargill and Continental are privately held firms, so they are exempt by law from having to reveal the same fiscal information that other firms must.

In 1972 the Department of Agriculture negotiated an infamous sale of grain to Russia that still is costing consumers and farmers, but that turned out to be a sweet deal for the grain oligopolists and for the Soviets. The Russian grain deal offers a rare glimpse of how favored corporations farm the government for a bounteous harvest. As one soured farmer put it. "The Department of Agriculture is just a one-stop shopping center for the grain corporations."

First, the grain corporations maintain a domineering presence in the Department of Agriculture's Export Marketing Service (EMS), which is the government's center of grain-trade activity and regulation. Grain officials shuttle back and forth between industry and government. In the few months surrounding the Russian grain deal, for example, five top USDA grain administrators either came from or went home to Continental, Bunge, Dreyfus and Cook, four of the big six grain traders.[10] One of these commuters, Clifford Pulvermacher, denied that any of this government-industry closeness could be construed as collusion: "It's a matter of people living together, and jointly trying to get a job done."

They did a job on all of us in the spring and summer of 1972. From the start, the grain traders were involved in the sale to the Russians. Clarence Palmby was the head of EMS at the beginning of government negotiations, and he traveled to Moscow in April with the U.S. trade delegation. Just prior to going, Palmby had been offered an executive post at Continental Grain Corporation's New York headquarters. Palmby did not accept at that time, but he did buy an apartment in Manhattan. During the Russian trip, Palmby took a couple of days on his own to tour that country's wheatfields—and observed first-hand that Russia would have to import large amounts of grain to meet its needs.

In May, after returning home, Palmby resigned his government position and accepted the offer to join Continental. Within a couple of weeks, Russian grain officials were in this country to negotiate directly and privately with the grain companies, and Clarence

Palmby was wining and dining them for Continental. By June 1, the Russians had signed contracts to buy $7.5 million worth of U.S. grain—$5 million of it from Continental Grain.

From mid-June to early July of 1972, a great deal of negotiating was underway. An official Russian trade delegation was meeting in Washington with USDA and White House officials to work out credit terms that would allow Russia to purchase at least an additional 7.5 million bushels of American grains over the next three years, with no top limit on total amount bought. The U.S. government would handle the financing. The actual purchases, USDA officials had told the Russians, would have to be made from the grain corporations, so the Soviets also had delegations of buyers negotiating with the top grain firms, primarily in New York, Washington and Minneapolis. A few U.S. government officials and a handful of grain-firm executives were the only Americans aware of this high-level dealing. The transactions were not made public until mid-July.

The government and top grain firms knew (1) that Russia was going to buy massive amounts of grain, (2) that this country would have the only grain to buy, and (3) that the value and price of this country's 1972 grain crop would rise substantially. They did not share this information with independent competitors of the grain oligopoly (including farmer-owned grain cooperatives), nor with grain farmers who were beginning to harvest their 1972 crop, nor with American consumers and taxpayers, who would foot the bill.

Knowledge is power, and such closely held economic knowledge is cash. This secrecy conferred a considerable subsidy on the grain giants. Continental, Cargill and the few other firms that were aware of the coming sale rushed out to the Southwest in June to buy wheat.

Farmers in these early-harvesting states were unin-
formed of any grain dealings going on back East, so
they sold their wheat to the grain traders for about
$1.25 a bushel. Three months later, after news of the
big grain deal had been made public, that same wheat
would have paid $2.25 to the farmer.

In a concise report on the grain deal, Al Krebs found,
"Throughout the southwest and the early-harvesting
midwestern states, 20 to 25% of the 1972 wheat crop
was sold by the middle of July."[11] In Oklahoma alone,
the withholding of information by USDA cost wheat
farmers some $47 million. It will be a long while before
farmers in that part of the country forget being short-
changed by their government, and they still remember
the contorted explanation of their Secretary of Agriculture: "Farmers didn't lose money because of early sales,
they just didn't make the additional money they might
have made."

Gouging farmers is an indirect subsidy. The grain
traders also had a direct subsidy that made the Russian
deal especially lucrative to them. The government was
setting the price of U.S. grain sold abroad, and generally
that price was a bit lower than the price paid for the
same grain in this country. In order to encourage exports, the government subsidized the difference between
the high domestic price and the lower foreign price. The
subsidy usually added a few pennies a bushel to the
international sales of the grain corporations.

With the massive purchase of wheat by Russia, however, the price of U.S. grain skyrocketed. Yet, USDA
held the foreign price of U.S. grain at the same low
level. The difference between the price at home and the
price abroad expanded from 6¢ on July 8, when the
Russian deal was publicly announced, to a peak of 47¢
on August 25, when the government finally stepped in

to halt the spiraling subsidy. In those few weeks, the grain oligopoly collected more than $300,000,000 in export payments from the taxpayers.

Even the manner in which USDA cut off the give-away reveals the kind of favoritism that is commonly shown corporate power. August 24 was to be the last day of the taxpayers' largesse, but that turned out to be the longest day in grain history. The grain firms are in a position to finalize a foreign sale and register it for subsidy at the time most advantageous to them—which is to say they can hold off as the subsidy climbs, finally registering their claim when the subsidy peaks. Many appeared to be doing just that when it was announced rather suddenly on August 25 that the free ride was over.

Worried that such precipitous action had caught the corporations by surprise, USDA officials ruled that any grain registered for subsidy through September 1 would be treated as if it had been registered on August 24—making it eligible for the full payoff of 47¢ a bushel. In that week, 282 million bushels of wheat were registered, costing taxpayers $132 million.

Cargill, the largest grain exporter in the world, was a major winner in the Russian deal, and showed even fancier footwork in the effort to profit from the taxpayers. In a report to Senator Henry Jackson, the Senate Subcommittee on Investigations claimed to have evidence that Cargill sold wheat to its own wholly owned subsidiary in South America. The company collected an export subsidy (up to 47¢ a bushel) on this bogus "sale." The South American subsidiary sold the grain to another subsidiary in Europe, which made a final sale to a second party for a profit. Under the tax laws of this country, the profits made by foreign subsidiaries of American corporations are sheltered from taxation by our government as long as the profits remain abroad. Apparently, this international shuffling was all accomplished on paper, with the wheat never leaving the ship on which it originally had been loaded.

The grain giants have retorted that they failed to make much money on the Russian deal, but even if that can be believed,* it deceptively ignores the total impact of that historic transaction. The Russian sale was massive, and the government subsidies made it profitable to the traders, but much more significantly, that sale greatly inflated the profitability of subsequent grain sales that they made.[12] In fact, 53% of the grain registered for subsidies that summer were sold to countries other than Russia, and the General Accounting Office found that the big traders had profits on those sales ranging from 2¢ to 53¢ a bushel.[13] The grain firms themselves figure a profit of 1.6¢ per bushel to be good.

The corporations understood from the start that a Russian sale of such magnitude, coupled with worldwide shortages, would balloon grain prices to their advantage. So anxious were they to make that happen that they even sold the wheat to Russia at tremendous discounts, ranging to 9¢ a bushel. In a matter of weeks, the price of U.S. grain doubled. And as the oil giants and sugar corporations have taught us, there are enormous profits to be reaped in such price leaps.

The Russians were the only other winners in the deal. With their own wheat crop a failure in 1972, and with literally nowhere else to turn for grain but to the United States, the Russians hardly had much of a bargaining position. But they stung our bargainers badly. Not only

* As privately held firms, there is no public information available on sales and profits they had in 1972, and subsequent investigations of their role in the Russian wheat deal have relied on information supplied by the firms themselves.

did they get wheat at bargain-basement prices, but they even got the United States to handle the financing at a cheap rate. And, not only did they haul off enough of our supplies to meet their 1972 needs, they had enough for export to Eastern Europe and enough to build a stockpile for 1973.[14] As a crowning irony, in January of 1974, when U.S. grain supplies were running low because of exports, a Russian official offered to sell back some wheat to help tide us over until our new crop came in.

The great grain robbery is more than an embarrassment. More than any other single force, the grain deal with Russia wrecked the American food economy, and we have yet to put it back together. It badly depleted our supplies of grains, setting off an inflationary food-price spiral that has left both farmers and consumers in desperate shape, while middlemen have profited.

That has not been an uncommon result of government programs and policies. Public officials tend to view private interests as though they were inseparable from

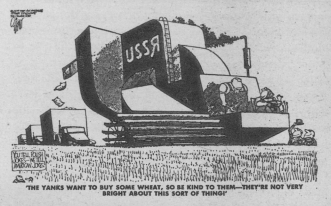

'THE YANKS WANT TO BUY SOME WHEAT, SO BE KIND TO THEM—THEY'RE NOT VERY BRIGHT ABOUT THIS SORT OF THING!'

Pat Oliphant. © *The Denver Post*. Reprinted with permission of the *Los Angeles Times* Syndicate.

public interests. As succinctly expressed in a 1973 editorial by the *Des Moines Register*:

> USDA relations with the grain trade, the pesticide makers and other businesses selling to farmers or buying from them are cozy. People like Butz who have been on both sides of the arrangement see nothing wrong, but it IS wrong if the purpose of government is to serve all the people, not special interest.[15]

The Promised Land

"The promised land for agriculture is near at hand," enthused Secretary Butz in a 1973 speech. This was not a revival for farmers—he was addressing the National Agricultural Advertising and Marketing Association, and he was telling them about the goal of American farm policy. The audience was significant, for such food executives are the chosen ones of the promised land, and the agencies of government are hard at work to deliver dinner unto them.

For years, agricultural legislation has been referred to as the "farm program," implying that it was designed to serve farmers. With the rise of consumer concern about food issues, the 1970 legislation was altered in title to imply service to both farmers and consumers—it is called "The Consumer Agricultural Food Protection Act of 1970." In truth, agricultural policy for at least the past two decades has been shaped to serve the marketing needs of corporate middlemen, without once having to mention them in a piece of legislation. At its present point of evolution, there are three primary tenets to America's agricultural policy: (1) get government out of agriculture; (2) produce for export markets; and (3) eliminate small competition.

GET THE GOVERNMENT OFF THE FARM. A basic thrust of agricultural policy is to eliminate government's involvement, leaving farmers to the workings of the "free" market. The idea is to terminate government programs that manage farm production—such programs as the one that buys excess grain production, storing it for sale in lean years, and the one that takes farm acres out of production in order to prevent market gluts. "Get the government off the farmer's back" is an often-spouted slogan that may have a nice ring to it on the banquet circuit, but in the real world it means that farmers and consumers alike surrender essential decision-making power over supplies of basic foodstuffs to oligopolistic food firms.

Senator Herman Talmadge of Georgia is chairman of the Senate Agriculture Committee. "I am a conservative man," he said in 1973. "The idea of getting government out of agriculture is basically very appealing to me. But I would be a traitor to the people of my state and nation if I were a participant in such a scheme."[16] What prompts such strong feeling?

In the first place, the food economy must have some kind of supply management at the farm level. Dispersed and competitive, farmers in this country have little control over the amount that they produce, and in years of decent weather they produce tremendous amounts of food. The constant threat, and the frequent result, is that farmers produce more than will be bought, thus producing a market glut and extremely low prices to farmers. In short, American farmers regularly have the capacity to produce themselves out of business.

Supply management is an integral part of the American economy. General Motors does not manufacture more Chevrolets than the market will bear—if auto demand slacks, GM simply lays off workers and either slows down the assembly line or shuts it off entirely, as it did for a period in 1974 and 1975. The price of Chevrolets, therefore, never drops and frequently goes up, as did the 1975 models. That makes a mockery of supply-and-demand mechanisms. It occurs because General Motors is a monopolistic giant, able to exercise total control over the supply of its products.

In fact, supply control at the farm level is much less pervasive than in other areas of the economy—but it is more visible and consequently subject to greater criticism. Doctors, for example, limit their numbers, and hence their competition, by restricting enrollment in medical schools. Similarly, plumbers, veterinarians, electricians, and other groups limit their supply below demand to assure a good price for their work.

Such manipulation is done privately and quietly, and it limits competition. Since the days of the New Deal, control of farm production has been handled by the public and in the open, and its purpose has been to preserve competition. The latter approach makes more sense, especially considering that food is the commodity being managed. Whether the issue is a peach marketing order, a set-aside of productive wheat acres or storage of grain in reserves, those ought to be public decisions rather than private, with full access to the decision-making process by all elements of the public.

That is not the approach of government in the new food economy, however. Now, government policy is shifting supply management of farm goods from public hands to private hands. "We seek to keep the Government out of agriculture and place decision-making in the hands of rational entrepreneurs," said the Secretary of Agriculture in a 1973 message.[17] "Rational entrepreneurs" is another way of saying that consumers and workers and even family farmers are irrational. In 1974, a USDA official expressed the view that the time was at hand for questions about farm production "to be moved away from dependence on the decisions of an increasingly urban-oriented Congress."[18] Again and again in 1973 and 1974, the speeches of Agriculture Department officials pointed to the rising political power of urban and suburban consumers as a major reason for reducing the public's access to decisions about farm production.

Having been cast out on the "free market," family farmers certainly are not sanguine. With no public regulation of their productive capacity, they foresee periods of boom and bust, and they wonder how to survive the busts. The Department of Agriculture admits that putting farmers on the free market means that they will experience "worldwide fluctuations" in demand and that their prices will "become more volatile."[19]

Agriculture officials in Washington, who regularly draw a check from the taxpayers, tell farmers that they must view this new freedom from "protection" as an "opportunity." In one breath, an assistant secretary of Agriculture told a farm group that in the new order of things each farmer must respond to signals of demand from world markets, that only their own forward-thinking management would protect them from the "ups and downs" of the market place. In the very next breath, this public servant told farmers that markets were changing on a daily basis, with doors opening and closing so fast that "what might happen next, no one can tell."[20] Good luck, and good-bye.

The farmer has been put on the free market alone. The giant firms that sell supplies to farmers are not operating in a free market, and there is a steady and steep rise in the farmer's costs—even in those years that

the free market is a bust. Nor is there a free market
between the farmer and the consumer. When farm
prices are high, the oligopolistic processors, marketers
and exporters are able to pass those costs right through
to the consumer. When farm prices are low, as they
normally will be, these middlemen are able to keep
consumer prices high and to reap inflationary profits.

The middle sector also is the long-run beneficiary of
any policy that weakens public control over production,
since that sector increasingly is taking charge of farming and monopolizing productive capacity. As that happens, they will not want government having any say
over the amount of food to be produced—just as
General Motors wants no public control over the pace
of the automobile assembly line. The difference is that
this is dinner being monopolized.

Dr. Don Paarlberg, USDA's chief economist, recently took consumers to task for not applauding the
new free market policy that takes the government out of
production management. "Now we have removed this
artificial increase in consumer prices," he boasted, "by
becoming competitive in world markets."[21] There are
no cheers from consumer quarters for the simple reason
that consumers had reasonable and stable prices under
the old system of public management, whereas the new
system has produced a one-third rise in food prices in
its two-year history. And the shift to world markets
gives American consumers much less control over food
prices in the marketplace, since multinational food
firms can use foreign demand to bid up domestic prices.

Another major element of supply management has
been public purchase and storage of excess grain production in years of abundance, with the option of selling
from this reserve in times of scarcity. This idea is at
least as old as the Bible. The government is now out of

the grain-storage business. Does that mean there is no storage of grain? No, it means that storage is now in private hands.

This sell-out was accomplished under the rationale that government storage of grain held farm prices artificially low—whenever the price of corn started rising, went the argument, government would sell corn from its storage bins and lower the price farmers were getting. It was said by agriculture officials in Washington that "rational entrepreneurs" ought to hold and manage any reserves. They did not mean farmers.

Family farmers do not have any long-term capacity to hold massive reserves of grain, nor do they have the capital resources necessary to construct such storage facilities. That capacity and those facilities are controlled primarily by the giant corporations that sell U.S. grain in international markets. A study by agricultural economists at Purdue University found that 56% of the storage capacity for grain in major U.S. ports was held by the big six international grain traders.[22] Grain used domestically is held primarily by such feed firms as Ralston Purina and Cargill and increasingly by such bakers as Continental Baking (ITT) and Campbell Taggart.

Under the new policy of putting grain surpluses in the hands of oligopolists, neither farmers nor consumers have any access at all to the decisions of how much shall be stored, when it will be released and at what price. By this twist of public policy, the public interest is left to the caprice of multinational corporations. Defenders of the grain corporations cite the savings to taxpayers if corporations bear the cost of storage, but those firms are not treating storage costs as a charitable contribution. These firms are oligopolies, and every bit of their storage costs are added into the price of grain, as is a profit margin they take for performing the service.

BIDDING FOR DINNER. "Food is the new currency," Senator Hubert Humphrey said joyously at an international soybean conference in Munich. Suddenly, raw materials again are the major factors in international power balances—the Arabs may have their oil, but we have food. "Everyone is talking about the power the Arab world has with its oil reserves," said Assistant Agriculture Secretary Yeutter in 1974. "I don't think that—over the long haul—I'd trade their oil reserves for this country's agricultural power."[23]

Therein lies another major tenet of today's agricultural policy: the world is one giant market waiting to be sold U.S. food products. "Peanut butter," whispered an agricultural official in the ears of the Southeastern Peanut Shellers Association in 1974. "Virtually no one outside North America knows about it. This is a marvelous marketing opportunity in a protein-hungry world."[24]

The primary rationale for this policy is that we have an agricultural abundance that can be sold profitably abroad, thus expanding American markets and improving our balance-of-payments position. The Secretary of Agriculture tempted Congress in 1974 testimony with the prospect of "more than 3 billion increasingly affluent consumers who live beyond our borders." That's a lot of peanut-butter sales, goes the argument, and they will help us buy imported cameras, shoes, automobiles, television sets, and even oil—"Food for Crude" is a favorite phrase of USDA officials.

It is suggested that the United States has a "comparative advantage" in the production of many food products, especially feed grains, wheat and soybeans.

Indeed we do. Our advantage is that we are by far the world's major supplier of each of these. For example, the United States produces about 75% of the world's soybeans, and 87% of the world's exports of raw soybeans come from here.[25] If food is the new currency, as Senator Humphrey asserts, then we are the Rockefellers of the world.

Touted in the name of family farmers, this policy of food exports is implemented through corporations. Farmers do not make the sales to Japan and Germany and Egypt. Farmers sell to the likes of Ralston Purina and Cargill, and those firms make the sales in the foreign markets that have been opened through the diplomatic efforts of the U.S. government. The balance-of-payments position of this country *is* improved, but a major share of that improvement ends up in the corporate till, rather than on the farm.

It is the farmer that takes the risk of exports, for the government has urged him to produce to capacity on the assurance that the government will keep the foreign demand steady. Farmers plant in the spring on the basis of USDA projections of demand. But these "experts" have been less than infallible at estimating U. S. demand, and downright wrong on a world scale. In fact, their estimates proved so wrong so often that in 1974 the Department switched to a plan of listing a possible range of supply-and-demand figures, from low to high. Instead of predicting a demand for 6 billion bushels of corn, the Department now predicts something like 5.5 billon to 6.5 billion. USDA officials say they fully expect the actual demand to fall within their predicted range two out of three times.

When they are wrong on the short side of foreign demand, it is the farmer who has to eat the error. If that demand drops, it is too late for farmers who already

have their crops well underway. The export corporations, however, are not fazed, for they have the flexibility to buy less from farmers and avoid suffering any
loss. And it is instructive that these corporations do not
for a moment rely on USDA predictions—the giant
exporters of grain, for example, have such an effective
worldwide network to obtain information that agents of
our CIA, according to *Business Week*, "often wine and
dine the company's traders to pick their brains."[26]

At times it appears that the CIA is running our export program, for food shipments are being used as an
extension of some of the worst aspects of American
foreign policy. The Secretary of Agriculture offered
this summation of food as a powerful weapon to be de-
ployed in geopolitics: "In a world in which a bad mon-
soon or an insect invasion can shake governments; in
a world in which foodstuffs can be used increasingly to
trade for dearly-sought energy supplies—in such a
world, the great influence of American agriculture
moves to the front burner."[27]

According to Chilean sources, when Salvador Allende was President there, the United States refused to
sell Chile vitally needed wheat, even though Allende's
government was offering cash. It was a political decision. Stephen Rosenfeld, writing in the Spring 1974
issue of *Foreign Policy,* said that less than a month after
the 1973 military coup that toppled Allende, the United
States approved a sale of wheat to the new Chilean
government; this sale was much larger than the one
Allende sought, and it was on credit.[28]

Secretary Butz claimed in 1973 that the earlier sale
of wheat to Russia was part of the deal for the Vietnam
peace settlement, and food concessions appear to have
been among the offerings to Arab leaders in exchange

for lifting the oil embargo. Our food abundance is being used as a bargaining tool to get what our government wants from other countries. Food has made us "the real peace broker in the world," the Secretary of Agriculture gloated.[29] Such international arrogance has gotten us in trouble before, and it is less endearing now that food is our chosen weapon.

Credit might be available to a favored military dictatorship, but not to countries that simply are hungry, with little strategic value to us. Our food export policy is no Food for Peace effort, no Share the Wealth program. This is for cash. Our food abundance goes to the highest bidders, which is another way of saying "Them that's got is them that gets." Only the industrialized countries have the cash to compete, and they are the ones least in need. In 1973–1974, half of our total exports of food went to the two most affluent areas of the world outside of the United States—Western Europe and Japan.

Because the affluent countries are regular customers, they get preferred treatment, which is to say they get dinner first. Government officials again and again have stressed the necessity of being a "reliable" supplier to these reliable buyers, even when that means cutting back on domestic supplies for American consumers, and even when it means world food needs will not be met. The policy is strictly business—it is not concerned with developing equitable access to food supplies, but of developing this country's access to foreign markets.[30]

Countries with the greatest need, but the least cash, are left standing on the outside, looking in. Oh, if there is a major food disaster in one of those countries, if their starving masses get on our evening news shows, then the government will send emergency shipments of grain, along with a covey of government photographers to snap hungry foreigners gratefully eating American charity. But for the everyday food needs of hungry nations, no special concessions are available to help them buy in the marketplace. Under current policy, the government makes no long-term, low-interest credit sales to help less affluent countries compete against the industrialized powers for a square meal from Uncle Sam's overflowing larder. "Hunger is relative," grumped Secretary Butz in 1974, "if your larder is empty, you cut back some."[31]

There is an obvious need for a carefully thought-out export policy. In the first place, as the primary producer of basic foodstuffs in the world, we have a responsibility to develop an equitable means of distributing our abundance. That is not an argument for a massive, worldwide giveaway of food, but it is an argument for a better system than letting only the highest bidders be the eaters. This is food, not some luxury item.

It is essential, too, that a food-export policy be publicly implemented, rather than turned over to oligopolistic corporations. The full public—consumers and farmers, as well as middlemen—must have control of American food supplies. That requires a system of publicly held food reserves, with adequate safeguards to protect the prices of both farmers and consumers.

There ought to be more moral authority behind our export policy than a crass effort to penetrate foreign markets for big American business. An export policy based on greed, imperialism and guilt may gain foreign-exchange credit for this country, but it does not do us credit as a people. It is possible to have both foreign exchange and humanitarianism, and that combination of American values ought to be the basis of our food export policy.

GET BIG OR GET OUT. The Japanese have focused their farm programs and policies directly on small farmers. Operating on only two to three acres each, these farmers have responded with a whopping foodgrain yield of 4,500 pounds per acre. That is about 50% better than we do in this country, where government has prized bigness of scale and technology—and our foodgrain yield is 3,050 pounds per acre.[32] Giantism is not essential. We could, like the Japanese, do just as well on much smaller units if our machinery and systems and credit mechanisms were to be focused on the little guys.

In a neat self-fulfilling prophecy, government encourages bigness by discouraging smallness, and as small entrepreneurs are displaced, government points to the remaining giants as an inevitable trend. Small-scale operators, no matter how efficient and productive, are not welcome in the halls of government and are not treated as legitimate clients of farm agencies erected in their names and supported by their taxes.

In fact, "small" seems to be a downright offensive term to most agricultural officials. "I went to see my county agent to see what help he could be to me," said a small dairy farmer in Pennsylvania, "and when I told him I only had a little place, just milking twenty-five cows, he drew back from me like I'd walked in with a disease."

Dr. Ned Bayley, former head of agricultural research at the Department of Agriculture, confided in 1969 that the march of technology, which is supposed to give people more choices, has given them fewer and has marched right over many productive farmers: "We have narrowed their choices to two: either get *with* the new production efficiency technology as we are developing it, or get *out* of farming business. These are not very inspiring alternatives."[33]

That expression of concern makes Dr. Bayley a uniquely sensitive public servant, for most of his colleagues are anxious to dismiss any smallness from agriculture. "They're going to help us out all right," a family farm representative said of government officials, "—right out of farming." At no time has that intention been made plainer than in 1973, when the Department of Agriculture and the Bureau of the Census teamed up in an ill-fated attempt to alter the official definition of a farm.

These overseers of the new food economy decided among themselves that any farmer making less than $5,000 a year in farm sales was no longer fit to bear the appellation "farmer"—even if his sole occupation and sole source of income was farming. Specificially, these little enterprises were no longer to be counted in the Census of Agriculture, which is taken every five years. The $5,000 cut-off level advocated by the Department of Agriculture would count out 56% of all the farms in America.[34]

The government was seeking to deny a majority of farmers the title of their occupation. In fact, the government apparently was seeking to deny their very existence, for it is likely that they no longer would have been eligible for USDA programs that are available to farmers who bear USDA's official stamp of approval. It was an effort by the Department of Agriculture to put a majority of its own constituents out of sight and out of mind. Fortunately, the scheme was detected early enough to draw the ire of some powerful congressmen and force the bureaucracy to withdraw it. But the attitude that pushed the redefinition has not been withdrawn, and there is little doubt that the plan will surface again.

For small farmers, 1973 was not a good year; their government officials seemed hell-bent on eliminating them. The Rural Development Act, passed by Congress in 1972, had authorized $45 million to be expended over three years in a special research and extension program focused in part on small farmers.[35] It was a promising piece of legislation, with the potential to help adjust technology to the small farmer's scale of operations, to help them shift to crops in which they could be more competitive, to help them develop effective bargaining mechanisms, to help them maximize their efficiency through cooperative practices and to help them get better marketing information and access.

But it did not help them at all. The USDA's budget requests in 1973, 1974 and 1975 have sought zero funds for the small-farm provision. USDA officials argued before congressional budget committees that there was no need for a special focus on small farmers, as they could be lumped in with the total rural development "problem." The provision has never been funded, and small farmers continue to be treated by government as a problem rather than as a resource.

It does not have to be that way. Ironically, U.S. government agriculturalists at work in the developing countries of the world are coming to the conclusion that farm productivity and efficiency can reach its maximum on extremely small farms. The crucial element is whether farmers have access to the necessary support systems. Writing in *Foreign Policy* magazine in 1974, James Grant reported, "The average small farmer in Northeast Asia has become far more productive per acre than his counterpart in the Indian or Pakistani

Punjab, primarily because the entire rural support system—credit and marketing institutions, agricultural extension, farm technology, and broadly available health and educational facilities—is designed to serve the small farmer with an average holding of just over two acres."[36]

Ted Owens, an official with the Agency for International Development, wrote in a 1974 *Washington Post* article that very small Egyptian or Taiwanese farms can out-produce even giant American farms on a per-acre basis. There is no secret formula involved, no magic technique that makes such productivity possible on such tiny plots (2 acres). It is simply that the farm support systems in those countries are adapted to farmers, rather than *vice versa*. As Owens wrote: "The improbable feature of small farm systems to Americans is the use of small-sized farm machinery and tools to supplement human effort, not replace it, to increase the amount of work farmers can do rather than drive them off the land."[37]

Even where farm-support systems in this country have traditionally focused on small-scale enterprise, government policy in recent times has been to divert them toward bigness. Farmer cooperatives, for example, are unique institutions that offer family farmers one of their best hopes for survival, and they offer consumers some measure of competitiveness in a marketplace now monopolized by a few food corporations.

The idea of farmer cooperatives, which are publicly sanctioned by the Capper-Volstead Act of 1922, is that family farmers can own and democratically control their own marketing institutions or can come together for the purposes of bargaining collectively. It is, in short, a mechanism designed to give the little guy a fighting chance against the overwhelming market power of middlemen.

But cooperatives have not held much favor in the Department of Agriculture since the days of Harry Truman, and the cooperative approach certainly has not been a significant tenet of farm policy. For example, in the Secretary of Agriculture's budget presentations to Congress over the past five years, setting forward the elements of his farm policy, there has been no reference at all to farmer cooperatives, no indication that these unique institutions fit importantly in USDA's approach to the food economy.

In fact, USDA's Farmer Cooperative Service, which is the primary federal agency charged with cooperative development, has a budget of only $2.3 million. On the relative scale of things, that is half the sum budgeted for the National Agricultural Library, and it is .024% of USDA's total appropriation. For all the good that little dab has done, it would make more sense to distribute it directly to this country's 2.9 million farmers—at least that would assure each of them about 90¢ worth of actual benefit.

Cooperatives are important to USDA officials only to the extent that a few of them have grown massive and taken on the trappings of the corporate food giants. If a cooperative dominates markets, as Sunkist and Ocean Spray do, then it is big business and can walk in the front door of the Department of Agriculture. The giant cooperatives are run by professional management hired from the same ranks as corporate managers, and their touch with the average farmer that supposedly owns and controls the co-op is about as warm as Del Monte's computerized touch with its average shareholder.[38]

Government officials have encouraged farmer cooperatives to abandon the "movement" aspects of their operation and to devote themselves strictly to business. That means abandoning farmers, particularly small farmers, and concentrating on organizational growth and market expansion. "Your challenge," Secretary Butz emphasized at Sunkist's 1974 annual meeting, "is to continue to expand the gigantic market which you have already built."

Helping Out

It is comforting to think that the problem with government is one official or one administration. "If only we could get shuck of Earl Butz . . ." goes the thinking. But it is not enough. Butz can go, but that does not diminish the power that food oligopolists exert over government.

The issue is corporate power, and your power. They have too much; you have too little. Republicans have not fought that imbalance, but neither have the Democrats. It was a Democratic Senator, supported by a flock of liberal Democrats, who used family farmers as a shield to urge the government payoff of $10 million to five chicken processors. It was Democratic Secretary of Agriculture Orville Freeman (1961–1969), not Earl Butz, who first took up the chant "get the government out of agriculture" and who laid the groundwork for doing it. Agricultural research appropriations are made each year by Congress, virtually without questioning who benefits from the expenditure, and those congressional committees are chaired by Democrats.

Previous Democratic administrations have shown more compassion than Republican administrations for the fate of those in the food economy who are displaced by corporate technology and systems, but they have shown no more willingness to fight the displacers. Democrats have urged rural development, job retraining and other social programs to help ease the pain of displacement, without facing the harder question of whether displacement ought to be allowed in the first place. Rather than "Adapt or die," the Democrats have offered "Adapt or be retrained."

In 1971, when the U.S. Senate voted on the nomination of Earl Butz to be Secretary of Agriculture, Senator Hubert Humphrey rose in qualified opposition: "I oppose the nomination of Dr. Butz, not because of his former agribusiness ties," said Humphrey. "We have large agribusiness firms in my State that are good firms; I am not trying to give them a hard time." Why did he oppose the nominee? "I oppose Dr. Butz because I do not believe he will fight for the farmer."[39]

That is too little, too late. You cannot fight *for* the farmer unless you are willing to fight *against* monopolistic food firms. Fighting for farmers and consumers alike means giving those firms "a hard time," but few in government have shown any inclination to get in the way of corporate power.

CHAPTER IX

Business as Usual: Corporate Influence on Government

Food firms get what they want from government because they are there to get it. The dominant processors, distributors and retailers of food maintain a constant and powerful presence in the Capital, and there is no food-related legislation, federal regulation or bureaucratic action that escapes their imprint.

The classic view of the lobbyist, as depicted in the Thomas Nast cartoons—a corrupt, shadowy figure, pockets stuffed with money, lurking in the nether corridors of government—is no longer apt. As one lobbyist assured a *Washington Post* interviewer, his way of life is hardly the constant whirl of "bottles, blondes and bribes" that many people imagine.[1] Far from it. Food power is applied to government today with finesse.

Capital Power

Within eight blocks of the White House there are 14 Washington offices of food corporations and three Washington offices of trade associations that represent food corporations. Other food firms have locations

Downtown Washington, D.C.—A Walking Tour of Food Power Within Eight Blocks of the White House

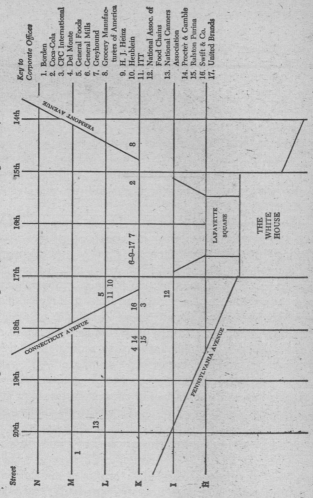

Key to
Corporate Offices

1. Borden
2. Coca-Cola
3. CPC International
4. Del Monte
5. General Foods
6. General Mills
7. Greyhound
8. Grocery Manufac-
   turers of America
9. H. J. Heinz
10. Heublein
11. ITT
12. National Assoc. of
    Food Chains
13. National Canners
    Association
14. Procter & Gamble
15. Ralston Purina
16. Swift & Co.
17. United Brands

throughout the Nation's Capital, but just these seven-
teen offices account for well over $100 billion worth of
food power—more than a tenth of this country's total
Gross National Product.

Recognition of that wealth is the first step in understanding the nature of corporate influence in the making
of food policy. These voices do not have to speak
loudly. The essence of business power in Washington
is its legitimacy. The presence of food firms is not as
"lobbyists," but as businessmen—leading citizens
quietly articulating a viewpoint from a position of economic and political strength. It is sophisticated, and it
is effective.

Rarely are these firms found out in the open. In 1973
and 1974 there were four major congressional hearings
dealing with the issue of monopoly power as a factor in
rising food prices. Corporations were not present as
witnesses at any of these public forums, although they
had been asked to participate in at least three of the
four. The staff of the Senate Select Committee on Small
Business conferred directly with officials of Ralston
Purina, Del Monte, and Safeway to request their appearances at public hearings in December of 1973. All
of the firms refused, though Del Monte submitted written questions to the chairman of the committee, request-
ing that he ask them of witnesses who were critical of
the food industry.[2]

Food firms were conspicuously absent again from a
1974 hearing of the Joint Economic Committee, which
was inquiring into the expanding profits of middlemen.
The firms had refused an invitation to testify. Did that
mean their side was not heard? No. During the public
hearing, the chairman of the subcommittee let slip the
information that he had breakfasted with several of the
food executives that very morning.[3]

There is nothing illegal about this, nor is it heavy-handed. There would be no request at breakfast to lay off the food industry, nor any hundred-dollar bills slipped under the chairman's toast. It simply would be an opportunity for big business to make its position known directly, personally, comfortably, and off the public record.

Business enjoys that opportunity day in and day out. This constant presence is the second major step in understanding food power in Washington. These firms are here full time, in many guises, and they are personally involved at every stage of the decision-making process. Professor Jimmy Johnson of American University made a study of lobbyists recently and found that at least 800 of the country's largest 1,000 corporations have some kind of direct representation in Washington.[4]

"Every time you get a new agency or another set of regulations that affect business," says Professor Johnson, "you get more corporate offices setting up shop here in Washington."[5] Food corporations increasingly favor this direct presence, which literally is an extension of the corporation into Washington. Through its "vice-president for governmental affairs," a corporation can have a full-time executive and staff looking to its interests—and the whole thing can be treated as a legitimate cost of doing business when it comes time to figure the company's income taxes.

As powerful as the lobbyists are, it is the Washington law firm that remains the major voice in governmental affairs for specific corporations, representing their clients before government agencies. These peculiar institutions —with names like Covington & Burling, Hogan & Hartson, Arnold & Porter, and Wilmer, Cutler & Pickering —hold millions of dollars worth of retainers to bend government to the will of food firms. These lawyers are specialists in governmental affairs, in knowing which lever to pull and when—many have worked in the government agencies that regulate their clients, and many are from offices on Capitol Hill. They know what they are doing.

These firms are large,* often with well over 100 lawyers, and they each have divisions stocked with legal talent specializing in antitrust legislation, FDA regulations or other specific aspects of government involvement in food matters. A highly competent and conscientious lawyer left one of these big firms in 1974 to work on the FTC's investigation of the food industry. He joined the Bureau of Competition, which is that agency's arm for enforcing the antitrust laws of the country. "I was stunned when I got here," he said. "There were more lawyers in my old firm than there are in the whole Bureau of Competition."

Not only are food firms represented individually in Washington, but also they have banded together in such powerful groupings as the National Association of Food Chains, National Canners Association, and Grocery Manufacturers of America. The wealth and geographic dispersion of their membership give these associations easy access into decision-making centers of Washington and enormous influence over the day-to-day business of government. Grocery Manufacturers of America (GMA), for example, has such billion-dollar-

---

* There are, for example, about 150 lawyers at Covington & Burling, and their food clientele includes Campbell Soup, Procter & Gamble, Nabisco, Carnation, National Brewing, ITT's Continental Baking (Wonder Bread, Hostess cakes, etc.), Green Giant, and Foremost Dairy. One of their lawyers serves as the general counsel of the National Canners Association; a former Covington lawyer is the number-two staff executive of Grocery Manufacturers of America; and another left Covington to become general counsel of the Food and Drug Administration in 1971.

plus companies as Procter & Gamble, Esmark, General Foods, Kraftco, Unilever, Ralston Purina, R. J. Reynolds, Coca-Cola, Nestlé, Scott Paper and Standard Brands among its 150 members. The power of the National Association of Food Chains (NAFC) in Congress is directly attributable to the fact that its largest 20 members alone total $40 billion in sales each year and have stores in practically every congressional district in the country.

These lobbies have the staffs and resources to keep up with every governmental action—not just staying broadly informed on major food issues, but paying attention to detail. The GMA has created three councils of its membership that meet regularly with the FDA, FTC and USDA. These are not low-level staff meetings, but regular opportunities for top food executives to sit down with the top government executives who make decisions affecting their businesses. For example, the chief officers of General Foods, Kraftco, Nabisco, Gerber, Heinz, General Mills, Hershey, Quaker and Pillsbury serve on the GMA council that meets several times a year with the FDA Commissioner and other top FDA officials.[6]

In an excellent 1971 article on GMA, *National Journal* said that Mary Gardiner Jones, then an FTC commissioner, "describes the meetings with GMA's council as an opportunity to explore the thinking of the commissioners and for the commissioners to get an understanding of business problems." That's all there is to it —nothing unseemly. It is simply that food corporations have the wherewithal to be where most of us cannot be, to exchange views and information directly and privately with top government officials, and generally to tend to their business in Washington.

The industry associations not only serve as the eyes

and ears of food middlemen in Washington, but they also frequently serve as the voice. At times this is necessary because of the onerous nature of what the firms want to say. For example, the National Canners Association (NCA), rather than individual canning corporations, has taken the industry lead in opposing bargaining rights both for family farmers and for farm workers. This tactic presents a united front by the canning industry, but it also saves individual firms the embarrassment of publicly taking such a negative position.

Del Monte, Campbell Soup, Hunt-Wesson, Heinz and other giants of the canning trade spend millions of dollars each year to promote public trust in their products and to create a favorable image of their industry. One 30-second evening news report of Heinz testifying against the obvious economic need of migrant farm workers or small tomato growers would undo a great deal of the public's good will toward Heinz. Thus, it would seem to be the better part of valor to let NCA carry the burden.*

GETTING THEIRS, BLOCKING YOURS. Joseph Danzansky, the president of Giant Food Stores, was elected top officer in the National Association of Food Chains in 1973. In his inaugural address to his supermarketing colleagues, Mr. Danzansky complained that food retailers had no government official they could point to

* This is not to say that individual firms hesitate to make their positions known in other ways; they just do it less publicly. In 1970, for example, the U.S. Senate was considering the long-overdue step of extending coverage of unemployment compensation to farm workers. Del Monte, which has 42,000 of these seasonal laborers at work in its fields and canneries, sent a telegram to a key committee member, categorically opposing the extension of this basic protection to farm workers. The corporate view prevailed, and these workers still are without full unemployment coverage.

as their own.[7] Cynics suggested that there were dozens of officials at FTC, FDA, USDA and Congress that the supermarketeers justifiably could claim as their own, but Danzansky insisted that they needed a full-time government advocate. Subsequently, NAFC executives met privately with the Secretary of Commerce and 25 other top-ranking department officials to urge creation of the post of food-chain ombudsman. As reported by *Supermarket News,* Danzansky asked the Commerce Department "to act as an advocate of the industry within the Federal Government and thus eventually to bolster its profit, harking back to the department's historical position as the Government's business advocate."[8]

At the very time that Mr. Danzansky and the food chains were maneuvering to get their own special advocate, they were working very hard to keep consumers from getting one. Since 1970, consumer organizations and others have been supporting legislation that would establish an independent agency to represent consumer interests before other federal agencies and courts. The expressed need for an institutionalized consumer advocate is that individual consumers have neither the time nor the resources—as corporations do—to represent themselves in numerous proceedings before the agencies of government.

Food firms have not seen the merit of that proposition, and they have been in the forefront of a vigorous lobbying effort by big business to keep the Consumer Protection Agency from ever opening its doors. In fact, when the original legislation failed at the last minute by a tie vote of the House Rules Committee on December 2, 1970, it was Grocery Manufacturers of America that was credited with the bill's defeat.

The consumer-protection bill is one of the infrequent

"big issues" that amasses the full strength of food power in Washington, and it offers an insight into another purpose of the trade association—that of rallying the industry and focusing its effort. GMA was one of the earliest of Washington's trade groups to see that this consumer legislation would in fact go a long way toward protecting consumer interests, thus posing a serious challenge to corporate interests. "YOU'D BETTER READ THIS," began a GMA memorandum to its membership in 1970, sounding the call to rise in opposition to the consumer legislation.

The GMA tactic, as Andrea Schoenfeld explained in *National Journal,* was not to take the politically untenable course of opposing consumer interests, but to draft an alternative bill and to put it forward in the name of consumers. The GMA bill, which was backed by all business interests in Washington, proposed the creation of a Consumer Affairs Service that had none of the effective provisions of the genuine article. Since 1970 was an election year, this tactic gave congressmen a way of voting against the consumer-protection agency without appearing to be against consumers. GMA's alternate was never intended to gain passage, but simply to draw enough votes to prevent passage of the other bill. It worked.

In 1971, the consumer-protection act again was moving toward passage. Industry interests defeated the legislation this time by attaching so many compromising amendments that consumer organizations felt compelled to withdraw support from their own bill.

By 1974, public support for consumer-protection legislation had grown and the composition of Congress had changed to the point that it seemed industry would be unable to prevent passage any longer. Even the threat of a presidential veto and dire warnings from food firms that the legislation would cause them to raise their prices did not keep the House from passing the bill by a 3-to-1 margin. It even became apparent that industry's opposition was weakening, with Montgomery Ward, Zenith, Polaroid, Motorola and other corporations switching to support of the bill.

But the food industry held firm. Using peer-group pressure, GMA and NAFC were able to keep the individual food corporations in line and maintain a united front. Bob Kuttner, of the *Washington Post,* reported that several supermarket chains had considered backing the bill, but deferred to industry solidarity. "We take a very low profile on this," a Safeway executive told Kuttner. "We're coordinating our position with the food chains association."[9] That preservation of unity won the food firms another year of grace, for the Senate fell two votes shy on September 19, 1974, of shutting off a Senate filibuster that industry backers were waging against the bill.[10] Despite a decisive victory in the House and a 64-to-34 favorable vote in the Senate, the public will was thwarted one more time by the strategic application of corporate food power.

That power does not go home when a major battle is over. It stays in touch with official Washington, dealing regularly with the small matters that do not attract public notice, and always staying on top of the larger issues. In 1973, Senator Philip Hart and others successfully maneuvered a piece of legislation through Congress requiring conglomerates to report information to the FTC on each of their lines of business. It seems like a small matter, simply asking a giant like ITT, for instance, to tell the public how much of its profit in any given year was derived from telephones and how much was derived from Twinkies.

These corporations, however, are notoriously reticent

about disclosing any information to the public. When this bill was passed, they did not simply sigh "win a few, lose a few"; they fought its implementation at every step. In 1974, for example, the firms succeeded in getting the House Appropriations Committee to delete most of the money budgeted for the reporting program and to limit the amount and kind of information that could be requested. It required major legislative fights on both floors of the Congress to restore most of what had been achieved in 1973. And now, the big corporations are fighting implementation of the law by tying it up in the courts.

While the food lobby never goes home, it frequently brings "home" to Washington. GMA's chief lobbyist, for example, does not always go into a congressional office alone, but frequently is accompanied by the executive manager of a food firm with a plant located in that congressman's district. And when Del Monte fought Senate legislation that finally would extend overtime-wage benefits to seasonal workers, the letters of opposition did not come from the San Francisco headquarters or the Washington office, but from plant managers in the several states where Del Monte canneries are located.

Campaign contributions are another tool that can be used to keep elected officials alert to the corporate presence. Corporate funds cannot legally be contributed to political campaigns, but it is legal for firms to establish nonpartisan committees to which corporate executives may voluntarily contribute for ultimate disbursement to candidates.

Campaign contributions by these corporate committees are not necessarily large, but they are strategically placed. Del Monte, for example, has major plant operations in 17 states, and the Del Monte Voluntary Nonpartisan Good Government Fund was active in each of them in 1972.[11] Chuck Neubauer and Donna Marx, reporters for *Chicago Today,* took a look at the Del Monte fund's disbursements for Illinois races in 1972.[12] The corporation has four canneries, a can manufacturing plant and a distribution warehouse in that state.

The reporters found that the fund paid out nearly $3,000 to 20 Illinois campaigns, including those of the governor, one Senator, four U.S. Representatives and nine state representatives. All but one of the state representatives receiving money from the Del Monte fund were from districts where Del Monte has plants, and four of them were on the agriculture committee of the state legislature. "We give where we do business," Del Monte's midwest division manager bluntly told the reporters. Though the contributions were small, it does not take much money to run for the legislature. "I'd certainly remember anyone who gave me $100 or so," one legislator said.

Remembrance probably is all that is sought with these campaign contributions, but that is a great deal. It affords the company welcome access into important offices when it is necessary to explain the industry side of some proposed legislation, or when the company is in search of sponsors for legislation that it deems worthy.

CLOAKS OF LEGITIMACY. The corporate presence sometimes is disguised, appearing at a congressional hearing or publishing a report on some issue of public importance under one of several cloaks of technical expertise.

The Committee for Economic Development, for example, is an organization that frequently is heard from in Washington, asserting authoritative positions on a wide range of economic issues. Its voice "is listened to by the nation's decision-makers and thought-leaders," says one of its officers.[13] But it is no independent economic analyst—it is an organization of more than 200 of the country's major corporate powers. Its purpose, according to a 1974 letter seeking industry contributions to its work, is to apply "sound business judgment to the analysis of critical economic and social issues of national, local and international concern."

In 1974, CED issued a widely publicized statement detailing the need for a new U.S. farm policy.[14] There was, however, little that was new in the policy. The statement was expressed in terms of consumers and farmers, but written in the corporate interest. It called for all-out farm production, more efficiency on the farm, continuing integration of the agricultural sector, increased exports to "friendly" countries, and the fostering of a market economy. Also, it accepted without question the "inevitability" of fewer farmers, calling for welfare programs and food stamps to ease their transition off the farm. In short, the "new" farm policy of CED is more of the same old policy of the past 20 years, merely shifting industrialization and monopolization into high gear.

The statement reflected corporate interests because it was written by corporate executives. The farm policy subcommittee of CED is made up of the chief executive officer of Independent Bancorporation, Franklin National Bank,* Kraftco, Deere & Company, Green Giant, Ralston Purina, Del Monte, Universal Foods, Pillsbury, H. J. Heinz, Quaker Oats and CPC International. The staff director for the group was John Schnittker, who

* Not only are bankers playing a major role in shaping farm and food policies, but this bank happens to have collapsed financially, finally going into receivership in 1974. If Franklin National is unable to manage its own affairs, why should anyone consider it competent to dabble in farm policy?

was Undersecretary of Agriculture during Orville Freeman's tenure at USDA.

Farmers and consumers could expect no relief from such a conclave, and that is exactly what they got. Yet, the national press treated the CED policy statement as though it were the independent analysis of unbiased economists. If those 12 corporations had issued the statement in their own names, the public response would have been much more skeptical. By using CED to enunciate the corporate view, the policy statement gained an unmerited aura of legitimacy.

In 1969, the Consumer Research Institute was created in Washington for the purpose of conducting research on food issues affecting consumers. It has a respectable advisory board of academics, and it has undertaken some major studies of consumer issues at the request of government agencies. For example, when FDA proposed guidelines for nutritional labeling, the agency turned to CRI to come up with label designs and to test-market them—an effort that is estimated to have cost the institute $100,000.

CRI is the creation of Grocery Manufacturers of America. It is not made up, as its name might suggest, by a group of consumers doing research, but is an institute doing research on consumers. A glance at its board of directors tells you that it actually stands on the opposite side of the counter from consumers: Kraftco, Grand Union supermarkets, Good Housekeeping, Heublein, J. Walter Thompson advertising agency, Quaker Oats and others. No consumer organization is involved, and they are hardly convinced of the scientific integrity of its work: "Consumers wouldn't trust what CRI did even if it was good," said the former head of Consumer Federation of America.

One of the most prominent scientific fronts for the

food industry is the Nutrition Foundation, which poses as an independent body of researchers and educators that develops and disseminates "authoritative information on nutrition."[15] In fact, it is a tax-exempt organization to which food corporations can contribute and get back scientific rationalization for the products of their industry. The Foundation is created and supported by such nutritious brands as Adolph's meat tenderizer, Coca-Cola, Hershey, International Flavors and Fragrances, Knox Gelatine and Eli Lilly.

The basic position of the Foundation is that food corporations have manufactured nutritious food, but the public does a poor job of eating: "Notwithstanding the high quality of the food supply, poor eating patterns and a lack of understanding of the basic principle of nutrition are prevalent among all socio-economic levels of the population," is the way it was put in their 1969–1970 annual report. Accordingly, the Nutrition Foundation "is working closely with industry, federal and state agencies, and universities to develop nutrition programs and materials to help establish good eating patterns for everyone."

Such outfits are common in Washington, and they give the corporate position a public credibility that it otherwise would be unable to command. It is an effort to buy legitimacy, and to some degree it works. Large corporations have the resources to create these organizations, and there seems to be plenty of scientific and economic technicians who are willing to pull the corporate load.

TIES THAT BIND. Joseph Califano used to be a senior staff aide in President Lyndon Johnson's administration; now he is a Washington lawyer, handling such business as Coca-Cola. Bryce Harlow directed Procter

& Gamble's Washington office before joining President Nixon's staff in 1969; now he is back at Procter & Gamble.[16]

The corporate presence in Washington sometimes *is* government, and the shifting of executives back and forth can leave the observer dizzy. Ralston Purina offers the classic example of sitting on both sides of the government desk. Mr. Hal Dean, who is the chief executive of Ralston Purina, served as chairman of the GMA council that sometimes met with Secretary of Agriculture Clifford Hardin. When Hardin was dismissed from his government position in 1971, he found a home as a vice-president and board member of Mr. Dean's corporation. In turn, Ralston Purina board member Earl Butz became the new Secretary of Agriculture.

This phenomenon is not unique to the Department of Agriculture. Michael Jacobson and Robert White reported in *The Progressive* that the Food and Drug Administration is also a haven for industry executives: "Twenty-two of the fifty-two top officials have worked for regulated industries or organizations that cater to those industries."[17] The House Intergovernmental Relations Subcommittee found in 1969 that of 49 high-ranking FDA officials who had recently resigned, 37 joined or served as consultants to firms that FDA regulates.

It seems at times that government is little more than a training base for the executives of regulated industries. Dr. Ogden Johnson resigned as director of FDA's Office of Nutrition in 1974 to become vice-president of Hershey Foods. Richard Lyng, who headed USDA's meat-inspection program, left in 1973 to become the chief lobbyist of the American Meat Institute, a trade association representing the largest meat firms. These are the more visible samples of a government-to-indus-

Rupe. 1971. National Farmers Organization. Reprinted with permission.

try turnover that occurs regularly at lower staff levels. There are plenty of FTC and FDA lawyers who will confide in private that they are working in these regulatory agencies only to gain experience and contacts that will make them more valuable to industry or to the Washington law firms that represent industry.

When food executives are not being invited to become government, they are being asked to consult with it. The hodge-podge of advisory committees that surrounds every division of every branch of every agency of government is replete with corporate representatives. There was an advisory committee at USDA, for example, to assure public involvement in the making of agricultural research policy. In 1972 and 1973, this 11-member committee had no consumer and no labor representation, and it had only token representation of family farmers. The "public" represented on it was Del Monte Corporation, the Nutrition Foundation, Crown Zellerbach Corporation, Curtice-Burns, Inc., Peavey Company Flour Mills, and other giants of the food industry.

In 1973, when the House Agriculture Committee was considering the farm bill, Representative George Brown moved to expand the size of this research advisory committee and to require that new members be chosen from a broader public than corporations. The thought of consumers, farmers and workers being involved in policy-making, even to this insignificant degree, did not appeal to the chairman of the committee, Representative W. R. Poage, who long had been a supporter of corporate policies in agriculture. He had a better idea: he moved to eliminate the advisory committee altogether. And that is what happened to the National Agricultural Research Advisory Committee.

On occasion, the food industry and the government

come together in curious joint ventures. In 1974, the USDA and HEW produced a booklet titled "Food Is More Than Just Something to Eat," designed as an educational piece to improve the diets of women of child-bearing age. But the government had a partner in preparing and distributing the booklet—Grocery Manufacturers of America. In fact, GMA was a full partner, having picked up half of the $200,000 price tag.[18] Why are food manufacturers allowed to participate when they have a clear proprietary stake in any publication advising consumers on nutrition? Simply because they have the money to chip in and because they always are close enough to government to assert their interests.

When the National Commission on Productivity undertook a study of the food industry, it turned out that the food industry was the primary studier. Of the 33 nongovernmental, nonacademic participants, half were from major food corporations and their industry associations.[19] The seven-member meat panel had one academic representative and six meat packers—Armour, Swift, Hygrade, Hormel, Wilson and Oscar Mayer. No cattlemen and no consumers.

This corporate participation in governmental affairs is standard practice, and it is their wealth that puts them there. They can afford the lobbyists, lawyers and consultants. Other groups do not have the same ease of access that such wealth affords, nor do they make such a deep impression on government policy. The corporate presence in Washington is pervasive and constant, and it has produced a virtual merger of the public and private sectors of the food economy.

Official Washington is a city of endless cocktail parties, where a few political notables, herds of lobbyists

and masses of congressional interns, State Department
secretaries, Capitol elevator operators and lesser lights
can be seen on practically any given evening. These are
crowded affairs, with people clustered in a series of
disorderly scrums——one around the hors d'oeuvres,
one around the bar and others around the political
notables that show up.

In February 1974, Wakefield Seafoods—a subsidiary
of Hunt-Wesson, which in turn is a subsidiary of
Norton Simon, Inc.—hosted such a party. It was a
cocktail reception, held in an imposing room of the
Senate Office Building, and it was attended by some
500 guests, including Agriculture Secretary Butz, White
House aide Peter Flanigan, presidential consumer advisor Virginia Knauer, Transportation Secretary Claude
Brinegar and such Senators as Percy, Scott, Buckley,
Humphrey, Weicker and Thurmond. Huge quantities of
delicious Alaskan king crabmeat were served and ap-
preciatively consumed ("Best food that's been seen in
the Senate for a hundred years," pronounced a 23-year-
old Senate elevator operator, who was eating his way
through law school at such occasions). In fact, the
affair was so fine, the political notables so glittering,
that it made the *Washington Post*'s society page the next
morning—the highest accolade for a Washington party.

The occasion, according to a 26-page press release
that was available and widely ignored that evening, was
a plea for special legislation that would protect such
fish processors as Wakefield, Del Monte and Heinz from
foreign fishermen. In particular, the firms were urging
that the government hold foreign fishing fleets out of
waters within 200 miles of our shores. Pointedly, the
guest of honor at the Wakefield reception was Senator
Warren Magnuson, who is chairman of the Senate

Commerce Committee, the one that considers such legislation.*

The Wakefield affair is instructive—there is both less and more than meets the eye at such parties. First, fewer than a dozen of the 500 people reaching for the hors d'oeuvres could have explained in any detail what the occasion was about. And, while Senator Magnuson undoubtedly was pleased to be honored, there is hardly a congressman around whose support can be had for a crab claw and a scotch. This was no pressure event, no hard sell by the food industry.

But on the other hand, there was more to it than a free crabfeed. The significance of the event lies in the easy affability of it all. The food giants have the money to put on such an affair, and they have the prestige and power to draw policy-makers to their party. Food firms also have amiable lobbyists in Washington who can attend the party and take the opportunity to chat briefly and informally with the chairman, the Secretary of Agriculture or the presidential advisor. Government is not simply a matter of putting a bill in the hopper and letting the legislative process run its course, as taught in the civics texts. It is a matter of personalities regularly relating to each other—not just what you know, but who you know.

If you had walked into the Wakefield party you would have recognized right away that the public and private sectors know each other on a first-name basis—if not like friends, certainly like business associates. This business-sponsored party, both gracious and purposeful, is typical of the corporation-government relationship: always keeping in close touch with each other.

---

* Later, in September of 1974, the Senate Commerce Committee favorably reported the 200-mile-limit legislation, and it awaits action by the full Senate.

On his way out of the party, clutching a napkin full of hors d'oeuvres that he said was for his driver, Secretary Butz assured Jeannette Smyth of the *Washington Post* that it was not the mounds of Alaskan crab that had drawn him to the Wakefield reception, it was the mixture of congressmen and food-industry executives who were there to eat it: "I got more work done here than I do in an afternoon," he said.[20]

CHAPTER X

Eat Your Heart Out

Clement Freud, an eminent gastronome and author from England, was in this country in 1973, touring and speaking. He appeared on a late-night television talk show, where he was asked his impression of American food—"uniformly clean" was the judgment.

That is a fair summation of where we are being taken by the monopolization and industrialization of the food economy, and it is a harsher judgment of us than of our food. Our meek acceptance of giantism, of technologies and of corporate systems has cost us more than eternally rising prices and deteriorating quality. We are paying with our individuality, our self-sufficiency, and our ability to exercise basic control over something as essential as dinner. We are trading economic power for illusory convenience, economic humanism for culinary security—all in the name of some ill-defined "progress." It is leaving us as bland as our food.

Food oligopolists at this very moment are industrializing the American food experience, totally eliminating the human touch. From harvesting machinery to wrapped vegetables, from boxed beef to automatic checkout counters, food comes virtually untouched, with the only active hands being yours, digging deeper into your pocket to pay for every bit of this depersonalization.

Agricultural economists are quick to dismiss any questioning of industrialization in the food economy. "You've already got it in the other sectors," snorted an economics professor at Iowa State University, "and it's just natural that you're going to get it in food." It is not natural at all, nor is it desirable. Food is one of the few real things left in our lives. It nourishes and pleases us in a way that automobiles and television sets cannot— it literally is part of us. To industrialize food, to make it conform to technologies and systems, is to industrialize ourselves and finally to surrender the quality of our lives to the mass-produced standard of big business. Food cannot be assembled like a telephone, and there is no reason it should be. If anything ought to be real in our lives, ought to be left to nature rather than being simulated by corporate technicians, it is food. Monopolistic conglomerates cannot make our telephones work; why should they be arrogant enough to think that they can handle dinner? More to the point, why should we be dumb enough to let them?

THE DEPERSONALIZATION OF DINNER. Food is life's basic, with values that are cultural, physiological and economic. From the family farm to the mom & pop store, from haggling with the butcher to serving a favored family recipe, food is a major factor in both our personal and community identities. That cultural value is being disregarded as dinner is converted to just another disposable product to be manufactured uniformly and sold impersonally. Make it cheap and turn it over; get 'em in and get 'em out, taking their money as they pass. That is an abrupt restructuring not only of the economic system, but of people's way of thinking about food and of their power over it. It reduces people to consumption units, and it has no nobler motive than economic greed.

There can be no doubt of the need for technologies and business systems, but they should be made to conform to human scale, to enhance our humanity rather than diminish it. As Barry Commoner wrote in *The Closing Circle,* "Ecological survival does not mean the abandonment of technology. Rather it requires that technology be derived from a scientific analysis that is appropriate to the natural world on which technology intrudes."[1] That is not, however, the relationship that is becoming predominant in the food economy, where technologies and systems are dictating the shape of things and forcing people to make the adjustment.

The food-delivery system is being taken beyond people. Every stage is being automated, for no better reasons than that it *can* be automated and that it means higher profits in the middle. Supermarkets displaced the independent butchers, and now they are eliminating their own meat cutters. Push that bell at the meat-counter in the near future and chances are there will be no answer. The reason is that the supermarkets, the major beef packers and the Department of Agriculture have joined in a concerted effort to shift to a system they call "boxed beef."[2]

Instead of meat cutters at the store, the beef is cut, boxed and frozen at centralized processing facilities in the Midwest and Southwest, then shipped to supermarkets. According to the National Association of Food Chains, roughly 80% of all "fresh" meat at supermarkets by 1977 will be boxed—meaning frozen and pre-packaged.

What is the rationale for this technological innovation? Simply to cut out labor and reduce cost. But there is no clear evidence that it is much cheaper, since the costs of vacuum-packaging and freezing cancel any labor savings. Instead of paying for people, consumers will be paying for technology, and they can expect less for their money. The freezing technique means that consumers pay meat prices for water, which evaporated naturally under the fresh-meat system but is frozen into the beef under the centralized method—the *Washington Post* found that a 20-ounce package of frozen beef patties weighed 18 ounces when defrosted.[3] Even if cost savings exist through boxed beef, there is no reason to believe that they will be passed on to consumers, and no government agency is willing to insure that consumers will share in the savings.

Nonetheless, industry and government officials are eager to implement "a completely centralized cutting and packaging system," and shoppers can expect to get it. It means having to take the uniform cuts of beef, frozen and packed in boxes, with no butcher behind the glass to grind or cut it to individual needs, and it means no one is there to hear complaints—those will have to be directed to the machinery in Des Moines.

About the only human touch that remains in today's cavernous supermarkets is at the checkout counter, but even that promises to be short-lived, for the industry is moving now to adopt "one of the most revolutionary technological advances of modern history," as one wide-eyed grocery executive put it.[4] It is the automated checkout. Instead of a person ringing up your groceries, it will be the Sperry-Univac Accuscan or the IBM 3660 Supermarket System.

These computers will not read out the prices to you, like the checker does, but instead will silently scan a "universal product code" that is printed on each food label. This code is a series of vertical bars that tells the computer what the product is, who made it and what it costs. Unfortunately, you have to be a computer to read it—the code tells the shopper nothing. That would not be significant except for the fact that industry also intends to eliminate the old practice of putting the price on individual products. To find what an item costs, shoppers will be asked to look to a price marked somewhere on the shelf or to go to a central place in the store. The president of Pathmark stores says that the missing price is no problem since shoppers know some prices from memory anyway. The only other option is to accept what the computer prints out—"People are going to be asked to trust a machine," admitted an official of the National Association of Food Chains, lamely adding, "They've learned to with banks."[5]

Already, major food manufacturers are coding their labels to conform to the computer checkouts, and stores throughout the country are beginning to convert to the automated systems. The conversion is expected to be virtually complete by 1980. This particular step to further depersonalize the grocery business will not come cheaply, costing about $150,000 per store, or an estimated $5 billion for the entire industry. Of course, that total sum will be added to your grocery bill. You will pay more, and in return you will have machines in the place of people.

Why? The bait to consumers is that the electronic "checkers" will be much faster than the human version, thus shaving a couple of minutes off the time that customers have to wait in line. It is doubtful that two or even three minutes makes up for the depersonalization that results, but it is academic anyway, since the supermarkets intend to use the speedier systems as an excuse to eliminate some of their checkout counters. Joseph Danzansky, whose Giant Food stores are changing now to the computerized system, says that the average number of checkout aisles in his chain will fall from eight to six.[6] They hope to be able to maintain current speed of checkout, not increase it.

So desperate is the Pathmark president to sell consumers on the new technology that he has cited the advantage of quieter stores, pointing to cash registers "which are now silent, except for a barely audible 'Click' or 'Beep.' "[7]

The main argument put forward is that automated checkouts will save on labor costs at the store, eliminating manual checking of grocery stocks (the computer keeps a running tab of supplies) and eliminating manual stamping of prices on packages. In fact, however, no one seems to know whether any cost savings will be achieved. Of course, the computer firms promise sizable savings, but are unwilling to guarantee them, and grocery executives estimate savings for the industry to be from $90 million to $370 million a year, which is so broad a range as to be meaningless. And again, even if there are any savings to the industry, it is difficult to believe that the supermarkets would ever pass it along to shoppers. Even the National Association of Food Chains, which supports adoption of the computerized systems, will say only that they are "very hopeful" that the new technology might eventually "result in cost reductions of such magnitude as to have a downward pressure on prices."

Finally, the food chains hold out the promise that their new equipment assures "fool-proof ringup," with total elimination of error at the checkout counter. Those who have ever wrestled with computer billing systems —which is everyone in the country who has a telephone or a credit card—can only shake their heads quietly at that assertion. And when the central computer breaks down from time to time, as computers have a way of doing, that store will just have to shut its doors until a technician from IBM's regional headquarters can be detailed to fix it.

But even if these automatic checkouts were able, as claimed, to eliminate all pricing errors, to cut checkout time in half and to weigh the produce to within 1/100 pound, they still would represent a false efficiency, a long step away from human satisfaction—which is why there is an economy in the first place. Usually, technology is introduced on the excuse that it somehow will make our life richer, more rewarding; but this "advancement" by the food industry cannot make that promise. If one thing is clear about grocery shoppers, it is that they want *more* personality in the system, not less.

Virginia Knauer, the President's in-house consumer, embraced the automatic checkouts in 1974: "I think computers have become a way of life," she said. "People are used to it." What she does not seem to comprehend is that they are used to computers because they have had no choice but to get used to them, and they will have to get used to these or go hungry. The adoption of computerized checkouts is an industrywide movement, occurring throughout and at once. In other words, the big stores have colluded, with the acquiescence of government, to do this.* [9] Safeway and Kroger

---

* There even was a "smoke-filled room" aspect to this collusion. The standard symbol used as the universal product code was selected by an industry committee made up of representatives from Del Monte, General Foods, Greenbelt Co-op Stores, H. J. Heinz, Procter & Gamble, Red Owl Stores, Safeway Stores and Winn-Dixie Stores, plus an attorney. These nine people met in a closed session on a March weekend in 1973 to

and A & P and Giant and all the rest are putting them in now, without asking shoppers whether they want them. And once the chains have invested $5 billion in them, the machines are there to stay.

Even when food firms have recognized that consumers would like to have some element of humanity in their economic dealings, they have dealt with that emotion by exploiting it, offering merchandising gimmicks in place of substance. In most areas of the country, for example, truck farmers have sought a market for their produce by opening their own roadside stands. In recent years, these farmers' markets have become quite popular, as consumers have sought some relief from the remoteness of supermarkets and shopping centers.

First National Stores (Finast, they call themselves) noticed the popularity of farmers' markets in Massachusetts. So they set up an imitation farmers' market by placing cases of fruits and vegetables on their parking lot, shading them with brightly colored beach umbrellas. The effort was not to respond to consumer needs, but to milk those needs, and maybe to drive the real farmers' markets off the roads—*Supermarket News* reported that Finast hoped their ersatz market "will give independent fruit and vegetable stands a run for their money."

Having eliminated the authentic mom & pop groceries, bakeries and butcher shops, food chains now offer blatant counterfeits. A & P, for example, opened "Butcher Shoppes" in some of its stores in 1974, at-

choose the code for the entire food industry. No public interest was represented, though the public interest is dramatically affected. The private session, according to *Supermarket News,* was held "amid secrecy worthy of Henry Kissinger," with various reports putting the meeting place on a boat in the Atlantic, on an airplane, in New York, in Washington or in Chicago.

tempting to cash in on the public feeling for nostalgia. These are cute places, staffed by a couple of meat-cutters who wear straw hats, colorful aprons and garters on their sleeves. A report in *Supermarket News* marveled at the novelty of these little shoppes, noting that they had "an 8-foot counter, over which the two meatcutters on duty and the customers can talk to each other."

Throughout the food economy, efficient and productive people are being displaced by the technologies of the oligopolists. It is more than an economic consideration—such things as the desire to eliminate labor costs. It is a pervasive attitude, shared by big business and government officials, that things would be much neater, would work more smoothly, if only there were no people to contend with. This attitude is coupled with a big-business fascination with technological gadgetry.* Together, they have produced massive technological displacement in the food industry.

First, farm workers were replaced by crop chemicals and harvesting machinery; then they were followed into the packing sheds and processing facilities by new technology and routed from those jobs. Then farm owners were displaced as this technological "imperative" continued to require capital rather than people. The Department of Agriculture points proudly to the decline in the farm population over the last thirty years, saying

* Maybe you have wondered who buys those intricate telephone systems that you sometimes see advertised—the phones that can dial numbers from memory, that can be hooked to an intercom so you can walk freely about the room and continue to hear and talk to your party, and so forth. Big business buys those. There is hardly a corporate officer in a major firm who would be content with a regular phone. A complex instrument on your desk has become a more prestigious corporate symbol than a key to the executive washroom.

that technology has "freed" those people to do other things.

People being displaced from farms today are good farmers. They do not want to be "freed," and it makes no economic sense to displace them. Only 5% of the population in the United States today lives on the farm. Shall that go to 1%? How low? Why are we pursuing a policy of taking productive people off the land?

What are these people "freed" to do? USDA never faces that one. "Nowadays no one is forced to milk cows or work 365 days a year," boasted the Undersecretary of Agriculture in 1974. "With opportunities open to them, more people are making other choices."[10] They have no choice but to make other choices, and what are those opportunities he speaks of? Jobs are being eliminated throughout the American economy, and people are finding nowhere to go.

Even if they are lucky enough to get a job in the city it offers little of the satisfaction and meaning that farming held, and chances are it is being eliminated too. Over the years, farm women have been "freed" to become checkout girls at supermarkets. Now they are being freed from that task by automatic checkout. "We do not intend to eliminate our checkout personnel," Joseph Danzansky protested. "They will still be needed there to bag the groceries."[11] That makes them assistants to a computer. And how long before there will be automatic baggers? One gets the uneasy feeling that they would replace customers if they could.

Seven blocks from the Capitol building in Washington, D.C., stands a vestige of this country's food past. It is a farmers' market—one of many that used to be the centers of food activity in Washington. This one still is in operation. Called the Eastern Market, it has two produce stands, a cheese stand, four pork-and-beef stands, two poultry stands, a bakery and a fish stand, all independently owned and family-operated. On weekends, about a dozen farmers from the area back their trucks up to the curb and display their produce, eggs and poultry for sale under the outdoor shed.

Directly across the street from Eastern Market is a Safeway, one of the chains that monopolize 72% of the grocery sales in the Washington area. Food at the Safeway is not cheaper, nor is it anywhere near the quality of that available across the street. The selection of meats, produce and dairy products is much more varied at the Market. It takes no more time to shop at the Market than it does at the Safeway, and it is a much more satisfying experience.

At the Market, you can buy butter by the inch if you want it; you can get fish that is caught fresh daily and fileted in front of you; you can pick through the bushel baskets of fresh greens to choose the ones that please you, fresh-killed chicken, with honest-to-goodness flavor, is always available, and it comes in enough ways to meet your individual needs—as fryers, roasters, stewers, capons, whole, in pieces and even gizzards and hearts; you can buy just one pork chop or just one-quarter pound of ground beef—they are not prepackaged.

The meat stands at the Eastern Market have no plans to sell frozen beef, boxed in Des Moines, nor do their butchers wear funny hats and cute butcher costumes. The Market is not installing computerized checkouts—in fact, the produce sellers and the farmers outside under the sheds still hand your change to you from their apron pockets.

The Eastern Market makes all kinds of sense. This country could choose to base its food economy on that type of marketing system and do much better than we do now with giantism and oligopoly. As it is, Eastern Market is the aberration. The Market has had to weather attempts to tear it down and finally may have to be designated a historic site to protect it from those who would replace it with a parking lot. Of course, its success and its very existence is an embarrassment to supermarkets in the Washington area. The place does a booming business, mainly because the people there sell food at competitive prices and treat customers as human beings. At the Thomas Calomiris produce stand in the summer of 1974, Mrs. Calomiris added two free peaches to the four I had picked out. "Take these," she said. "They don't look as nice as the ones you bought, but they will taste the best." Indeed they did.

THE MCDONALDIZATION OF AMERICA. We cannot remake dinner without remaking ourselves. Not only are hams becoming uniformly bland, but so is American taste. Not only are local beers disappearing, but so is local identity. Not only is the greasy spoon being sterilized and franchised, but so is the spirit of entrepreneurship. We are becoming what we eat.

As Calvin Trillin relates delightfully in his book, *American Fried*, wherever you travel in the country today, the food you eat is the same.[12] Ask a local booster of Austin, of Fresno, of Birmingham, or of Rochester where to get a good meal, and chances are you will be directed what Trillin calls the "Maison de la Casa House," probably revolving atop the city's tallest bank building. You will eat a prefrozen imitation of Continental cuisine, when you know perfectly well that somewhere in the vista below you there is the finest Mexican food, exquisite fried chicken, or an excellent German kitchen willing to serve you. Your taste buds atrophy and the local food spots go out of business, while the revolving fraud cites your presence as evidence of widespread consumer demand for prefrozen dinners.

While homogenized, uniform meals have not come as a result of our demand, we have accepted them, passively assured their domination of our food economy. We are a nation built on self-reliance, but we are letting ITT teach our children that breakfast is a fortified cake; we are letting General Foods convince us that Cool Whip topping is fresh, even though it is a nondairy product and requires chemicals to maintain its "freshness"; and we are letting Shakey's pizza parlors gloat that "others feed you fast, we feed you fun," without raising the point that none of them feed us well.

Driving down the interstate highways anywhere in the country on two to eight lanes of uninterrupted boredom, an occasional green sign looms at an exit, proclaiming in uniform lettering: FOOD—GAS. It's an appropriate combination. You may need both. There on one side of the exit road is the gasoline oligopoly, offering to tank up your car at a high price; on the other side is the fast-food oligopoly, offering to tank up your family at the same high price. It's dull, but you take it. Pay the price. Get back on the interstate. You make the rest of the trip puffed, but hardly satisfied. Your children think that the thing you ate is what a hamburger is all about. And the food chain rings up your money. It is self-reinforcing monopoly.

It is not just on the interstates. This oligopolistic force extends into our neighborhoods, homogenizing uniqueness and standardizing tastes. "McDonald's is right in your neighborhood," says the company's annual report. It is no idle boast, for the firm has some 3,000 stores located almost everywhere. This $1.5 billion giant has a greater impact than merely intruding into America's diverse neighborhoods with its neon uniformity and trash-strewn presence. Its unerring sameness alters our perception of food. Mimi Sheraton, writing in *New York* magazine, reported that the fish caught for McDonald's Filets O'Fish sandwiches is treated on factory ships to stay white and to be both odorless and tasteless.[13] It is then frozen and shipped to a central plant, where it is cut into shape, thawed, breaded, refrozen and shipped to golden arches throughout the world. "Tastes crisp, doesn't it?" asked a fish-processing official as Ms. Sheraton sampled the final product. "How could I be the one to tell him," she asked, " 'crisp' is not a taste?"

McDonald's even advertises a guarantee that its teenage personnel* will say "Thank you" when you buy from them. That is this company's idea of the human touch—uniformed waitresses repeating "thank you" with the same regularity and depth of feeling that you get from the green light at a highway toll booth. Forcing the McDonald's crew to be polite (or lose their ill-paid jobs) does not increase our sense of humanity, but it must certainly lessen theirs.

The McDonald's standard is conformity. Their buildings look the same, their food tastes the same, their people act the same. They even operate a training center in Illinois, called Hamburger University, to make sure that their management and hamburgers in Toledo *are* the same as those in Phoenix. It is that conformity that they are selling—wherever you are, you can be sure

---

* McDonald's hires part-time workers almost exclusively, mostly teenagers and students. This allows the company to pay the lowest possible wages, with few benefits. In fact, the U.S. minimum-wage law has certain exemptions that allow less than full protection for part-time, student employees. In Congress and in the Department of Labor, that exemption is known unofficially as the McDonald's Rule.

that a meal at McDonald's will be uniformly clean. There is not much chance of your getting food poisoning at these places, but neither will you get excited.

That is a silly trade-off, and we are silly to make it. Is the pioneering spark so dead in the American people that there is any real need to flee to the security of the golden arches? If we are unwilling to take the remote chance of getting food poisoning in order to assure variety and value in our dinner, then we are as weak as the taste we get.

Small entrepreneurs in tens of thousands of restaurants have lent character, quality and identity to their distinct towns and neighborhoods. Everyone knows some of these places, and all of us have our favorites. Jimmie's Cafe in Washington, D.C., Johnny's B-29 just outside Thackerville, Oklahoma, and The Smokehouse in Denison, Texas, are three great places that always will linger in my mind and be a part of me. There is no food poisoning in these places, just good eats and good people.

Now, however, these places and our communities are being nationalized—not by government, but by corporate power. "Fast-food chains are replacing the vanished neighborhood bar, ice-cream parlor and restaurant," wrote Joseph Morgenstern in *Newsweek*. "They're replacing the vanished neighborhood."[14] With their cleaply manufactured edibles, their far-reaching advertising budgets and their deep-pocket financing capability, these chains can move anywhere, cut their prices and drive local enterprise out of business. It is happening in localities across the United States, and it steadily is transforming regional uniqueness into national uniformity. Our neighborhoods are not vanishing, they are being vanquished.

We have been lucky. Family farmers, independent

food producers, mom & pop stores and neighborhood restaurants have worked long hours every day and made economic sacrifices to keep the places going. But oligopoly power is putting unbearable pressure on these independent enterprises, and it is harder now than ever before for the family operation to make a go of it. The family's kids show little inclination to take on the burden of fighting these oligopolies.

There used to be a place on Capitol Hill called Spicer's, located in the basement of a town house near the Senate Office Building. It made the best fried chicken in Washington, never cooking it in advance or putting it under lights to stay warm. The chicken came crisp and delicious right out of the fryer, so hot you had to wait several minutes for it to cool on your

---

THE ALL-AMERICAN MENU—AN ENDANGERED SPECIES

Fisherman's Platter	$2.25
Bar B Q Chicken	2.25
Beef Stew	1.95
Veal Cutlet, two veg.	2.15
Hamburger Steak, two veg., gravy & onion	1.95
Open Face Roast Beef Sandwich	2.35
Meat Loaf, two veg.	1.95
Pork Chops, two veg.	2.55
Ranchburger Platter	1.49
Spaghetti & Meatballs	1.65
Franks & Beans	1.50
Cold Platter	2.25
Hot Turkey	2.05
Stuffed Cabbage	2.25

Soup	.45	Sodas & Ice Tea	
Onion Rings	.50	Large	.25
French Fries	.30	Small	.15

---

plate. They served lima beans, shelled fresh every morning. With draft beer and a country-music juke box, the place was an oasis to Southerners working at the Capitol—sometimes a Southern Senator's entire staff could be found at Spicer's.

Spicer's closed in 1969 when the family retired and no younger person was there to keep the doors open. It was an irreplaceable loss. You could, however, go to Boone's Lunch Counter at Eastern Market and get fried chicken that was very good, if not up to the top quality of Spicer's. But Boone's shut down in 1974 when that family retired. The only fried-chicken place still in the neighborhood is a Col. Sanders franchise. It's hardly the same.

This scene is being repeated over and over again in thousands of neighborhoods as the old folks are retiring or dying. We have assumed that they always were going to be there. These small entrepreneurs, who have given us an alternative to giantism and monopoly, are about to disappear—abruptly. Only corporations are there to pick up the pieces, and to consolidate them. McDonald's opened 445 new outlets in 1973, and had another 120 under construction at year's end.[15] It is the McDonaldization of America.

LEAVE IT TO THEM. Food executives, both in business and in government, have encouraged people to leave dinner to them. We have gone along with that to the point that we now are dependent on oligopolists. Few Americans know anything about food anymore—they do not know how to produce it, how to process it, and increasingly they do not even know how to prepare it.

Two generations ago we were a country of farmers, and even people in cities often had a garden and maybe a cow and some chickens. Today, we wouldn't know our way around a farm, and we are losing our way around the kitchen. Corporations tell us in their advertising that we should not try to mess with fried chicken, rather we had best stick to the safer, surer method of Shake 'n Bake. And how can a simple homemaker hope to get through the week without relying on all eight varieties of Hamburger Helper? Dessert, of course, simply cannot be considered without a supply of Fruit Helper on hand.

It's as though no one this side of Julia Child or Craig Claiborne should dare attempt any meal that does not come in a convenience package, premeasured, prespiced and preferably precooked. Trust us, implore the corporations, and we'll see you through a lifetime of culinary convenience. It won't be much good or good for you, but it will involve no work, no risk, no sweat. "That's where we're at," wrote Tom Donnelly in the *Washington Post.* "Any tattered old copy of the *Fannie Farmer Boston Cooking School Cookbook* will tell you where we've been."[16]

Having left dinner to them, they have given us giantism and monopoly power. That has not even produced "efficiency," which is the stated goal of the food experts. But if giantism and monopoly could produce efficiency, in the narrow sense that these technicians use it, why should that be the standard for dinner? How many of us want "efficient" carved on our tombstones as a summation of our existence? It has to be the lowest rung on the ladder of human values, yet it has become practically the sole measure of economic performance, allowed literally to dictate the nature and substance of the food system. Is it efficient to have a food economy that produces a steady rise only in prices and corporate profits, while employment, competition, taste, choice and nutritional value steadily decline?

Our faith in experts has hardly been well rewarded. Speaking of one group of experts in 1972, John Kenneth Galbraith said, "If all agricultural economists were laid end to end, it would be a good thing." His exact meaning may be obscure, but his tone of distrust and irreverence is healthy. Economics is not a science, no matter how hard economists try to convince us otherwise, and the fact that some people have degrees naming them economists need not mean that they are experts on the economy—at least not in the sense that they know what to do, or even know what is going on. They are to the economy what weathermen are to the weather. It is time to stop saluting these people.

If we will not assert ourselves over dinner, then when will we? It is argued that the economic changes in the food industry are nothing to worry about, since the same change has already taken place in most other areas of our economy. Precisely. If our family cars are being recalled, if our gasoline supplies are being manipulated, if our headache remedies are being deceptively advertised, if our home appliances are being shoddily made, if our computerized charge accounts are being jumbled—why should we now turn dinner over to that same way of doing business?

WHAT DO YOU WANT FOR DINNER? About a hundred press releases a week are issued from the Department of Agriculture, heralding everything from major policy positions to 4-H Club citations. Late in the summer of 1973, one of these releases caught the attention of the Co-Directors of the Agribusiness Accountability Project, Susan DeMarco and Susan Sechler. It announced that Secretary Butz would appear for one hour at a

HERMAN FENSTERHABEN, ECONOMIST, BETHESDA, MARYLAND: I would not in principle oppose the idea of slowing down the staples market by passing an across-the-board bread tax. I do not agree, however, with those in the Administration who believe we could encourage a stricter adherence to the American work ethic by imposing an additional surcharge on day-old bread. My own suggestion to the Administration was that pump-priming be based on a softened private sector, with productivity reduced toward the goal of having parity reflected in the adjusted G.N.P., on the basis of real dollars or 1939 dollars, whichever came first, but that seemed too neo-Keynesian for the post-Keynesians, not to mention the reverse.

USDA-sponsored "Harvest Happening" at Tysons Corner Mall, a shopping center in the suburbs of Washington, D.C.

The "Happening" was to be one of those staged press events, giving Butz a forum to tell a few startled shoppers what a great buy food is. This appearance among Tuesday-afternoon shoppers also would be cited later as evidence of the Department's concern for and contact with American consumers. It was to be a simple hour— a brief address by the Secretary, ten minutes of questioning from an audience of curious onlookers, a picture-taking session with Butz milking a cow named Raquel, then coffee for everybody.

DeMarco and Sechler, however, saw to it that the "Harvest Happening" would have more substance than the Secretary intended. With food prices out of control and with consumer organizations unable to get so much as a meeting with USDA's top brass in the past, it was time for consumers finally to have their hour with Earl Butz.

Eight local and national consumer groups were organized by the Agribusiness Project to attend the Tysons Corner event. With the public and the press looking on, the Secretary's field trip to the suburbs was turned into a brief but serious questioning period on his food policies. There were more hard questions than answers, as he ducked, waffled and bluffed his way through any question more specific than "Why does food cost so much?" Finally, the consumer advocates asked Butz to agree to meet with them in a private discussion of their economic concerns, just as he frequently meets with corporate interests. "Well, you get in touch with us," he dodged. "We'll have you meet with someone." The consumer representatives did not let him get away with it this time, continuing to ask for their meeting until he finally had to relent. Consumer groups would get their meeting. Grimfaced, he abruptly terminated the questioning and stalked off to milk Raquel.

The significance of the "Harvest Happening," is not in what it taught USDA, though Secretary Butz has not been back to Tysons Corner, but in what it taught consumer groups. First, the fight for dinner finally has to come down to the fundamental level of economic structure. Underlying the issues of food prices, nutrition, taste and choice is the economic and political power that is built on the oligopolistic structure of the food industry. At Tysons Corner, for the first time, consumer representatives were coming to grips with the structural issues of food economics.

Second, the mystique of economic expertise, which makes most people hesitant to question food policies and programs, was pierced. At Tysons Corner, the emperor was wearing no clothes, and consumers found that they could tell him that. It is possible to fight back against government officials, corporate executives and economists.

If bigger is not better, neither is it inevitable. The giantism of today's food economy is not the result of some mystical dialectic marching through history. Rather it is an economic system devised and implemented by and for private interests. Other systems could be devised and implemented—systems that respond to a broader public interest. "There is nothing inexorable about the trend toward large-scale agriculture," admitted Dr. Don Paarlberg, USDA's top economist. "With a representative government, the people can have any kind of agriculture they want."[17]

The last point was glibly tossed out, but it is not without a solid kernel of truth. People *can* make a difference if they are willing to take on the fight. Consumers, family farmers, workers and independent business people have a common stake in the structure of the food economy, and together they can amass enough political and economic strength to be the decisive force in shaping that economy. Our food future is not an economic question—it is a political question.

People must intrude into the political process that determines food policy. That means national legislation and elections, but it also means many small efforts that are narrowly focused. "Politics" is meant here in the generic sense of policy decisions that have public impact. Congressional passage of legislation creating the Consumer Protection Agency is one of those decisions, but so is an individual determination that the family will go no more to McDonald's.

It has not made the national news, but there are people all over the country who are fighting against various aspects of corporate food power and achieving significant successes:

• The Crystal City Restaurant was a neighborhood institution in the DuPont Circle area of Washington, D.C., for more than 30 years. In 1973, the restaurant burned, and the Chaconas family chose to retire rather than rebuild. The neighbors were stunned shortly thereafter to learn that Gino's, the fast-food chain, was negotiating a long-term lease on the property. The lower- and middle-income people who live in the DuPont Circle area feel a strong neighborhood identity, and the area is architecturally and socially distinctive. The coming of Gino's was an unwanted and unwarranted intrusion into this community.

The residents took action, forming "The Ad-Hoc Committee to Prevent Ginocide." There were Ginocide petitions, pickets, block parties and even T-shirts as the residents rallied to prevent what one termed "burger blight." In their best corporate manner, Gino's detailed an executive to becalm the agitated residents. There was no need to fear Gino's, he soothed; "We understand your market area." "That's 'neighborhood,'" said the residents, with their worst suspicions confirmed.

The political effort of the community forced the corporation to drop its plans. Shortly afterward, a French family opened a restaurant at the Crystal City site, and the individuality of the neighborhood has been assured.

• The indomitable spirit of Jim Witvoet has yet to win out over Chicago officials, but neither has the bureaucratic spirit of the officials prevailed. Witvoet is a farmer who has been fighting city hall for ten years over the right to sell his produce directly to consumers, without a middleman. On Saturday mornings, he backs his truck up to the curb of West Randolph Street in the same area where his father and grandfather used to sell. The Randolph Street farmers' market used to be located there until the city banned it ten years ago as a traffic obstruction. The neighbors flock to buy from Witvoet.

"We're in sympathy with his cause," said a lawyer for the city government, "but he has to tune himself with progress." The "progress" that the lawyer is upholding requires consumers to pay 96¢ for a dozen ears of corn at the supermarket, while Witvoet sells his home-grown ears at 60¢ a dozen. He has amassed scores of tickets (unpaid), spent time in jail (unremorsefully), and even been acquitted in a jury trial (understandably).

• While Chicago is trying to push the last farmer off its streets, other cities are inviting farmers to town. From Bangor, Maine, to Seattle, Washington, people are creating and supporting farmers' markets as one of the most effective means of by-passing food oligopolies. More than 100 cities are revitalizing old markets or establishing new ones, and both farmers and consumers are flocking to the places.[18]

• Tired of high-priced, low-quality bread, people of Minneapolis formed a cooperative bakery. The bakery is just one part of a community-owned and cooperatively run enterprise that also includes several food stores and a restaurant. The whole operation began five years ago with a $50 loan. By eliminating profit, by getting no-interest loans directly from residents of the community, by hiring no management and by employing low-paid volunteer workers, they are able to provide high food value for little money. "We started out with nothing but our wits and a spirit of cooperation," said a co-op member, "and built from them a true alternative to bad food and exploitative jobs. If we can do it, anybody can."

• Jean Farmer lives in Bloomington, Indiana, where she organized a countrywide campaign to get junk foods out of the schools. They were being sold by vending machines in the hallways, and kids were allowed to buy either the hot lunches from the school or soda and snacks from the machines. After a two-year effort, she won. The school board voted in 1974 to offer only food that "makes a significant contribution to the students' nutritional needs."

• Ms. Farmer has not been alone in her concern with junk foods in the schools. When a science teacher in New Haven, Connecticut, became principal of an elementary school there, one of his first actions was to ban the sale of junk foods in the school and to send a note home encouraging parents to pack nutritional items in their children's lunches. You still can buy candies and cakes from vending machines at Cornell University, but you also can buy apples from them. About 50 bushels a week are sold from just one machine in a classroom building.

The structure of the food economy is too important an issue to be left to corporate interests and government economists. A broader public must get involved in decisions that affect them so directly and significantly. It might be that the full American public would choose giantism, but that decision ought to be made deliberately and thoughtfully by them, rather than waking up too late to a *fait accompli* by the food giants.

If the American people were to opt for a more human scale of food economics, there are tools at hand to help them get it. A place to start would be the family farm. There is much greater productivity from 1,000 family farmers tilling 600 acres each than there is from 10 corporate-controlled farmers tilling 60,000 acres each. And there is no question that the many are more competitive than the handful. If competitiveness and high productivity produce the best food and the most reasonable prices, then it makes sense to focus our agricultural-support systems on the smaller units most able to deliver these qualities.

Our support systems, now directed toward marketing corporations, could be shifted to family farms. Land-grant colleges, for example, should attend to the technological needs of smaller-scale farmers, as the *Des Moines Register* urged in a 1973 editorial: "The agricultural colleges could do more to increase total farm output in this country by concentrating on these [smaller-scale farmers] in research and extension work than by continuing to devote most of their efforts to the big farmers."[19] More and cheaper credit could be made available to family farmers, with special low-interest loans to help young people amass the capital needed to enter farming. Farm organizations themselves could begin to act as bargaining agents between their membership and the farm-supply corporations, negotiating for tractors and other equipment designed to meet the scale of operation and capitalization of independent family farmers. The Federal Trade Commission ought to get enough resources and public pressure to take long-overdue action against farm-supply oligopolies, restoring some measure of effective price competition in those industries.

There is a great deal that can be done to free the market-place, allowing the family farmer's productivity and competitiveness to reach consumers. At the very least, the existing antitrust laws could be dusted off and put into action on an industrywide basis. Special attention must be given to the anticompetitive effect of vertical integration into farming, and we should pass such legislation as the proposed Family Farm Act, which would prohibit corporate control of farming. We could require food middlemen to bargain collectively with farmers, thus restoring some balance to the power relationship that is forcing farmers to merge into corporate systems or go out of business.

Regional marketing of farm produce could be encouraged, lowering transportation costs and giving farmers access to greater marketing options. The procurement power of the federal government, now spent primarily on the products of oligopolistic middlemen, could be used to purchase directly from farmers and farmer cooperatives.

These are just a few of the elements of a program that would help us restore the family farm to a position of national resource. There is nothing radical or even new about them. They require no major wrenching of the existing economic order. If we want to have family farms, even small family farms, we can have them. It is not that we lack solutions, but that we have lacked the will.

There is a point at which people must say "No more." Big-business technologies and systems will push you around to fit their needs until you finally refuse to be pushed. That refusal can be intense, such as Jean Farmer's stand in Bloomington or Jim Witvoet's stand in Chicago. Or it simply can be a low-keyed refusal to sit still for wrapped fresh vegetables at your supermarket, or a series of pointed questions about food power directed to candidates for public office.

You do not have to make a nuisance of yourself (though we need more "nuisances" willing to penetrate the pretensions of corporate and government officials). You do not even have to be a "better" citizen (though we need many more people willing to stand publicly and fight food oligopolies). But at the very least, you have to be a human being, willing to ask "Why?" whenever big business and government demand that you adjust to their version of progress, and willing to say "No!" if the answer does not satisfy you.

For years, middle-class people have heard about hunger and poverty in this country but have never felt any kinship with the plight of the poor. Middle- and upper-income people have stood in supermarket lines with low-income people who have paid at the register with stamps rather than cash. But that has been them, not us.

Finally we are learning that it *is* us. We're just relatively better off, a notch or so higher. When beef prices go high at the supermarket, we shift from steak to hamburger, while the poor shift from hamburger to beans. But all of us are shifting, while food corporations are profiting and expanding their market control. Oligopolistic food power is not something that affects only a few of us. It is not just a matter of 1,000 farmers a week going out of business, nor just a matter of Cesar Chavez making a courageous fight with farm workers. It is our fight too, our dinner. You have no more power over the price of Del Monte string beans than a farm worker has over the wage he will get for picking those string beans.

If we are going to make a difference in any aspect of our lives, perhaps the place to start is here, with corporate food power. Unlike automobiles and telephones, the monopolization of dinner is not yet complete. There remains time to fight back. If we choose it, we *can* have family farms, independent processors, mom & pop stores, family restaurants, nutrition, good taste and fair food prices.

Appendices

A. Supermarkets
B. Profits & Concentration
C. Profits & Advertising
D. Corporate Contract with Farmer

APPENDIX A

Financial Information on the Top Twenty Chain-Store Supermarkets, 1973

Supermarket Chain	1973 Sales (in millions)	% of All Grocery Sales	% of All Chain Supermarket Sales	Net 1973 Profit (After Taxes)	1973 Return on Shareholder Equity
1. Safeway Stores	$ 6,773.7	—	—	$86,271,000	13.2
2. A&P	6,747.7	—	—	12,227,000	2.0
3. Kroger	4,204.7	—	—	29,916,000	7.6
4. Acme (American Stores)	2,320.3	—	—	18,063,000	9.0
Top 4 Total	$20,046.4	20.4	36.3		
5. Lucky	2,290.5	—	—	32,344,000	18.9
6. Jewel	2,219.6	—	—	36,336,000	13.8
7. Winn-Dixie	2,109.7	—	—	42,720,000	19.2
8. Food Fair	2,092.1	—	—	2,131,000	1.6

9. Grand Union	1,494.0	—	—	2,309,000	—	1.5
10. Supermarkets General	1,333.8	—	—	7,739,000	—	10.9
Top 10 Total	$31,586.1	32.1	57.3			
11. National Tea	1,252.6	—	—	(18,342,000)	—	—
12. Stop & Shop	1,083.0	—	—	8,860,000	—	12.2
13. Allied	1,035.9	—	—	4,281,000	—	9.9
14. Fisher Foods	868.8	—	—	9,435,000	—	16.8
15. First National	859.6	—	—	(14,858,000)	—	—
16. Albertson's	852.5	—	—	9,138,000	—	17.7
17. Colonial	827.2	—	—	11,114,000	—	13.7
18. Giant*	669.1	—	—	7,438,000	—	12.3
19. Publix**	650.0	—	—	not available	—	na
20. Arden-Mayfair	642.1	—	—	(17,970,000)	—	—
Top 20 Total	$40,326.9	40.9	73.1			

* Giant figures from *Fortune*. "The 50 Largest Retailing Companies." July 1974. p. 120.

** Publix figures for 1973 not available. These are 1972 sales.

Sources: *Supermarket News*. "Public Chains Report Net Up 40% in '73 Recovery." July 1, 1974, p. 1.

APPENDIX B

Average Net Profits after Taxes for 85 Food Corporations, Grouped by the Degree of Their Market Concentration

Group	Concentration Range (4-firm)	Number of Firms	Net Profits	
			Simple Average	Weighted Average[1]
I	Below 40%	21	7.5%	6.2%
II	40–49%	32	9.5	9.2
III	50–59%	15	13.2	12.9
IV	60% and above	17	14.2	15.1

[1] Weighted by company sales.

Source: Federal Trade Commission. "The Structure of Food Manufacturing." Technical Study No. 8. National Commission on Food Marketing. June 1966. Table 5. Page 204.

APPENDIX C

Profit Rates of Food Manufacturing Firms Associated with Levels of Industry Concentration and Advertising-to-Sales Ratios

Advertising-to-sales ratio (Percent)	Associated net firm profit rates as a percent of stockholders' equity[2]				
	1.0	2.0	3.0	4.0	5.0
Four-firm concentration:[1]					
40%	6.3	7.4	8.5	9.6	10.7
45	8.0	9.1	10.2	11.3	12.4
50	9.3	10.4	11.5	12.6	13.7
55	10.3	11.4	12.5	13.6	14.7
60	11.0	12.1	13.2	14.3	15.4
65	11.4	12.5	13.6	14.7	15.8
70	11.5	12.6	13.7	14.8	15.9

[1] The average concentration ratio (weighted by the company's value of shipments) of the product classes the company operated in 1950.

[2] Other variables influencing company profitability were held constant at their respective means. These variables were the firm's relative market share, growth in industry demand, firm diversifica-

tlon, and absolute firm size. Profit rates are averages for the years 1949–52.

Source: Bureau of Economics, Federal Trade Commission. "Economic Report on the Influence of Market Structure on the Profit Performance of Food Manufacturing Companies." September 1969, p. 7.

APPENDIX D
Sample Contract Between Chicken Processors & Producers

MARYLAND
BROILER GROWERS AGREEMENT

THIS AGREEMENT, made this _____ day of _____, 19___, between _____, a Maryland Corporation of _____, Maryland, hereinafter referred to as _____ and _____ of _____, hereinafter referred to as GROWER.

In consideration of the mutual covenants herein contained, the parties agree as follows:

It is the intent and purpose of the parties hereto that this Agreement shall provide the terms and conditions upon which GROWER, acting as an Independent Contractor and not as a partner, agent, or employee of _____ shall house, feed and care for the broiler chicks for _____.

I. _____ agrees:

　　A. To furnish approximately _____ broiler chicks to the GROWER to be raised under this contract.

　　B. To furnish to the GROWER all supplies such as feed, fuel, medications, vaccines, chicks, litter, sanitation and insurance necessary for the production of broilers.

　　C. To determine when the flock is to be moved and notify the GROWER of the proposed movement date.

　　D. To maintain adequate records of all supplies such as feed, fuel, medication, vaccines, chicks, litter, sanitation and insurance and to provide GROWER with an accounting of them at settlement.

II. GROWER agrees:

　　A. To provide Housing and Equipment as listed on Schedule A attached and to provide utilities, and labor to care for and properly raise the chicks under this Agreement.

B. To notify _____ if there is any disease, parasitism, or noticeable change in the health of the flock.

C. To keep all records necessary for the proper care of the flock as directed by _____

D. To be present or represented when chicks are delivered and during the catching and movement of each flock and to be responsible for the raising or moving of equipment ahead of the catching crew to insure the proper care of his equipment and for the reduction of bruises and fecal contamination.

E. To pay _____ for any birds from the flock used by the GROWER with the authorization of _____.

III. It is further agreed by _____ and GROWER that:

A. _____ shall have the right for itself, its agents, and employees to enter upon, over and into the lands and premises of the GROWER where the said flock is or shall be located, pursuant to the provisions of this Agreement, at such time as _____ may deem necessary to inspect the flock. If, in the judgment of _____ the GROWER is not satisfactorily performing his obligation under this Agreement with reference to the maintenance, treatment, feeding and care of the flock at anytime, _____ shall have the right to charge the GROWER with any necessary expenditures to accomplish such purpose.

B. It is understood and agreed that all supplies such as feed, chicks, medications, etc. furnished by _____ are, and shall remain the sole and exclusive property of _____

C. The GROWER accepts full liability for the payment of any and all applicable Federal and State taxes and for all applicable taxes for Unemployment Compensation, Old Age Benefits or Workmens Compensation Insurance now or hereafter imposed by any governmental agency, as to himself and persons engaged in the performance of this Agreement. Said taxes shall be paid directly by the GROWER and shall not be chargeable to _____.

D. _____ shall not be held responsible for damages to the GROWER caused by delay or failure to perform hereunder when such delay or failure is due to fire, strikes, acts of God, legal acts of public authorities or delays or defaults due to labor, feed or fuel shortages by reason of fire, which cannot be forecasted or protected against.

E. This Agreement may be cancelled by either party hereto giving written notice thereof before said flock covered by this agreement reaches 7 weeks of age. Such cancellation to become effective when flock is moved.

IV. It is further agreed by _____ and GROWER that:

A. _____ will pay to the GROWER as full compensation for growing services performed by the GROWER for _____ an amount based on:

    1. The "Prime Cost" of the flock (The prime cost is determined by dividing the farm weight of poultry moved into the total invoiced retail cost of all supplies such as feed, medications, fuel, chicks, vaccination, insurance, litter and sanitation.)

    2. The 20 Flock "Average Prime Cost". (The average prime cost is the total invoiced retail cost of all supplies as defined in paragraph 1 above, divided by the total farm weight for the 20 flocks. The 20 flocks will include the flock being settled in addition to the preceding 19 flocks settled.)

Any flock with a prime cost of 1.0¢ or more over the "average prime cost" will be excluded in computing the average prime cost.

    3. The "Selling Price" is determined by using the USDA Poultry Report published on Monday at Newark, N.J. for the week in which final movement of the flock occurs. The average of the New York US Grade A and Plant Grade weighted average price will establish the "selling price."

    4. The "Processed Meat Cost" is calculated by taking the "Average Prime Cost" for the 20 flocks, divide by a standard yield of 73% and add 7.25¢ standard processing cost per dressed pound.

    5. The "Processed Meat Cost/Selling Price Differential" as outlined on Schedule B attached represents the "Base Contract Payment" per net pound.

    6. The "Net Pounds" are determined by taking the farm weights of poultry moved, at processors scales,

less USDA weights condemned (after converting to live weights using the formula below).

(*a*) Divide total head condemned into carcass weight. (This gives the average dressed weight of each bird condemned.)

(*b*) Multiply the average dressed weight per bird times 1.15. This will give you the average live weight per bird condemned.

(*c*) Multiply the average live weight of birds condemned by the number of head condemned for the following causes: Tuberculosis, Leukosis, Tumors, Sept. & Toxemia, Synovitis, Air Sac. The total of these will equal the condemnation deduction on your flock settlement.

The plant caused condemned for bruises, cadavers, contamination, noeviscera and the parts condemned are not included in the condemnation deduction.

Example.—20 Flock "Averaging Prime Cost" 14.50¢ per live pound, ÷ 73% Standard Yield, + 7.25¢ standard processing cost per dressed pound = 27.11 "Processed Meat Cost" per dressed pound.

"Selling Price."—Prices reported by USDA for trucklot sales delivered to New York.

	Cents
U.S. Grade A—weighted average price	29.50
Plant Grade—weighted average price	28.50
Average	29.00

29.00¢ less Processed Meat Cost 27.11 = +1.89¢ per pound "processed meat cost/selling price differential." See Schedule B for "Base Contract Payment Per Net Pound" (2.315¢).

7. To the "Base Contract Payment" for each grower with a "prime cost" less than the "average prime cost" will be added the difference between the prime cost and average prime cost.

8. From the "Base Contract Payment" for each grower with a "prime cost" greater than the "average prime cost" will be deducted the difference between the prime cost and average prime cost.

Under no circumstances will less than $55.00 per 1,000 chicks started be paid to the grower with the following exception:

——————— will compensate the GROWER by an amount equal to $6.00/1,000 per week in the event of a loss due to acts of God (including but not limited to fire, windstorm, flood, and hail); however, in the event more than 2% of a flock dies as a result of the lack of oxygen and/or heat exhaustion when outside temperature is 95 degrees or less (as determined by either the official weather recording stations of the Federal Agency at Salisbury airport or at Wallops Island, whichever is nearer), the payment will be based on salable pounds of live poultry, moved from the farm.

9. The payment to the GROWER will be made within fifteen days of the day of the final movement of the flock from the farm. Any national or state holiday occurring in this time period may extend it accordingly.

IN WITNESS WHEREOF, the parties hereto have executed this agreement the day and year first above written.

———————————————— ————————————————

(Grower)

———————————————— ————————————————

(Witness)   (Witness)

SCHEDULE "A"

General housing and equipment specifications

Grower must meet the following requirements:

(*a*) 8/10 square foot per bird floor space.

(*b*) Round tube feeders or auger-pan feeders, minimum 18 pans per thousand chicks.

(*c*) 1 gallon water jug per hundred chicks for first 10 days.

(*d*) 32 feet of water space per thousand chicks.

(*e*) Round wire pens around each stove.

(*f*) 750 chicks per stove.

(*g*) Pen size of 2,000 chicks or less.

(*h*) Winterize house as prescribed by serviceman.

(*i*) Maintain dirt at proper level.

(*j*) Restrict other fowl from the premises.

(*k*) Provide a proper disposal unit, incinerator or pits.

(*l*) Provide properly maintained roads from county or state road to and around broiler houses. To pay tow charges incurred by Owner due to improperly maintained roads.

(*m*) Furnish one 24″ pedestal fan per thousand birds to equivalent fan capacity to maintain proper broiler comfort in summer.

(*n*) Exclude any wild birds from broiler house.

(*o*) Adequate emergency power to maintain favorable conditions for broilers during outage.

Schedule B

Processed meat cost/selling price differential:			Base contract payment per net pounds
+$2.76	$3.00	....	$2.50
+2.51	2.75	....	2.450
+2.26	2.50	....	2.405
+2.01	2.25	....	2.360
+1.76	2.00	....	2.315
+1.51	1.75	....	2.270
+1.26	1.50	....	2.225
+1.01	1.25	....	2.180
+ .76	1.00	....	2.135
+ .51	.75	....	2.090
+ .26	.50	....	2.045
+ .01	.25	....	2.00
0		....	2.00
− .01	.25	....	2.00
− .26	.50	....	1.955
− .51	.75	....	1.910
− .76	1.00	....	1.865
−1.01	1.25	....	1.820
−1.26	1.50	....	1.775
−1.51	1.75	....	1.730
−1.76	2.00	....	1.685
−2.01	2.25	....	1.640
−2.26	2.50	....	1.595
−2.51	2.75	....	1.550
−2.76	3.00	....	1.50

Source: U.S. House of Representatives. Hearings before the Antitrust Subcommittee of the Committee on the Judiciary. "Family Farm Act." Sample contract supplied by USDA at the request of Rep. James Abourezk. March 22 and 23, 1972. Serial No. 28. Pages 36–39.

Sources

There are precious few sources of information on the issue of monopoly power in the food economy. There are two primary reasons for this dearth—first, public agencies and the press have done a poor job of monitoring the food economy, and, second, food corporations are notoriously tight-fisted about releasing even the most innocuous information.

Thousands of research publications are churned out by the U.S. Department of Agriculture and by colleges of agriculture each year, but only an unmeasurable fraction of them relate even slightly to the structure of the food system. In 1966, the National Commission on Food Marketing recommended that Congress require an annual report from the FTC on the competitive structure of the food economy, but Congress has yet to take such an obviously necessary step. Not only have we failed to take action against food monopolies, but we have failed even to find out who they are and what they are doing to us.

This book pulls together bits and pieces of information that are scattered through government documents, industry publications, academic studies and the popular press. Heaviest reliance has been placed on the publications of USDA's Economic Research Service, the Federal Trade

Commission, the National Commission on Food Marketing's technical studies, and such industry periodicals as *Feedstuffs, Business Week, Supermarket News* and *The Wall Street Journal*. In addition, the book draws heavily from the files of the Agribusiness Accountability Project and on interviews with dozens of people throughout the country who are involved in food and economic issues.

Listed below is a partial bibliography and a resource guide for those who want additional information on issues discussed in this book.

Books, Reports, and Hearings*

1. John M. Blair. *Economic Concentration: Structure, Behavior & Public Policy*. New York: Harcourt Brace Jovanovich, Inc. 1972. 742 pages.

2. Susan DeMarco, Susan Sechler. AAP *Report on the World Food Situation*. Washington: Agribusiness Accountability Project. March 1975.

3. Federal Trade Commission. *Economic Papers*, 1966–1969. Washington: Government Printing Office (GPO). 1970. 313 pages.

4. Federal Trade Commission. *Economic Report on the Baking Industry*. Washington: G.P.O. November 1967. 120 pages.

5. Federal Trade Commission. *Economic Report on Discount Food Pricing in Washington, D.C.* Russell C. Parker. Washington: GPO. March 1971. 18 pages.

* Mailing Addresses for Ordering Government Publications:

(1) Superintendent of Documents
U.S. Government Printing Office
Washington, D.C. 20402

(2) U.S. Department of Agriculture
Washington, D.C. 20250

(3) U.S. SENATE
Name of committee or Senator
Washington, D.C. 20510

(4) U.S. House of Representatives
Name of committee or Representative
Washington, D.C. 20515

6. Federal Trade Commission. *Economic Report on Food Chain Selling Practices in the District of Columbia and San Francisco.* Washington: GPO. 1969.

7. Federal Trade Commission. *Economic Report on the Influence of Market Structure on Profit Performance of Food Manufacturing Companies.* Washington: GPO. September 1969. 50 pages.

8. Federal Trade Commission. *Economic Report on the Structure and Competitive Behavior of Food Retailing.* Washington: GPO. 1966. 372 pages.

9. Martha M. Hamilton. *The Great American Grain Robbery & Other Stories.* Washington: Agribusiness Accountability Project. 1973. 313 pages.

10. Marshall Harris. *Entrepreneurship in Agriculture.* Iowa City: The University of Iowa Agricultural Law Center. Monograph No. 12. 1974. 163 pages.

11. Jim Hightower, Susan DeMarco. *Hard Tomatoes, Hard Times: The Failure of the Land Grant College Complex.* Cambridge: Schenkman Publishing Co. 1973. 268 pages.

12. Michael Jacobson. *Nutrition Scoreboard: Your Guide to Better Eating.* Washington: Center for Science in the Public Interest. 1973. 102 pages.

13. Michael Jacobson and Joel Anderson. *The Chemical Additives in Booze.* Washington: Center for Science in the Public Interest. 1972. 38 pages.

14. Linda Kravitz. *Who's Minding the Co-op?* Washington: Agribusiness Accountability Project. 1974. 148 pages.

15. National Commission on Food Marketing. *The Structure of Food Manufacturing.* Technical Study No. 8. Washington: GPO. June 1966. 292 pages.

16. National Commission on Food Marketing. *Organization and Competition in Food Retailing.* Technical Study No. 7. Washington: GPO. June 1966. 568 pages.

17. National Commission on Food Marketing. *Studies of Organization and Competition in Grocery Manufacturing.* Technical Study No. 6. Washington: GPO. June 1966. 270 pages.

18. North Central Public Policy Education Committee. *Who Will Control U.S. Agriculture?* Urbana, Illinois: University of Illinois Cooperative Extension Service. Special Publication 27. August, 1972. 56 pages.

19. North Central Public Policy Education Committee. *Who Will Control U.S. Agriculture? A Series of Six Leaflets.* Urbana, Illinois: University of Illinois Cooperative Extension Service. Special Publication 28. March 1973.

20. Victor K. Ray. *The Corporate Invasion of American Agriculture.* Denver: National Farmers Union. 1968. 103 pages.

21. William G. Shepherd. *Market Power & Economic Welfare: An Introduction.* New York: Random House. 1970. 302 pages.

22. F. M. Scherer. *Industrial Market Structure and Economic Performance.* Chicago: Rand McNally and Company. 1970.

23. U.S. Congress. House Antitrust Subcommittee. Hearings, Serial No. 28. *Family Farm Act.* 92nd Congress, second session. March 22 and 23, 1972. Washington: GPO. 1972. 165 pages.

24. U.S. Congress. House Committee on Government Operations. Hearings. *Packaging and Labeling Matters.* 91st Congress, 1st session. June 3, 4 and 5, 1969. Washington: GPO. 1969. 232 pages.

25. U.S. Congress. House Subcommittee on Monopolies and Commercial Law. Hearings. Serial No. 15. *Food Price Investigation.* June, July 1973. Washington: GPO. 1973. 740 pages.

26. U.S. Congress. Joint Economic Committee. Consumer Economics Subcommittee. Hearings (Not yet published) on the Farm-Retail price spread. May 21, 1974.

27. U.S. Congress. Senate Commerce Committee. Hearings. Serial No. 93–78. *Federal Trade Commission Oversight.* 93rd Congress, 2nd session. March, May 1974. Washington: GPO. 1974.

28. U.S. Congress. Senate Select Committee on Small Business. Hearings. (Not yet published.) *Corporate Giantism and Food Prices.* December 10, 11, 12, 1973.

29. U.S. Department of Agriculture. Agricultural Research Service. *Consumer Products by Design: A Report on New Foods, Fabrics and Materials from Agricultural Research.* Agricultural Information Bulletin No. 355. Washington: GPO. June 1972. 71 pages.

30. U.S. Department of Agriculture. Economic Research Service. *Entrepreneurial Control in Farming.* Marshall Harris. ERS No. 542. Washington: USDA. February 1974. 20 pages.

31. U.S. Department of Agriculture. Economic Research Service. *Input Requirements of the Food Industry.* John E. Lee, Jr. Prepared Speech for the National Agricultural Outlook Conference. Washington: USDA. February 21, 1973. 13 pages.

32. U.S. Department of Agriculture. Economic Research Service. *Interrelations in Our Food System.* William T. Manley and Donn A. Reimund. Prepared speech for National Agricultural Outlook Conference. Washington: USDA. February 21, 1973. 10 pages.

33. U.S. Department of Agriculture. Economic Research Service. *The One-Man Farm.* Warren R. Bailey. ERS-519. Washington: USDA. August 1973. 12 pages.

34. U.S. Department of Agriculture. Economic Research Service. *Synthetics and Substitutes for Agricultural Products: Projections for 1980.* William W. Gallimore. Marketing Research Report No. 947. Washington: USDA. March 1972. 64 pages.

35. U.S. Department of Agriculture. Packers & Stockyards Administration. *Final Ruling on Proposed Regulations on Packer Control of Custom Feedlots.* Marvin L. McLain, Administrator. Washington: USDA. May 14, 1974. 60 pages.

36. Harrison Wellford. *Sowing the Wind.* New York: Grossman Publishers. 1973. 384 pages.

Periodicals

1. *Antitrust Law & Economics Review.* Quarterly (P.O. Box 6134, Washington, D.C. 20044). Frequent and generally excellent articles on monopoly power in the food economy.

2. *Business Week*. Weekly. Frequent articles on food and farm industries, quarterly financial data on major corporations, and special features on individual firms in the food industry.

3. *Des Moines Register.* Daily. The most comprehensive, in-depth coverage of agricultural issues by any newspaper in the country. Has excellent investigative reporters both in Washington, D.C. and in Des Moines.

4. *Directory of Corporate Affiliations.* Annual (National Register Publishing Company, Skokie, Illinois). Subtitled "Who Owns Whom?", this directory lists the major subsidiaries of 3,400 U.S. Corporations.

5. *Feedstuffs.* Weekly (Miller Publishing Company, Box 1289, Minneapolis, Minnesota, 55440). Thorough coverage of the grain industry and of governmental policies affecting it.

6. *Forbes.* Bi-weekly. Occasional articles on food and farm industries. Its annual directory issue, usually published May 15, has useful financial data on major corporations.

7. *Fortune.* Monthly. Occasional articles on food and farm industries. Its annual listing of top 500 U.S. corporations, and its listing of the second 500 U.S. corporations, has useful financial data.

8. *The Kiplinger Agricultural Letter*. Bi-weekly. A subscription-only newsletter from Washington that both forecasts and reports developments in agricultural policy.

9. *Supermarket News.* Weekly (Fairchild Publications, 7 East 12th Street, New York, NY. 10003). Comprehensive reporting on the food retail industry and of governmental actions that affect it.

10. *Marketing and Transportation Situation*. Quarterly (USDA, Economic Research Service, Washington, D.C., 20250). Regular reports on the difference between what farmers are paid for food and what consumers are charged.

11. Annual Reports of corporations. Issued at various times during the year by individual firms and obtainable by writing directly to them. Contains very general corporate data, but sometimes has useful information on the firm's organizational structure, its product lines and its broad plans for the future.

Organizations

1. Agribusiness Accountability Project
   1000 Wisconsin Avenue, N.W.
   Washington, D.C. 20007

2. Arkansas Community Organization for Reform Now
   523 W. 15th Street
   Little Rock, Arkansas 72202

3. Center for Community Change
   1000 Wisconsin Avenue, N.W.
   Washington, D.C. 20007

4. Center for New Corporate Priorities
   1516 Westwood Boulevard, Suite 202
   Los Angeles, California 90024

5. Center for Rural Affairs
   Post Office Box 405
   Walthill, Nebraska 68067

6. Center for Rural Studies
   1095 Market Street
   San Francisco, California 94103

7. Center for Science in the Public Interest
   1779 Church Street, N.W.
   Washington, D.C. 20036

8. Children's Foundation
   1028 Connecticut Avenue, N.W.
   Washington, D.C. 20036

9. Community Nutrition Institute
   1910 K Street, N.W.
   Washington, D.C. 20006

10. Consumer Federation of America
    1012 14th Street, N.W.
    Washington, D.C. 20005

11. Consumers Union of United States, Inc.
    256 Washington Street
    Mt. Vernon, New York 10550

12. Federation of Southern Cooperatives
    Epes, Alabama 35460

13. Highlander Center
    Box 245A, RFD 3
    New Market, Tennessee 37820

14. Movement for Economic Justice
    1609 Connecticut Avenue, N.W.
    Washington, D.C. 20009

15. National Catholic Rural Life Conference
    1312 Massachusetts Avenue, N.W.
    Washington, D.C. 20005

16. National Consumers Congress
    1346 Connecticut Avenue, N.W.
    Washington, D.C. 20036

17. National Farmers Organization
    Corning, Iowa 50841

18. National Farmers Union
    P.O. Box 2251
    Denver, Colorado 80201

19. National Sharecroppers Fund
    1346 Connecticut Avenue, N.W.
    Washington, D.C. 20036

20. People's Warehouse
    205 Eleventh Avenue, S.
    Minneapolis, Minnesota 55415

21. Rodale Press
    33 E. Minor Street
    Emmaus, Penna. 18049

22. Small Towns Institute
    P.O. Box 517
    Ellensburg, Washington 98926

23. Southern Regional Council
    52 Fairlee Street, N.W.
    Atlanta, Georgia 30322

24. United Farm Workers, AFL-CIO
    P.O. Box 62
    Keene, California 83531

Notes

Chapter I

. Federal Trade Commission (FTC). "Economic Report: Discount Food Pricing in Washington, D.C." Russell C. Parker. March 1971. pp. 15, 17.

2. U.S. Department of Agriculture (USDA). Economic Research Service. "Market Structure of the Food Business." Marketing Research Report No. 971. September 1972. p. 97.

3. *Antitrust Law & Economics Review*. "Price Discrimination Cases in the Retail Food Industry." Summer 1970 (Vol. 3, No. 4). p. 84. This is a reprint of an internal memorandum from two staff attorneys to the Chief, Division of Discriminatory Practices, Federal Trade Commission, dated June 18, 1969.

4. National Commission on Food Marketing. "Organization and Competition in Food Retailing." Technical Study No. 7. June 1966. Especially Chapter 5, "The Role of Mergers in Changing Market Structure," pp. 97–128. Also, Chapter 7, "Economies of Scale in Food Retailing."

5. National Commission on Food Marketing. "Food from Farmer to Consumer." Final Report. June 1966. p. 72.

6. "Price Discrimination Cases." *Op. cit.* p. 85.

7. National Commission on Food Marketing. "Organization and Competition in Food Retailing." *Op. cit.* p. 38.

Chapter II

1. John Kenneth Galbraith. *Economics and the Public Purpose.* Boston: Houghton Mifflin Company. 1973. p. ix.

2. A. C. Hoffman. Statement before U.S. Senate Select Committee on Small Business. Hearings on "Corporate Giantism and Food Prices." Dec. 10, 1973. p. 2.

3. William G. Shepherd. *Market Power and Economic Welfare: An Introduction.* New York: Random House. 1970. pp. 108–9.

4. *Ibid.* pp. 110–111.

5. Dr. Russell C. Parker. Unpublished testimony before Consumer Economics Subcommittee of the Joint Economic Committee. May 21, 1974. p. 4.

6. Federal Trade Commission. *The Structure of Food Manufacturing.* Technical Study No. 8 of the National Commission on Food Marketing. June 1966. pp. 43–48. See Figure 8, 44.

7. Parker. *Op. cit.* p. 4.

8. National Commission on Food Marketing. *Op. cit.* Final Report. June 1966. p. 94.

9. Federal Trade Commission. "Enforcement Policy with Respect to Product Extension Mergers in Grocery Products Manufacturing." May 15, 1968. Included in: U.S. Congress. House Subcommittee on Monopolies. Hearings. "Food Price Investigation." 93rd Congress, 1st Session. June, July 1973. p. 415.

10. National Commission on Food Marketing. Final Report. *Op. cit.* p. 95.

11. Beatrice Foods Company. "Quarterly Letter to Stockholders." May 31, 1971. p. 5.

12. U.S. Bureau of the Census. Current Business Reports. "Monthly Retail Trade." June 1974.

13. U.S. Congress. House Subcommittee on Monopolies. Hearings. "Food Price Investigation." 93rd Congress, 1st Session. June, July 1973. p. 156.

14. *Chain Store Guide, 1974: Directory of Supermarket, Grocery and Convenience Store Chains* (National Association of Food Chains).

15. U.S. Congress. "Food Price Investigation." *Op. cit.* Table 2-6. pp. 437–440.

16. Metropolitan Market Studies, Inc. "1973 Grocery Distribution Guide." 1973. 164 pp.

17. National Commission of Food Marketing. *Food Retailing.* *Op. cit.* Table 5-3. p. 104.

18. *Ibid.* pp. 104, 125.

19. *Ibid.* pp. 103–125.

20. Parker. *Op. cit.* pp. 7–19. And, U.S. Congress. "Food Price Investigation." *Op. cit.* pp. 156–159.

21. See: U.S. Department of Agriculture. Economic Research Service. "Input Requirements of the Food Industry." John Lee, Jr. February 21, 1973. p. 1.

22. Federal Trade Commission. *Food Manufacturing. Op. cit.* pp. 81–83.

23. Information drawn primarily from materials assembled by the Agribusiness Accountability Project in 1973 from such sources as Del Monte annual reports, industry press, interviews and files of the Securities and Exchange Commission (10–K forms).

24. *Who Will Control U.S. Agriculture?* North Central Regional Extension (NCRE). Kyle, Sundquist, Guither, "Who Controls Agriculture Now?–The Trends Underway." University of Illinois. Urbana. Special Publication 27. August 1972. p. 9.

25. Safeway Stores, Inc. *Annual Report, 1973.* pp. 10–11.

26. Federal Trade Commission. *Food Manufacturing. Op. cit.* p. 57.

27. *Nation's Restaurant News.* "Food Producers Flex Restaurant Muscle." April 30, 1973. p. 1.

28. Federal Trade Commission. *Food Manufacturing. Op. cit.* pp. 202–210. See Table 5. p. 204.

29. Former President Richard M. Nixon. Press conference before National Association of Broadcasters. Houston, Texas. March 19, 1974.

30. USDA. Economic Research Service. "Marketing and Transportation Situation." MTS-192. February 1974. p. 2.

31. *Business Week.* "1973 Profits: A Year to Remember." March 9, 1974. p. 101.

32. UPI story on USDA marketing-margins report for August-September 1973. In: *St. Louis Post Dispatch,* October 29, 1973.

33. John O. Whitney, President, Pathmark Division of Supermarkets General Corporation. "The Food Distributor: Final Stopping Point Before the Table." Address at "A Seminar on Food from the Farm to the Table." Sponsored by Grocery Manufacturers of America. Washington, D.C. August 9, 1973. p. 18.

34. *California Farmer.* Robert Long. "A Banker Looks at California Agriculture." March 16, 1968. And, "Guest Editorial." July 6, 1968.

35. USDA. Economic Research Service. "Interrelations in Our Food System." William T. Manley and Donn A. Reimund. February 21, 1973.

Chapter III

1. *Supermarket News.* "Don't Run Scared Industry Told." October 29, 1973.

2. *Consumer Reports.* "Competition and the Price of Food." May 1974. p. 412.

3. Dr. Russell C. Parker. "Monopoly Causes of High Food Prices." Statement before U.S. Senate Select Committee on

Small Business. Hearings on "Corporate Giantism and Food Prices." December 10, 1973. p. 2.

4. Department of Labor. Bureau of Labor Statistics. "Employment and Earnings." June 1974. Table C-2.

5. *Business Week*. "Executive Compensation: Getting Richer in '73." May 4, 1974. p. 58.

6. *Des Moines Register*. "Calls Employee Dishonesty 'Dominant Business Factor.'" May 18, 1974.

7. *Who Will Control U.S. Agriculture?* Kyle, Sundquist, Guither. *Op. cit.* p. 8.

8. USDA. "The Farm Index." April 1973. p. 16.

9. *Business Week*. "The Spectacular Rise of the Consumer Company." July 21, 1973. p. 52.

10. USDA. Economic Research Service. "Marketing and Transportation Situation." May 1974. MTS-193. Table 6. p. 12.

11. *Idem*.

12. Dr. Michael F. Jacobson. *Nutrition Scoreboard*. Center for Science in the Public Interest. Washington, D.C. July 1973. p. 88.

13. *The Washington Post*. "Chipping Away at Fresh Potatoes." Deborah Sue Yaeger. July 7, 1974. p. K1. Also, *Fortune*. "P & G Secret Ingredient." Peter Vanderwicken. July 1974. pp. 76–77. Also, information on Pringle's cannister.

14. *Business Week*. July 21, 1973. *Op. cit.* p. 48.

15. *Fortune*. July 1974. *Op. cit.* p. 76.

16. *Los Angeles Times*. "Whatever It Is, It's Definitely Not Chocolate." Carole Agus. (*Newsday* syndicated article.) January 19, 1974. p. 1.

17. Westinghouse Broadcasting Company. Group W Productions. ". . . And the Rich Shall Inherit the Earth." January 22, 1973. p. 31 of transcript.

18. U.S. Congress. House Government Operations Committee. Hearings. "Packaging and Labelling Matters." June 3, 4 and 5, 1969. pp. 2–5.

NOTES

19. *Consumer Newsweek.* "Government Survey Shows Packaging Deception Still Rampant." June 18, 1973. In: U.S. Congress. "Food Price Investigation." *Op. cit.* pp. 280–282.

20. U.S. Congress. "Packaging and Labelling Matters." *Op. cit.* pp. 83–84.

21. *The Kansas City Star.* "U.S. Food a Relative Bargain." Nick Thimmesch (*Los Angeles Times* syndicate). Quoting George Koch, President, Grocery Manufacturers of America.

22. *Des Moines Sunday Register.* "Find Grocery Bill exceeds 16% of Pay." Philip W. McKinsey. (*Christian Science Monitor* News Service.) March 18, 1973. p. 4A.

23. *The Washington Post.* "Increasing Price of Food Causes Anger at the Supermarkets." Judy Luce Mann. July 27, 1973.

24. Federal Trade Commission. *Food Manufacturing. Op. cit.* p. 30.

25. U.S. Congress. "Food Price Investigation." Mueller testimony. *Op. cit.* p. 334.

26. "Rapping the System." Charles Mueller. *Antitrust Law & Economics Review.* Volume 3, No. 4. Summer 1970. pp. 27–28.

27. *Fortune.* "The Fortune Directory of the 500 Largest Industrial Corporations." May 1974. pp. 230–251.

28. U.S. Congress. House Committee on Interstate and Foreign Commerce. Hearings. "Statement of the Hon. Peter W. Rodino, Jr." July 2, 1974. Also, *Consumer Reports.* May 1974. *Op. cit.* p. 412.

29. *Milling and Baking News.* "FTC Reviews ITT Continental, Industry Marketing." February 5, 1974. p. 65.

30. Federal Trade Commission. "Economic Report on the Baking Industry." November 1967. p. 44.

31. *Milling and Baking News.* February 5, 1974. *Op. cit.* p. 82.

32. *Milling and Baking News.* "FTC Examines ITT Continental Marketing Strength." February 12, 1974. p. 40.

33. *Milling and Baking News.* February 5, 1974. *Op. cit.* p. 64.

34. *Idem.*

35. *Supermarket News.* "Supreme Courts Lets Stand Continental Baking Penalty." Penny Girard. Fairchild News Service (FNS). October 29, 1973. p. 28.

36. *The Southwestern Miller.* "Bakers in $45,000,000 Antitrust Suit." October 15, 1971.

37. Federal Trade Commission. Baking Industry Report. *Op. cit.* p. 69

38. *Milling and Baking News.* "Indict Arizona Bakers on Price Fixing." February 19, 1974.

39. National Public Affairs Corporation for Television (NPACT). "Washington Connection." March 27, 1974. p. 3 of transcript.

40. *Des Moines Register.* "Profit Boost Seen in Higher Bread Prices." George Anthan. February 26, 1974. p. 1.

41. *The New York Times.* "Days of 'Cheap Food' May Be Over." Morton I. Sosland. March 11, 1973.

42. USDA. Economic Research Service. "Interrelations in Our Food System." *Op. cit.* p. 10.

Chapter IV

1. *Advertising Age.* August 1971.

2. Consumer Nutrition Institute. "Weekly Report." September 28, 1972. p. 7.

3. Dr. Michael Jacobson and Rita Poretsky. "The Foodmakers." Center for Science in the Public Interest. 1973. p. 2fn.

4. Richard A. Ahrens, Ph.D. "Nutritional Health Changes Resulting from Changed Food Intake Patterns." Background paper prepared for The Changing Food Supply in America Conference, sponsored by the Food and Drug Administration. May 22, 1974. p. 1.

5. U.S. Department of H.E.W. "1968–70 Ten-State Nutrition Survey." Also, National Center for Health Statistics. "Health and Nutrition Examination Survey of 1971–72." Report prepared for U.S. Senate Select Committee on Nutrition and Human Needs. 1974.

6. *The New York Times.* "Nutrition Is Now a National Controversy." Jane E. Brody. August 27, 1973. pp. 1, 24.

7. *Ibid.* p. 24. Also, Robert Rodale. "What 'Convenience' Foods are Losing." *The Washington Post.* March 21, 1974. p. E14.

8. *The Washington Post.* "The Case of the Curious Convenience Food Comparison." Marian Burros. August 8, 1974. p. F1.

9. Dr. Alexander Schmidt. "How Safe Is the Food You Eat?" Interview in *U.S. News and World Report.* April 8, 1974. p. 39.

10. USDA. "The Farm Index." November 1972. p. 15.

11. Center for Science in the Public Interest, *et al.* Petition to Food and Drug Administration. August 1, 1974.

12. USDA. Economic Research Service. "U.S. Food Fat Consumption Trends." ERS552. April 1974. p. 20.

13. *The Washington Post.* "The Fun Food Fad and Balanced Meals." Phyllis C. Richman. February 28, 1974. p. F1.

14. Dr. Michael Jacobson. *Nutrition Scoreboard. Op. cit.* p. 82.

15. *The New York Times.* "If People Won't Eat the Healthful Foods, What Can Be Done?" Virginia Lee Warren. October 31, 1972. p. 48M.

16. *Washington Star-News.* "Bakers, Millers Urged to Enrich Products." Judith Randal. July 10, 1974.

17. National Academy of Sciences. "Proposed Fortification Policy for Cereal-Grain Products." 1974.

18. Senator William Proxmire. "Conflict of Interest in Vitamin Recommended Dietary Allowances." *Congressional Record.* June 10, 1974. p. S10177.

19. *Washington Star-News.* "Ignoring Additives in Our Food." Judith Randal. August 12, 1974. p. A12.

20. *The Washington Post*. "FDA: Looking to 'Future Shock'?" William Rice. August 1, 1974. p. K1.

21. Dr. Ferdinand Zienty. "Prospects in Food Additives." Unpublished paper delivered before American Institute of Chemical Engineers. March 19, 1974. p. 5.

22. *Des Moines Register*. "Long List of Additives a 'Shock to the Beer Lover.'" George Anthan. March 15, 1973. p. 7. Also, see "The Chemical Additives in Booze." Michael Jacobson and Joel Anderson. Center for Science in the Public Interest. 1972.

23. *Washington Star-News*. "Searching for Wine Without Additives." David Pursglove. August 21, 1974. p. E5.

24. Dr. Claude Frazier. *Coping with Food Allergy*. New York: Quadrangle. 1974.

25. *The Washington Post*. "Are We Becoming Paranoid About Additives in Food?" Dr. Ben F. Feingold. September 19, 1974. p. F1.

26. *Fortune*. "The Hysteria About Food Additives." Tom Alexander. March 1972. p. 64.

27. *The Washington Post*. "Nitrites vs. Scientists." Marian Burros. July 25, 1974. p. F1. Also, Consumer Nutrition Institute. Weekly Newsletter. "USDA Panel Issues Nitrite Recommendations." July 25, 1974. p. 6.

28. Frazier. *Op. cit.*

29. *Newsweek*. "My Turn." Alden Whitman. May 28, 1973. p. 15.

30. U.S. Congress. Senate Labor and Public Welfare Committee. Hearings. Part 4A. "The Role of Land-Grant Colleges." Testimony of Alice Shabecoff. 92nd Congress, 2nd Session. June 19, 1974. p. 2289.

31. *Harper's Magazine*. "Eight Months on Full Feed." Vance Bourjaily. March 1972. p. 74.

32. *Organic Gardening and Farming*. Letter from Mary-Charlotte Shealy. January 1974. pp. 18–19.

33. *Consumer Reports*. "Turkey Off the Assembly Line." November 1973. p. 664.

34. *Esquire.* "Cry the Beloved Country Ham." James Villas. May 1974. p. 136.

35. *Newsweek.* "Requiem for a Vestigial Organ." Shana Alexander. February 18, 1974. p. 34.

36. *Fortune.* "While the Big Brewers Quaff, the Little Ones Thrist." Charles G. Burck. November 1972. p. 178.

37. *Time.* "The Beer that Won the West." February 11, 1974. p. 73.

38. Burck, *Op. cit.* p. 106.

39. *Supermarket News.* "FTC Charges Coors." August 13, 1973.

40. *Canner Packer World.* "Soy Protein—Nutritious Answer to High Food Costs." Dr. Joseph Rakosky, Jr. May 1972. p. 10.

41. *The Bergen* (New Jersey) *Record.* "A Defense Is Offered for Lemon Cream Pie." Robert Feldberg. Interview with Robert Weiss, President, Morton Frozen Foods Division of ITT. August 13, 1971.

42. *Los Angeles Times.* "Whatever It Is, It's Definitely Not Chocolate." Carole Agus. (*Newsday* syndicated article). January 19, 1974.

43. *The New York Times.* "Beating the High Cost of Chocolate." Nadine Brozan. July 22, 1974.

44. USDA. Economic Research Service. "Synthetics and Substitutes for Agricultural Products: Projections for 1980." William W. Gallimore. MR Report No. 947. March 1972. Uses cited throughout report and in tables.

45. *Ibid.* p. 5.

46. Consumer Nutrition Institute. Weekly Newsletter. "USDA Approves Two of Three 'Alternate Foods.'" April 4, 1974. p. 8.

47. National Educational Television. "The Great American Dream Machine." Segment on Morton's Lemon Cream Pie. Marshall Efron and Penny Bernstein. January 6, 1971. Transcript.

48. Morton Frozen Foods. "Sales Bulletin. From: Robert J. Buck, Director of Advertising & Merchandising. Re: Unfavorable Publicity for Morton Lemon Cream Pies." February 1, 1971. p. 2.

Chapter V

1. Federal Trade Commission. *Food Manufacturing. Op. cit.* p. 68.

2. *Ibid.*, pp. 74–75.

3. U.S. Congress. "Food Price Investigation." *Op. cit.* p. 334.

4. Federal Trade Commission. *Food Manufacturing. Op. cit.* pp. 125–128. (see Table 9, p. 126)

5. Federal Trade Commission. "Economic Report on the Influence of Market Structure on the Profit Performance of Food Manufacturing Companies." September 1969. pp. 6, 7. (see Table 1-3)

6. Federal Trade Commission. *Food Manufacturing. Op. cit.* pp. 65–66.

7. *Ibid.*, p. 70.

8. *Ibid.*, p. 129.

9. *Fortune.* Burck. *Op. cit.* p. 107.

10. *Canner Packer World.* "Fifteen Reasons . . ." February 1974. p. 28.

11. Federal Trade Commission. *Food Manufacturing. Op. cit.* p. 69, fn. 21.

12. *Idem.*

13. *Fortune.* "P & G's Secret Ingredient." Peter Vanderwicken. July 1974. p. 79.

14. *Business Week.* "The Lower Birthrate Crimps." July 13, 1974. p. 50.

15. *Pacific Fruit News.* June 29, 1974. p. 5. Also, *The New York Times.* "A Label That's All in the Family." Gene Salorio. September 1, 1974.

16. National Commission on Food Marketing. "Studies of Organization and Competition in Grocery Manufacturing." Technical Study No. 6. June 1966. p. 18.

17. *Supermarket News.* "Cereals Fight Over Healthy Volume." August 12, 1974. pp. 6, 8.

Chapter VI

1. Response Analysis Corporation. "What the Public Says About Food, Farmers and Agriculture." RAC 3696. November 1973.

2. Earl Butz. Address before Joint Convention of Nebraska Stock Growers Association and Sandhills Cattle Association. Chadron, Nebraska. June 8, 1972.

3. Annual surveys by the U.S. Census Bureau show that roughly 50,000–100,000 farms folded each year during the past decade.

4. Center for Rural Studies. *People and Land.* "Tenneco Bids Farewell to 'Cottage Industry.'" Summer 1973. p. 9.

5. USDA. Office of Communication. "What's Happened to Food Prices?" April 1973. p. 14.

6. Roy N. VanArsdall. "Organization of the Agricultural Sector: Can the Family Farmer Compete?" In: "Proceedings of the Finance Sessions." The Eleventh Annual Agricultural Industries Forum. January 29 and 30, 1969. University of Illinois. Urbana, Illinois. p. 14.

7. *Who Will Control U.S. Agriculture? Op. cit.* "Issues in Concentration vs. Dispersion." Harold F. Breimyer and Wallace Barr. p. 19.

8. *Feedstuffs.* "Large Corporations' Role in Agricultural Production Will Involve More Coordination Rather Than Control." April 2, 1973.

9. USDA. Economic Research Service. "Economies of Size in Farming." J. Patrick Madden. Agr. Econ. Report 107. February 1967.

10. USDA. Economic Research Service. "The One-Man Farm." Warren R. Bailey. ERS-519. August 1973. p. 1.

11. *Ibid.* pp. 2, 12. Also, unpublished internal memorandum of the Exploratory Project for Economic Alternatives, Cambridge, Massachusetts. Bob Lightfoot. March 23, 1973.

12. U.S. Congress. "Food Price Investigation." *Op. cit.* FTC letter, citing Leonard W. Weiss. *Case Studies in American Industry.* pp. 432–433. Also, John Kenneth Galbraith. *Economics and the Public Purpose. Op. cit.* p. 46n.

13. *Who Will Control U.S. Agriculture?* Breimyer and Barr. *Op. cit.* p. 14.

14. *Feedstuffs.* April 2, 1973. *Op. cit.*

15. John Kenneth Galbraith. *Op. cit.* p. 73.

16. USDA. "What's Happened to Food Prices?" *Op. cit.* p. 14.

17. U.S. Congress. House Agriculture Appropriations Sub-Committee. "Hearings." 1972. pp. 328–329.

18. USDA. Economic Research Service. "Balance Sheet of the Farming Sector, 1973." Evans, Warren, Reinsel and Simunek. AIB-365. October 1973. Table 25. p. 30.

19. Shepherd. *Op. cit.* pp. 268, 289.

20. *Business Week.* "Riding the Farm Boom." October 27, 1973. p. 76.

21. *The New York Times.* Seth King. "Bigger Machines for Bigger Farms." June 18, 1972.

22. Westinghouse Broadcasting Company. ". . . And the Rich Shall Inherit the Earth." *Op. cit.* p. 19 of transcript.

23. *Antitrust Law & Economics Review.* Paul D. Scanlon. "FTC and Phase II: The McGovern Papers." Spring 1972. Volume 5, no. 3. Table 1, pp. 33–36.

24. U.S. Congress. "Food Price Investigation." *Op. cit.* See testimony of United Egg Producers, p. 193, and testimony of Harry Fortes, p. 223.

25. *Los Angeles Times.* Reuters. "Ralston Purina Co. Doing Well with Feed and Consumer Mix." November 24, 1973. p. 9.

26. *Business Week.* October 27, 1973. *Op. cit.* p. 76.

27. Glenn S. Hensley, editor. *Farm and Power Equipment.* May 1974. p. 3.

28. John R. Rarick. News Release. "Russian Tractors Plowing a New Market." June 28, 1974.

29. *The Kansas City Star.* AP. "Eastern Farmers Drive 'Red' Tractors." April 6, 1974.

30. *The New York Times.* Theodore Shabad. "Soviet-Made Tractors Get Tryout Upstate." April 24, 1974.

31. Federal Reserve Bank of Chicago. "Agricultural Letter." July 5, 1974.

32. Lavern Rison. "Where the Sixty Cents Goes." In *U.S. Farm News.*

33. USDA Undersecretary J. Phil Campbell. Excerpts from speech. April 25, 1974.

34. USDA. Economic Research Service. "Marketing and Transportation Situation." Quarterly. 1960 through 1974.

35. Food Action Campaign. "A Del Monte Company Town." 1973 (1000 Wisconsin Ave., N.W. Washington, D.C. 20007).

36. Artemus Ward. *The Grocers' Hand-Book and Directory for 1886.* Philadelphia. The Philadelphia Grocer Publishing Co. 1882. pp. 135–136.

37. Testimony of Sam Losito before the U.S. Senate Select Committee on Small Business. Unpublished hearings on "Corprorate Giantism and Food Prices." December 11, 1973.

38. Mushroom Processors Association. "Memorandum to Trade Staff Committee of the U.S. Tariff Commission." June 26, 1973. Investigation 332–72. p. 15. Also, Losito testimony. *Ibid.*

39. *The Wall Street Journal.* Francis L. Partsch. "Firms as Farms." May 2, 1972.

40. *The New York Times.* "Rise of Corporate Farming a Worry to Rural America." B. Drummond Ayres, Jr. December 5, 1971. p. 1.

41. *The Great American Grain Robbery*. Martha Hamilton. Washington: Agribusiness Accountability Project. 1973. pp. 13–14.

42. *Des Moines Register*. George Anthan. " 'Black Market' in Grain Cars." May 23, 1974. p. 1.

43. USDA. Packers and Stockyards Administration. Industry Analysis Staff. Arnold Aspelin and Gerald Engelman. "National Oligopoly and Local Oligopsony in the Meat Packing Industry." Abstract of paper presented at American Agricultural Economics Association. August 20, 1972, Table 1. p. 3.

44. USDA. Packers and Stockyards Administration. Marvin L. McLain, Administrator. Adoption of amendments to sub-section 201.2(m) and section 201.70a of the Regulations. May 14, 1974. p. 52.

45. USDA. Packers and Stockyards Administration. Dr. Gerald Engelman. "Potential Anticompetitive Effects of Packer-Custom Feeding." Testimony given at Des Moines, Iowa. February 26, 1974. p. 4.

46. USDA. Packers and Stockyards Administration. Dr. Gerald Engelman. "The Changing Structure of American Agriculture." Statement at the Graduate Institute of Cooperative Leadership. University of Missouri, Columbia, Mo. June 17, 1974. pp. 24–25.

47. *Feedstuffs*. "University Economists Express Concern about Concentration of Agricultural Production." April 2, 1973.

48. USDA. Economic Research Service. Manley and Reimund. *Op. cit.* p. 9.

49. Oren Lee Staley. Quoted in *The Washington Post*. "U.S. Policy Handcuffs Small Farmer." Nick Kotz. October 5, 1971.

Chapter VIII

1. Richard Rodefeld. "A Reassessment of the Status and Trends in 'Family' and 'Corporate' Farms in U.S. Society." Inserted in *Congressional Record*, May 31, 1973 by Senator George McGovern. Also, see National Farmers Orga-

nization *Reporter.* "Muzzling Effort Backfires; Witness Rid-
dles USDA Corporate Farm Study." March 1972. p. 1.

2. USDA. Economic Research Service. "Entrepreneurial Control in Farming." Marshall Harris. ERS No. 542. February
1974. p. 16.

3. Philip Raup. "Corporate Farming in the United States."
Journal of Economic History. March 1973. p. 290.

4. USDA. Packers and Stockyards Administration. Marvin L.
McLain. *Op. cit.* p. 31.

5. Federal Trade Commission. "In the Matter of United
Brands Company." Final Order. Docket No. 8835. May
14, 1974. Also see "Complaint," same case and docket
number, issued February 11, 1971.

6. *Business Week.* "Tenneco's New Strategy: Growing from
Within." August 3, 1974. p. 52.

7. Del Monte Corporation. "Five Directions for Growth in
the 1970's." Address by Alfred W. Eames, Jr. and Richard
G. Landis. San Francisco. May 27, 1971. p. 5.

8. USDA. Economic Research Service. Manley and Reimund.
Op. cit. p. 6.

9. Woody Guthrie. "Pretty Boy Floyd the Outlaw."

10. *Who Will Control U.S. Agriculture?* Breimyer and Barr.
Op. cit. p. 18.

11. USDA. Economic Research Service. Ronald L. Mighell and
William S. Hoofnagle. "Contract Production and Vertical
Integration in Farming, 1960 and 1970." p. 4.

12. *Feedstuffs.* December 12, 1970. p. 4.

13. U.S. Congress. House Antitrust Subcommittee. Hearings.
"Family Farm Act." Testimony of U.S. Undersecretary
J. Phil Campbell. March 22, 1972. p. 28.

14. USDA. Economic Research Service. John Lee. *Op. cit.*
p. 12. USDA. Economic Research Service. Manley and
Reimund. *Op. cit.* pp. 9–10. Center for Rural Affairs (PO
Box 405, Walthill, Nebraska 68067). "Who Will Sit Up
with the Corporate Sow?" 1974.

15. USDA. Economic Research Service. Manley and Reimund. *Op. cit.* p. 9.

16. U.S. Congress. "Family Farm Act" Hearings. *Op. cit.* pp. 36–39.

17. Harrison Wellford. *Sowing the Wind.* New York: Grossman. 1972. See chapter titled "Poultry Peonage." p. 101.

18. USDA. Packers and Stockyards Administration. Marvin McLain. *Op. cit.* p. 28.

19. ABC-Television News. "Food: Green Grow the Profits." Documentary broadcast December 21, 1973. pp. 46–49 of transcript.

20. Marcus v. Eastern Agricultural Association. 32 N.J. 460, 161A, 2d 247 (1960). Cited in USDA. ERS. Harris. *Op. cit.* p. 5.

21. USDA. Economic Research Service. Manley and Reimund. *Op. cit.* p. 6.

22. ABC-Television News. *Op. cit.* pp. 58–59.

23. *Who Will Control U.S. Agriculture?* Breimyer and Barr. *Op. cit.* p. 14.

24. U.S. Congress. "Food Price Investigation." *Op. cit.* Attachment 5. "Statement on Behalf of the National Canners Association. November 16, 1971." p. 568.

25. Family Farm Act Hearings. *Op. cit.* p. 28.

26. Annual reports of individual corporations. Also, *The New York Times.* "Food Makers Sample Diversification." Ernest Holsendolph. January 7, 1973.

27. Dr. George Irving. Quoted in *National Geographic.* "The Revolution in American Agriculture." Jules B. Billard. February 1970. pp. 184–185.

28. Westinghouse Broadcasting Company. *Op. cit.* pp. 43–44.

29. *The Wall Street Journal.* "Firms as Farms." *Op. cit.*

30. *The Wall Street Journal.* "Recipes for Profits." Bob Arnold. July 19, 1974.

31. Wellford. *Op. cit.* pp. 105, 106.

32. Dr. Jean Mayer. "Practice Makes Imperfect." Syndicated column (*New York News*) appearing in *The Washington Post.* March 15, 1973. p. G6.

33. ABC-Television News. *Op. cit.* pp. 9–11.

34. V. James Rhodes and Leonard R. Kyle. "A Corporate Agriculture." No. 3 of a series of six leaflets published by the North Central Region Extension Services. University of Illinois. Special Publication 28. Urbana, Illinois. March 1973. p. 2.

35. *The Washington Post.* "Drought." Dan Morgan. August 11, 1974. p. 1.

36. *Business Week.* "Crop Failure Down on the Conglomerate Farm." February 19, 1972. p. 81.

37. USDA. Office of Communication. "Farm Prices Fall While Marketing Margins Rise." June 24, 1974.

Chapter VIII

1. U.S. Congress. Senate Committee on Agriculture and Forestry. "Nomination of Earl Lauer Butz." 92nd Congress. 1st Session. November 17, 18 and 19, 1971.

2. A. C. Hoffman. *Op. cit.* p. 3.

3. *Hunger USA.* A Report by the Citizens' Board of Inquiry into Hunger and Malnutrition in the United States. Boston: Beacon Press. 1968.

4. Martha M. Hamilton. *Op. cit.* Chapter 10.

5. Del Monte Corporation. *Shield.* "Harry and the Middlemen." Winter 1973. p. 10.

6. U.S. Congress. Senate Committee on Agriculture and Forestry. "Poultry Indemnity Payments." Report No. 93-772. April 8, 1974.

7. U.S. Congress. House Committee on Agriculture. "Statement of Dr. F. J. Mulhern, Administrator, USDA Animal and Plant Health Inspection Service." April 10, 1974. p. 5.

8. Geneva (New York) Agricultural Experiment Station. *Annual Report.* 1967.

9. *The New York Times.* "If People Won't Eat the Healthful Foods, What Can Be Done?" *Op. cit.* p. 48M.

10. Hamilton. *Op. cit.* Chapter 5.

11. Al V. Krebs. "Of the Grain Trade, by the Grain Trade, and for the Grain Trade." In: Hamilton. *Op. cit.* Appendix VII, p. 289.

12. U.S. General Accounting Office. "Exporters' Profits on Sales of U.S. Wheat to Russia." B-176943. Feburary 12, 1974. pp. 15–16.

13. *Ibid.* p. 2.

14. *St. Louis Post Dispatch.* "U.S. Public the Clear Loser in Soviet Grain Deal." Joseph Albright. November 27, 1973.

15. *Des Moines Register.* "USDA-Agribusiness Complex." September 21, 1973. Editorial page.

16. *Los Angeles Times.* " 'I'd Be a Traitor If I Supported Nixon Farm Policies'—Talmadge." Herman Talmadge. March 9, 1973.

17. USDA. Address by Secretary of Agriculture Earl Butz. "It's a New Ball Game." December 17, 1973. p. 6.

18. USDA. Address by Assistant Secretary of Agriculture Clayton Yeutter. "Key Issues Facing Farmers in 1974." March 1, 1974. p. 7. USDA 562-74.

19. USDA. Remarks by Don Paarlberg, Director of Agricultural Economics. "Agricultural Trade and Domestic Adjustments in Agriculture." March 21, 1974. p. 4.

20. USDA. Address by Assistant Secretary Richard L. Feltner. "Breaking Barriers and Broadening Horizons." July 11, 1974. pp. 4–5. USDA 1900–74.

21. Paarlberg. *Op. cit.* p. 5.

22. Monte E. Juillerat and Paul L. Harris. "Grain Export Industry Organization and Facilities in the United States." Purdue Unversity Department of Agricultural Economics. August 1971.

23. Yeutter. *Op. cit.* p. 5.

24. USDA. Speech by Assistant Secretary of Agriculture Clayton Yeutter. "Agricultural Policy in the Years Ahead." June 11, 1974. USDA 1603–74. p. 7.

25. *Feedstuffs.* July 8, 1974. p. 23.

26. *Business Week.* "The Incredible Empire of Michel Fribourg." March 11, 1972. p. 84.

27. Earl Butz. Reprint of speech in *Feedstuffs.* July 8, 1974. p. 10.

28. *Foreign Policy.* "The Politics of Food." Stephen Rosenfeld. Spring 1974. p. 17.

29. Earl Butz. *Feedstuffs. Op. cit.* p. 10.

30. *National Journal Reports.* "World Food Conference Prompts U.S. Farm Policy Review." Daniel J. Balz. June 1, 1974. p. 808.

31. *The New York Times.* "Foreign Appeals for Food Raise Price Specter Here." Edwin L. Dale, Jr. May 13, 1974. p. 10.

32. *Foreign Policy.* "Development: The End of Trickle Down?" James P. Grant. p. 51.

33. USDA. Speech of Ned Bayley. "Agriculture Research: Arrows in the Air." September 10, 1969. p. 5.

34. USDA. Economic Research Service. "Concepts Involved in Defining and Identifying Farms." Richard J. Foote. June 1970. ERS 448. p. 110.

35. Rural Development Act of 1972. Title V. "Rural Development and Small Farm Research and Education."

36. Grant. *Op. cit.* pp. 51–52.

37. *The Washington Post.* "World's Lilliputs Hold the Answer to Famine Threat." Edgar Owens. October 13, 1974.

38. Linda Kravitz. *Who's Minding the Co-op?* Washington, D.C. Agribusiness Accountability Project. 1974.

39. Senator Hubert Humphrey. U.S. Senate debate on the nomination of Earl Butz. *Congressional Record.* December 2, 1971. p. S20163.

Chapter IX

1. *The Washington Post/Potomac.* "Six Persuaders." Rudy Maxa. March 10, 1974. p. 14. (Quoting Robert Gray of the public relations firm, Hill & Knowlton)

2. U.S. Congress. Senate Select Committee on Small Business. Hearings. "Corporate Giantism and Food Prices." Questions discussed by Senator James Abourezk. December 10, 1973.

3. U.S. Congress. Joint Economic Committee. Consumer Economics Subcommittee. Hearing. May 21, 1974.

4. *U.S. News & World Reports.* "Those Washington Lobbyists." April 29, 1974. p. 44.

5. *Idem.* Also see *Corporate Ambassadors to Washington.* Robert W. Miller and Jimmy D. Johnson. Washington: The American University. 1970.

6. *National Journal.* "Washington Pressures/Sophisticated GMA Lobby Represents Grocery Item Industry in Era of Consumerism." Andrea F. Schoenfeld. March 13, 1971.

7. *Washington Star News.* "Danzansky New Food Chains Chief, Hails Consumers." Philip Shandler. October 16, 1973.

8. *Supermarket News.* "Chains Ask Commerce Department Aide." FNS. July 15, 1974. p. 1.

9. *The Washington Post.* "Lobbies Fight Consumer Bill." Bob Kittner. 1974.

10. *The Washington Post.* "Consumer Bill Dealt 4th Defeat." Spencer Rich. September 20, 1974. p. A1.

11. Del Monte Voluntary Nonpartisan Good Government Fund. Reports filed in October 1972 with the U.S. General Accounting Office in Washington, D.C. Especially an October 4, 1972 report, ID No. NPOOOOAB. pp. 7–9.

12. *Chicago Today.* "Food Industry Joins Campaign Donors List." Chuck Neubauer and Donna Marx. September 21, 1973.

13. Fund-raising letter for CED sent to corporations by Robert E. Dewan, Chairman of the Board, S. S. Kresge Company. January 2, 1974. With attachments.

14. Committee for Economic Development. "A New U.S. Farm Policy for Changing World Food Needs." October 1974.

15. The Nutrition Foundation. "1969–1970 Report." p. 95.

16. *The New York Times.* "Musical Chairs in Business and Government." Michael C. Jensen. November 12, 1972. Section 3, p. 1.

17. *The Progressive.* "Company Town at FDA." Michael Jacobson and Robert White. April 1973. p. 49.

18. Consumer Nutrition Institute. Weekly Report. "Food Is More Than Just Something to Sell." March 7, 1974. p. 8.

19. National Commission on Productivity. "Productivity in the Food Industry." 1973. pp. 22–23.

20. *The Washington Post.* "Congressmen and King Crabs." Jeannette Smyth. February 7, 1974.

Chapter X

1. *The Closing Circle.* Barry Commoner. Bantam Books: New York. 1972. p. 187.

2. USDA. "Is Boxed Meat the Answer?" Address by Secretary of Agriculture Earl Butz to the Boxed Meat Seminar. Chicago, Illinois. July 5, 1974. USDA 1556-74.

3. *The Washington Post.* "Suppose the Butcher Vanished." Marian Burros. September 5, 1974. p. G1.

4. *The New York Times.* "Revolution Near at Check-Out Counter." John D. Morris. May 21, 1973.

5. *The Washington Post.* "Ringing the Robot Cash Register." William Rice. August 29, 1974. p. E16.

6. Joseph Danzansky. Speech before business and marketing professors. Catholic University. Washington, D.C. September 1974.

7. John O. Whitney. "The Food Distributor." Speech delivered at a seminar on food sponsored by Grocery Manufacturers of America. Washington, D.C. August 9, 1973. p. 11.

8. National Association of Food Chains. "Statement on the Development of the Universal Product Code—Electronic Check-stand Technology and Its Relationship to Consumers." February 1974. p. 3.

9. *Supermarket News.* "Group to Pick UPC Symbol." Nancy Brumback. March 26, 1973. p. 1.

10. USDA. Excerpts from a talk by Undersecretary of Agriculture J. Phil Campbell. April 11, 1974. USDA 953-74. p. 5.

11. Danzansky. Catholic University. *Op. cit.*

12. *American Fried.* Calvin Trillin. New York: Doubleday & Company. 1974.

13. *New York.* "The Burger That's Eating New York." Mimi Sheraton. August 19, 1974. p. 35.

14. *Newsweek.* "The Roadside Gourmet: Pop Goes for the Food." Joseph Morgenstern. September 25, 1972. p. 78.

15. McDonald's Corporation. "Annual Report." 1973.

16. *The Washington Post.* "Just Thaw It and Boil It, Ma, and to Blazes with the Old Way of Cooking." Tom Donnelly. 1974. p. B1.

17. USDA. "Farm Policy Implications and Alternatives." Don Paarlberg. Talk before 1973 National Agricultural Outlook Conference. February 21, 1973. p. 8.

18. Rep. Ed Mezvinsky has made a survey of farmers' markets operating around the country and has prepared a report that includes suggestions on starting such a market in your area. For a copy, write to Rep. Mezvinsky, House Office Building, Washington, D.C. 20515.

19. *Des Moines Register.* "Farm Research." Editorial. October 30, 1973.

Index

A&P (The Great Atlantic & Pacific Tea Company): 8, 25, 34, 45, 186, 215, 285

Adamy, Clarence: 24

Additives: 59, 62–64, 102–108, 111, 113–114, 118, 127–130, 132–134

Advertising: 31, 33, 54, 80, 89, 98, 109, 114, 122, 123–124, 135–153; Appendix C

American Association for the Advancement of Science: 110

American Bakeries Company: 79

American Bakers Association: 83

American Brands, Incorporated: 13, 15

American Cyanamid Company: 109

American Home Products Corporation: 13

American Meat Institute: 271

Anderson, Clayton & Company: 42

Anheuser-Busch (Budweiser): 17, 56, 123, 125, 135n, 142

Archer Daniels Midland Company: 130, 184

Artificial flavoring: 89, 103–105, 108, 111, 113–114, 132–134

Asparagus: 205–206

Bank of America: 45, 167, 170

Barr, Dr. Wallace: 158, 161, 198, 206

Bayley, Dr. Ned: 250

Beatrice Foods Company: 13, 15, 23, 56, 77, 149

Beef: 42–43, 50, 118, 184–187, 281

Beer: 104, 105, 121–125

Bell, William, Company: 129, 132

Boeing Company, The: 191, 215

Borden, Incorporated: 14, 17, 22, 30, 34, 36, 54, 56, 128, 138, 257

Bread: 78–85, 99-100, 302

Breakfast cereals: 17–18, 61–62, 92, 95–96, 98–99, 111–112, 136–137, 146, 148, 152–153

Breimyer, Dr. Harold: 158, 161, 198, 206

Bunge Corporation: 184, 232

Butchers: 281, 285, 288

Butz, Earl (Secretary of Agriculture): 43–44, 47, 62, 108, 136, 189, 201n, 218–219, 238, 244, 246, 253, 254–255, 275, 296; "Cowhand on the Potomac": 154–155

CPC International Incorporated: 13, 37, 257, 268

Campbell, J. Phil (Undersecretary of Agriculture): 51, 178, 207, 287

Campbell Soup Company: 15, 17, 36, 42, 56, 93, 135n, 143, 260n, 262

Campbell Taggart Incorporated: 36, 79, 82–83, 84, 243

Candy bars: 68, 126–127

Cargill, Incorporated: 29, 130, 150, 167, 173, 184, 191, 197, 201, 224, 227, 231, 235, 243, 245

Carnation Company: 17, 36, 69, 128, 260

Census of Agriculture: 250–251

Central Soya Company: 125–126, 130

"Cheap" food: 86

Chevron Chemical Company: 166–167

Chicken: 117–118, 201, 202–203, 210–211, 213, 225–228, 288

Clark, Senator Dick: 226

Clorox Company: 181, 191

Coca-Cola Company, The: 15, 17, 29, 34, 74, 135n, 146, 257, 261, 270

Committee for Economic Development: 267–268

Consolidated Foods Corporation: 13, 15, 36, 56, 149, 209

Consumer Federation of America: 87, 269

Consumer Protection Agency: 264, 300

Consumer Research Institute: 269

Consumers Union (Consumer Reports): 52–53, 118

Continental Grain Company: 184, 201, 231, 233

Cook Incorporated: 184, 232

Cooperatives: 251–252, 303, 304

Coors Brewing Company: 123, 124

Cornell University: 229–230

Covington & Burling: 259

Crocker, Betty: 37, 102, 149

Crystal City, Texas: 180

Danzansky, Joseph: 263, 283, 287

Deere & Company: 167, 168–170, 174, 268

DeKalb AgResearch, Incorporated: 167, 168

DeMarco, Susan: 10, 121, 296

Del Monte Corporation: 12, 17, 26–27, 31, 34, 42, 49, 61, 70, 71, 74, 102, 120, 138, 142, 152, 156, 159n, 180–181, 192, 195, 197, 204–206, 209, 224, 257,

258, 262, 266–267, 268, 273, 275, 284n, 306

Diversification: 208–209

Dole (Castle & Cook): 13, 42, 147, 182, 224

Dow Chemical Company: 159n, 167, 191

Dreyfus, Louis, Corporation: 184, 232

Eastland, Senator James: 226

Eggs: 193–194, 200

Entrepreneurship: 157, 162, 166, 187, 189, 190, 197–208, 289, 291–295; Appendix D

Executive salaries: 44–45, 55, 56–57, 71–72

"Experts": 245, 296, 299

Family farm efficiency: 156–157, 158–160, 188, 215, 251–252, 303

Farmer, Jean: 303, 305

Farmer bargaining: 180–181, 203–205, 206; Appendix D

Farmers' markets: 285, 287–289, 301–302

Farm share of food dollar: 41–42, 61, 177–178, 179, 180–181, 227

Fast food chains: 96–97, 130, 291–292

Fat: 47n, 96

Federal Extension Service: 170

Federal Trade Commission: 7, 8, 18, 20, 25, 30, 34, 35, 77, 137–138, 141, 144, 152, 194, 260, 265, 304; FTC monopoly overcharge study: 73, 75, 77, 125, 172–173

Feingold, Dr. Ben: 105, 107–108

Filberts, Mrs.: 67–68

First National Stores (Finast): 285

Food & Drug Administration: 94, 107, 109, 260, 261, 269, 271–273

Food Fair Stores: 25

Foreman, Carol: 87

Fortification: 99, 101

Frazier, Dr. Claude: 105, 107

Freeman, Orville: 254

French Company: 62, 67, 73

Freud, Clement: 278

Galbraith, John Kenneth, 12, 162, 296

General Aromatic Products: 131

General Foods Corporation: 13, 17, 34, 37, 56, 90, 111, 114, 135n, 139, 142, 144, 149, 209, 257, 261, 284n, 290

General Mills, Incorporated: 18, 22n, 37, 41n, 56, 60, 61, 62, 67, 96, 112, 113, 130, 152–153, 209, 257, 261

Gerber Products Company: 17, 138, 150, 152, 261

Getty Oil Company: 159n, 191

Giant Food Incorporated: 187, 262, 283, 285

Gino's Incorporated: 300

Givaudan Corporation: 132

Good Housekeeping: 143, 269

Grace, W. R., & Company: 37, 171

Great Western United Corporation: 37, 86

Green Giant Company: 37, 42, 120, 182, 260n, 268

Greyhound Corporation (Armour Food): 14, 117, 143, 184n, 186, 191, 224, 227, 255, 274

Grocery Manufacturers of America: 71, 257, 260n, 264, 266, 269, 271, 274

Ham: 119–120

Hamilton, Martha M.: 224

Harris, Dr. Marshall: 190, 198

Hart, Senator Philip: 76, 226, 265

Heinz, H. J., Company: 13, 38, 56, 62, 70, 73, 137, 143, 147, 211, 257, 262, 268, 275, 285n

Hershey Foods Corporation: 15, 68, 261, 270, 271

Heublein, Incorporated: 15, 38, 56, 147, 191, 257, 269

Hoffman, A. C.: 12, 220

Holly Farms (The Federal Company): 29, 35, 42, 227

Hormel, George A., & Company: 186, 274

Hostess cakes: 14, 81, 89, 100, 142

Humphrey, Senator Hubert: 244, 255, 275

Hunt-Wesson Foods (Norton Simon): 101, 143, 159n, 262, 275–277

Innovation: 4, 111, 140, 148, 153

International Harvester Company: 169, 170, 171

International Minerals & Chemicals Corporation: 155n, 167, 171

International Multifoods Corporation: 38, 42, 127, 148

ITT: 14, 79, 81–83, 89, 99, 119, 127, 134, 135n, 139, 141, 191, 214, 243, 257, 260n, 265, 290

Interstate Brands Corporation: 79

Iowa Beef Processors: 42, 184n, 186

Jackson, Senator Henry: 235

Jacobson, Dr. Michael: 91, 97

Jewel Stores: 34, 57, 187

Jones, Mary Gardiner: 261

Jukes, Dr. Thomas H.: 109

Kane-Miller Corporation: 38

Kansas State University: 229

Kellogg Company: 18, 112, 139, 146, 153

Kentucky Fried Chicken (Heublein): 97, 227

Knauer, Virginia (Presidential Consumer Advisor): 51, 284

Kool-Aid: 90, 147

Kraftco Corporation: 38, 56, 60, 68, 143, 144, 261, 268

Krebs, Al: 234

Kroger Company, The: 8, 24, 25, 34, 45, 186, 194, 197, 284

Kyle, Dr. Leonard: 187, 215

Libby, McNeil & Libby (Nestlé): 31, 101, 146

Ling-Temco-Vought (Wilson meats): 14, 184n, 186, 191, 224, 227, 274

Long, Robert W.: 45–46, 170
Low-income eaters: 71–73, 223, 305
Lucky Stores, Incorporated: 8, 35, 45, 57, 156

Marriott Corporation: 49, 120
McDonald's Corporation: 57, 97, 98, 290–292, 300
McHale, Secretary James: 161
Miles Laboratories, Incorporated: 130
Miller Brewing Company (Philip Morris): 122, 151
Mom & Pop stores: 4, 6, 279, 306
Monsanto Corporation: 127
Morton Foods (ITT): 14, 133–134
Mrak, Dr. Emil: 109
Mushrooms: 182

Nabisco: 57, 130, 260n
Nader, Ralph: 19–20, 76
National Academy of Sciences: 101
National Association of Food Chains: 24, 187, 230, 257, 260, 263, 265, 280, 282, 283
National Canners Association: 206–207, 257, 260n, 262
National Commission on Food Marketing: 7–8, 9, 21, 22
National Consumers League: 117
National Farmers Organization: 188, 197–198, 202, 218
National Farmers Union: 218
National Tea Company: 27
Nesheim, Robert O.: 101–102

Nestlé: 15, 39, 68, 110, 120, 261
Nitrates and nitrites: 107, 119
Nutrition Foundation: 270, 273

Ocean Spray Cranberries, Incorporated: 39
Ogden Corporation: 39, 224
Oscar Mayer & Company: 57, 186, 224, 274
Owens, Ted: 252

Paarlberg, Dr. Don (USDA Director of Economics): 242, 299
Pabst Brewing Company: 17, 123, 124, 125
Packaging: 65–68, 195, 230, 278, 295, 305
Parker, Dr. Russell C.: 20
Peaches: 204–205, 213
Peavey Company: 184, 273
Pepsico, Incorporated: 15, 17
Peter Paul, Incorporated: 126
Pet Incorporated: 13, 15, 39, 74, 101, 112, 128
Pillsbury Company: 15, 39, 42, 57, 201, 209, 227, 261, 268
Potatoes: 62–64, 183
Pringle's: 63–65
Processed food: 58–68, 73, 94–107, 215, 302
Procter & Gamble Company: 13, 62–66, 73, 146–147, 257, 260n, 261, 271, 285n
Proxmire, Senator William: 76, 101
Purex Corporation: 159n, 168, 191, 206

Quaker Oats Company, The: 18, 39, 56, 98, 101, 112, 143, 152–153, 209, 261, 268, 269

Ralston Purina Company: 12, 39, 42, 47n, 101, 118, 120, 130, 143, 155n, 162, 166, 167, 168, 171, 173–174, 182, 192, 193–194, 197, 199, 201, 208, 211, 216, 224, 228–229, 243, 245, 257, 261, 268, 271
"Relevant" market: 24, 79, 180, 185
Restaurants: 34–35, 36–40 (Table), 291–292, 306
Return on investment: 43–44, 77, 123n, 163–166, 190
Reynolds, R. J., Industries, Incorporated: 14, 261
Rhodes, Dr. James: 193, 196, 215
Riviana Foods Incorporated: 15, 40
Richard Rodefeld: 190
Royal Crown Cola Company: 17, 76–77
Rural development: 251–252
Russian wheat deal: 232–238
Rutgers University: 99, 230

Safeway Stores, Incorporated: 8, 12, 24, 27, 34, 35, 40, 57, 186, 194, 197, 258, 284, 284n, 288
Schlitz, Joseph, Brewing Company: 15, 17, 57, 123, 124, 125
Schmidt, Dr. Alexander: 94, 102

School lunch & breakfast programs: 89–90, 99, 130, 223
Sechler, Susan: 296
Seven-Eleven (Southland Corporation): 5–6, 31–34, 45
Seven-Up Company: 17, 74
Shepherd, Dr. William G.: 16, 18, 168
"Slack fill": 68–71
Small farmers: 249–254
Southdown, Incorporated: 122
Staley, Oren Lee: 188
Standard Brands, Incorporated: 13, 113, 126, 146, 261
Stokely-Van Camp, Incorporated: 31, 143, 147, 155n, 224
Stop & Shop Companies, Incorporated: 66
Sugar: 86, 94–96, 98, 99, 112, 133
Sunkist: 254
Superior Oil Company: 191, 210, 216
Supermarkets: 4, 5, 6–10, 12, 23–27, 31, 34, 41, 43–45, 56, 57, 149–153, 186, 280, 283–284; (electronic checkout), 285, 286; Appendix A
Supermarkets General Corporation (Pathmark Stores): 44–45, 281, 283
Swift & Company (Esmark, Incorporated): 34, 37, 107, 114, 184n, 186, 195, 197, 199, 209, 224, 228–229, 257, 261, 274
Synthetic foods: 126–132

Talmadge, Senator Herman: 239

Taste: 114–121, 125, 212, 290–291, 295

Tenneco Incorporated: 14, 155n, 156, 159n, 168, 169, 171, 191, 195, 208, 214, 216

Texas A&M University: 229

Textured Vegetable Protein (TVP): 131

Tomatoes: 115, 121, 211, 213, 230

Tractors: 168, 174, 215

Trillin, Calvin: 289

Turkey: 118, 200

Unilever: 14, 15, 17, 34, 40, 47n, 191, 261

United Brands Company: 13, 17, 40, 56, 159n, 186, 194–195, 257

University of California: 68, 109, 213

University of Florida: 115

University of Georgia: 213

University of Illinois: 213

Upjohn Company: 168, 171

Vertical integration: 28, 31, 32–33, 34, 44, 155, 186, 193–194, 196, 197–208, 305; Appendix D

Washington law firms: 259–260

Wellford, Harrison: 202, 212

Wheaties: 61

Whitely, Velma: 176–177

Williams Foods, Incorporated: 131

Winn-Dixie Stores, Incorporated: 25, 45, 56, 187, 284n

Witvoet, Jim: 301, 305

Wodicka, Dr. Virgil: 101

Wonder Bread (ITT): 14, 34, 79, 81–82, 135n, 141, 151

Yeutter, Dr. Clayton (Assistant Secretary of Agriculture): 244

About the Author

For five years, JIM HIGHTOWER was director of the Agribusiness Accountability Project, fighting for the idea that farmers should be independent, food marketers competitive, prices reasonable, and that food should be both good and good for us. A native Texan, Hightower also has been Legislative Assistant to former U.S. Senator Ralph Yarborough. He is author of numerous articles and of *Hard Tomatoes, Hard Times*, a book about the failure of food and farm research. Hightower is a forceful and frequent spokesman on the food industry before Congress and throughout the country.